Justice for Young Offenders

THEIR NEEDS, OUR RESPONSES

Mary E. Vandergoot

PURICH
PUBLISHING
LIMITED
SASKATOON, SK. CANADA

Purich Publishing Ltd.
Box 23032, Market Mall Post Office
Saskatoon, SK Canada S7J 5H3
Phone: (306) 373-5311 Fax: (306) 373-5315
Email: purich@sasktel.net
Website: www.purichpublishing.com

Library and Archives Canada Cataloguing in Publication

Vandergoot, Mary Ellen, 1956-
Justice for young offenders : their needs, our responses / Mary E. Vandergoot.

Includes index.
ISBN 1-895830-27-3

1. Juvenile justice, Administration of — Canada. 2. Juvenile delinquents — Canada — Social conditions. 3. Juvenile delinquents — Canada — Psychology. I. Title.

HV9108.V35 2006   364.36'0971   C2006-903432-X

Cover design by Duncan Campbell.
Cover photo by Andrew Douglas/Masterfile.
Editing, design, and layout by Donald Ward.
Index by Ursula Acton.
Printed in Canada by Houghton Boston Printers and Lithographers.

Publishers' Note: Most legal case citations are to CanLII (www.canlii.org), a not-for-profit organization initiated by the Federation of Law Societies of Canada, which provides free access to legal resources. All case studies are composites, and any similarity to actual persons is accidental.

URLs for websites contained in this book are accurate to the time of writing, to the best of the author's knowledge.

The publishers gratefully acknowledge the assistance of the Cultural Industries Development Fund (Saskatchewan Department of Culture, Youth and Recreation) in the production of this book.

I would like to dedicate this book to R. and S., two young people I never met, but whose names were in my appointment book. They never arrived for their appointments with me. I dedicate this book to them in recognition of their pain and loneliness, which each day reminds me of the youth who fall between the cracks and those for whom we never knew how or when to intervene. The tragedy of their untimely deaths continues to shake my spirit and inspired the writing of this book.

CONTENTS

ACKNOWLEDGEMENTS

I would not have been able to complete this project without the continual support, friendship, and love of my husband, Robin Hawrysh. He read many initial drafts, offered guidance, and listened to me for many hours while I grappled with the project. I could not have completed the book without his patience and confidence in me.

I also thank my family, especially my children and my mother, who encouraged me along the way. I also thank my friends and colleagues who encouraged me throughout this project.

I am very grateful that the Young Offender Team, Child and Youth Program, Mental Health and Addiction Services, granted me a temporary reduction in my hours so I could work part-time while I wrote the book. I am also indebted to the many young people, parents, and professionals with whom I was fortunate to work during my time with the Young Offender Team in Saskatoon.

I thank Karen Bolstad and Don Purich of Purich Publishing, of Saskatoon, who saw the value of publishing a book of this nature. Their vision, support, and guidance throughout the writing and editing stages of the book helped me articulate my ideas and complete the project to the best of my abilities. I also thank editor Donald Ward for his editorial assistance with the completion of this book. I am also grateful to Karen Bolstad for her skill in ensuring the accuracy of the text during the final stage of editing.

There are many individuals who supported this project and assisted me with refining the text. I would like to acknowledge the helpful feedback on earlier drafts of selected chapters that I received from my family, friends, and colleagues, including: Chris Johnstone, Dr. Debby Boyes, Dr. Patricia Blakley, Judge Sheila Whelan, Kearney Healy, Rhonda Woolsey, Bryan Barker, and Elinor Keter. I am also indebted to Russell Smandych, Department of Sociology, University of Manitoba, whose constructive and helpful comments during an earlier stage of the project were very valuable.

The views expressed in this book are entirely my own and do not necessarily reflect the opinions or views of the Saskatoon Health Region, where I have been an employee since 1998. In referencing a number of publications, I have attempted to represent or interpret the views of the authors in a manner that is accurate and reasonable; however, should there be errors in fact or interpretation, neither my reviewers nor editor should be held responsible; they are entirely of my own, albeit, non-intentional, making.

The case examples used in this book are constructed in such a way that the identity of any person or family cannot be made. Significant facts about their identities have been altered to ensure that their true identities remain hidden. I apologize for any unintentional harm that may be caused by experiences of déjà vu the reader may encounter during the reading of this book. I have, to the best of my ability, obscured the details and identity of all persons and their situations. Nonetheless, some of the experiences, or the descriptions of characteristics of persons, may be similar to persons the reader knows. This is because many of the experiences described in this book may ring true to personal experiences, for they are not uncommon in the lives of Canadian families. However, I would like to assure the reader that any similarities between the persons and situations described in this book and the personal experiences of the reader are entirely coincidental.

Toward a Disability Paradigm

Canadian society has a history of using the criminal justice system to address the social and mental health issues of youth. The assumptions behind this practice range from the well-meaning to the punitive. One line of reasoning is that youthful offending needs to be nipped in the bud, so young people must be involved with the justice system at an early age to prevent them from becoming hardened criminals. Alternatively, many children are in need of protection and should be involved with the justice system to be kept safe. Finally, some people reason that many youth are in need of mental health treatment, and involvement with the justice system is one way of ensuring that they get it.

These assumptions are based on the child welfare model of youth justice, or the notion of *parens patriae* — the state as parent. In this model, the youth justice system functions as a surrogate parent to wayward youth — especially those who are disconnected from family and other supports. The consequences of relying on criminal sanctioning to respond to the social and mental health issues of youth has led to a new social problem in Canada — the disproportionate representation of youth with intellectual disabilities and other mental health issues who are in the justice system.[1] Many young people who have been caught breaking the law meet the criteria for at least one mental disorder; one in five has a serious one, often coupled with concurrent substance abuse.[2] A large number have histories of victimization and neglect. Many have learning problems, or may even be illiterate. The most common mental disorders seen in young offenders include disruptive behaviour, mood and anxiety disorders, substance abuse and dependence, and cognitive and behavioural disorders related to fetal alcohol spectrum disorders and intellectual and learning disabilities.

9

In an ideal world, the major systems involved with youth in Canada — justice, education, and health — would be united and integrated in addressing the needs of youth who come to the attention of the law. Interventions would be aimed at deficits in the youth and their environment, while at the same time capitalizing on their strengths. The onus would not be on any one system, and the emphasis would not be on any one way of intervening. Minor offenders would be quickly and efficiently diverted from the justice system, while those accused of serious property and violent offences would be sent to specific programming, where the swift interplay of resources would rally around the youth and the family. Few serious offenders would occupy the attention of the youth justice system, and even then, multiple systems would participate in rehabilitation and reintegration.

In the real world, none of the major systems involved with youth in Canada can escape responsibility for perpetuating the neglect of youth with mental disabilities — in the educational system, in the health system, and especially in the justice system. Ignorance and lack of experience leave many people confused about cognitive disabilities. They have difficulty understanding someone else's restricted capabilities when they are not immediately apparent, as a physical disability generally is. Parents worry about the stigma associated with children who have been labelled with a cognitive disability, and are unsure how to advocate for them. But we seriously underestimate the quality of life these youth and their families must endure when their disabilities go largely undiagnosed and no continuous support is available to them.

In May 1998 the federal government announced a new strategy for youth in the justice system, outlining substantial changes to the *Young Offenders Act* of 1984. On April 1, 2003, new sentencing statutes for young offenders came into force, ostensibly ushering in a new era of Canadian youth justice.[3] I recall the days leading up to the enactment of the *Youth Criminal Justice Act* vividly. I was one of a team of psychologists who provided forensic mental health services to youth and their families. For months, we had been planning around the proposed changes and wondering how they might affect our work. We examined the letter of the law and sought counsel about aspects of it that might affect our practices or pose ethical and service delivery challenges for us. We examined our policies and shored up our resources, getting ready for the new era.

We had some substantive questions. Would the new legislation change anything for young offenders with mental disabilities? Would it change anything for youth with complex needs? Would it affect the availability of resources for young offenders with special needs?

We had reason to be concerned. Many of us had been working for years with families whose children did not fit the mould. I had also experienced it personally, raising a child with a disability. Through 20 years of advocacy, I had been a witness to the difficulty of finding appropriate services and support in the community.

A common difficulty for young adults with mental disabilities is finding companionship and engaging in social activities with others in their peer group. Many are economically marginalized, relying on social assistance, and they lack the knowledge and the resources to establish a social life. They make plans with similarly disorganized, socially and cognitively challenged youth, with little money and no reliable means of transportation. Among parents, there is always the fear that they may unwittingly do something antisocial and end up in the hands of the authorities.

The natural protectiveness of parents of these youth poses challenges of its own when adolescent or adult children demonstrate a degree of independence. We must gauge when to grant them freedom and when to rein them in. This leads us to question our role as parents and protectors, their human rights, their quality of life, whether we are doing the right thing in each instance or in our overall approach. Is it an indication of success when a child with a disability does not come into contact with the justice system? Perhaps it is an indicator that we are on the right track, given the high rate of young adults with cognitive disabilities in the correctional system. But our goals are much broader. Shouldn't they be? All parents wish for more than a marginalized existence for their children, a reasonable quality of life — certainly more than just keeping them out of jail.

It is not unreasonable to expect that a youth justice system should take account of a young person's level of maturity, provide appropriate support and assistance, and conduct its activities using developmentally appropriate procedures. Unfortunately, the system does not always recognize that a 12-year-old requires a different response than a 17-year-old. There is no set of principles that automatically comes into play. Someone — a parent, a social worker, or other advocate — must alert the system to these individual differences. And navigating the system once you're inside requires a set of sophisticated skills on the part of the young offender, the family, and others involved in the young person's life.

The system does not automatically recognize when a young person is suffering from a mental disability, either. Mental disabilities and illnesses tend to amplify normal tendencies in any developmental period, and people with intellectual disabilities have much greater difficulty than others in navigating the court system. Many are unnerved by unfamiliar situations. They are vulnerable to unrealistic thinking and anxiety. Some have social histories that include various forms of abuse. They may have strong emotional reactions to authority figures, and overreact to attempts to calm them. They often have difficulty understanding or remembering rules, or they may know the rules but not have the capacity to act on them. Some have difficulty comprehending what is expected of them, and continually fail to meet the expectations of their parents, teachers, and others.[4]

The dilemma facing the justice system is that the biological, social, and psychological characteristics associated with mental disabilities are directly and demonstrably related to the patterns of behaviour that place young people at risk to come into conflict with the law. Many young offenders I see in my practice present with stressful or traumatic life experiences, as well as unhealthy lifestyles that place them in danger of breaking the law and developing more serious mental health issues. When caught committing an offence, they are at the nexus between the justice, health, and education systems, and society is some distance away from coherent and ethical policies and practices in dealing with them. They pose a conundrum: on the one hand, we want to single them out for differential treatment; on the other hand, we fear that doing so may bias the system against them.[5]

There is a profound lack of understanding in Canadian society of the interplay between physical and mental health, between victimization experiences and mental health, and how mental disabilities can impair a youth's functioning. There are even those in the professional community who suggest that issues such as fetal alcohol syndrome, attention deficit hyperactivity disorder, and learning disabilities have no bearing on how youth should be treated in society or by the justice system. Masked as a plea to treat all with equal fairness, it is in fact an insidious form of discrimination against youth with mental disabilities, and it is rarely challenged. Unless we confront the mythologies surrounding mental disabilities and the actual as well as the anticipated stigmatization of afflicted youth, these young people will continue to be mistreated, misunderstood, and misrepresented.

Much youthful offending can be understood by grasping the nature of mental disabilities and how they affect the functional capacities of an individual. To advocate effectively for youth with diminished capacities, we need to adopt a disability paradigm. This will allow us, first, to satisfy the normal human urge to understand the cause of behaviours that puzzle or disturb us. Knowing that a particular youth meets the criteria for attention deficit hyperactivity disorder, for example, or a learning disability, helps us conceptualize the nature of the youth's difficulties, and can also assist in securing resources.

But diagnosis is only part of the paradigm; understanding the functional implications of the diagnosis is the other. Framing the youth's behaviour in terms of a disability will help parents and professionals alike determine the amount of control a youth has over his or her symptoms, and will help adults gauge appropriate expectations. This will lead, in turn, to anticipating problems and relapses.

A disability paradigm will also help people cope with the negative consequences of a youth's behaviour, providing metaphors and explanations about why a youth is having difficulties and resolving many of the issues of self-blame or failure experienced by parents and professionals working with troubled adolescents. When we know that inappropriate or noncompliant behaviour stems from more than mere wilful disobedience, we can to some extent rule out the view that the child is "bad" or has a "character defect."

A disability paradigm will help us reframe our perceptions, expectations, and responses. We will be able to shift our focus from intentionality to immaturity and diminished competencies. It is easy, when dealing with a noncompliant young person, to assume that their behaviour is deliberate and intentional. It is less easy to understand and take into account the many factors — physiological, intellectual, societal, historical, environmental — that may be affecting the young person's behaviour. But as our experience grows, we will become more skilled at discerning when a youth is trying to perform well but cannot.

Youth, too, will benefit from a disability paradigm. Identifying why they may be having difficulty with one or another behaviour doesn't mean they have no control at all. It does not relieve them of personal responsibility for their behaviour, but it does convey the message that others share that responsibility.

The challenges faced both by the system and by youth with mental disabilities can be further mitigated by a better understanding of developmental issues unique to the adolescent period, and a better understanding of the impact of cognitive, behavioural, and emotional disabilities in some youth who are in conflict with the law. Thus, both a disability paradigm and a developmental perspective are necessary for understanding the problems facing young offenders.[6]

The literature points clearly to the need for clearer and better research into the relevance of mental health and mental disabilities to the youth justice system.[7] There is international consensus that the identification of youth with disabilities within the justice system is relevant at virtually all stages of processing[8] — at the earliest stages when police and other adults are determining whether extrajudicial or judicial measures should proceed; when determining the direction for investigations and case strategies for justice workers; when explaining behaviour in a way that facilitates constructive interventions; when developing programs that meet the youth's rehabilitative, educational, and mental health needs; and when encouraging youth to reach their potential by protecting their educational rights and giving them the tools they need for a successful life. It can also help reduce delinquent behaviour in the community, identifying youth who are in need of services and then providing them.

A key concept in the developmental perspective is understanding the expectations adults should have for youth at different levels of maturity. Because we often remember our own adolescence in terms of emotions and processes rather than as a logical series of discrete, easily definable events, we tend to have a poor understanding of the developmental needs of adolescents, and our expectations create confusion about maturity. When are children mature enough to drive, purchase alcohol and tobacco, enter into contracts, provide consent for treatment, consent to sexual activity, collect welfare independent of their parents, be employed, apply for vocational programs, or have their own cell phone or credit card? Canadian provinces differ in the ages at which certain privileges are given, and even within jurisdictions there are contradictions.

When do children become adolescents, and when do adolescents become adults? The *Youth Criminal Justice Act* arbitrarily defines 12 to 18 years as the time frame for adolescence. When youth in Canada break the law and they are 12 years old or older, we can charge them. But most people would acknowledge that 12-year-olds are more like children than adolescents, and that many 19-year-olds are more like adolescents than adults.

Adolescence is a unique period in human development, fundamentally different from both childhood and adulthood. It is manifested as a gradual period of transition, a process of "soft" events with fuzzy boundaries. It is impossible to define its onset or its ending. Moreover, studies reveal that the timing of various transitions among adolescents may vary with health, social and cultural expectations, and economic conditions. Heredity, psychological trauma, diseases and infections, nutrition, exercise, learning experiences, and numerous other factors can affect the onset and timing of the various physiological, intellectual, emotional, psychological, and social processes that overtake youth as they grow up. While it is expected that people aged 12 to 18 are more mature than children, they are still less mature than normally functioning adults, and they are fundamentally different from adults in their issues and needs.

Given the differences in maturity among individuals, it is important that the justice system pay attention to the capacities of young offenders as they navigate the justice system. To be truly just, the youth justice system must be truly separate from any other, and it must ensure that youth and their families are able to participate in all aspects of the process.

I believe the justice system has the capacity to respond to these youth, and I know that many people working in the system hold the same belief. It is my hope that this book will provide professionals, students, and other people who are interested in the youth justice system with a better understanding of the challenges we face in navigating our way through the system that deals with young offenders in our society, particularly those with mental disabilities. The discussion bridges a number of disciplines, including adolescent psychology, developmental criminology, forensic mental health, and the law, for a multidisciplinary perspective is essential in developing approaches to youth justice. But I am not a lawyer. The book is not intended to provide legal authority or legal direction, but to provide understanding and guidance as to the special needs of young offenders based on their development, mental and physical capabilities, and cognitive functioning. The book also outlines practical, theoretical, and conceptual tools, based on clinical experience, to aid professionals in their dealings with young offenders and their families.

CHAPTER ONE

The Tip of the Iceberg

But criminal law is not the only means of bolstering values. Nor is it necessarily always the best means. The fact is, criminal law is a blunt and costly instrument — blunt because it cannot have the human sensitivity of institutions like the family, the school, the church or the community, and costly since it imposes suffering, loss of liberty, and great expense.

— Law Reform Commission of Canada
Our Criminal Law

When Canadians 12 years old and older violate the *Criminal Code of Canada*[1] (the *Code*) and other statutes, they may face criminal charges. All substantive criminal law applies to youth as well as adults, but the *Youth Criminal Justice Act*[2] (YCJA) essentially replaces for youth the sentencing provisions provided for in the *Code*. According to section 140 of the YCJA, "Except to the extent that it is inconsistent with or excluded by this *Act*, the provisions of the *Criminal Code* apply, with any modification that the circumstances require, in respect of offences alleged to have been committed by young persons."

The relationship between youth justice legislation and the *Code* is complex, and capturing the essence of the key provisions of the YCJA is a particular challenge for non-legal professionals. Judges play a central role in shaping the law, and the law governs their deliberations. At the same time, their decisions can change the law. When a decision is challenged, an appeal is launched. If a higher court finds the original trial judge to have been in error, a precedent is set. Cases and laws can be challenged all the way to the Supreme Court of Canada. Case law accumulates, and Parliament amends the *Criminal Code* on an ongoing basis. Tracking the changing laws of an evolving justice system can be a formidable task.

The *Code* According to the *YCJA*

The nature of the relationship between the *Youth Criminal Justice Act* and the *Criminal Code of Canada* is apparent in several recent cases. In *R. v. R. C.*[3], for example, the Supreme Court ruled that the *Code* must be interpreted using the principles set out in the YCJA. The appeal was based on whether a trial judge had erred in declining to order a DNA test on a youth who had been found guilty of a primary designated offence[4] as defined in the *Code*:

> The 13-year-old accused had stabbed his mother in the foot with a pen after she dumped dirty laundry on him during an argument about getting out of bed and going to school. He later struck her in the face with his fist and kept swinging until his uncle intervened. He pleaded guilty to assault with a weapon and breach of an undertaking. Assault with a weapon is a primary designated offence. Pursuant to s. 487.051(1)(a) of the *Code*, a court is required to authorize the taking of DNA samples from an accused convicted of a primary designated offence unless it is satisfied under s. 487.051(2) that the accused has established that the impact of the order on his privacy and security interests "would be grossly disproportionate to the public interest in the protection of society and the proper administration of justice." The trial judge applied the exception and declined to issue a DNA order. The Court of Appeal reversed this judgement and directed that a DNA order be issued.[5]

The Supreme Court overturned the appeal and restored the original decision on the grounds that the "taking and retention of a DNA sample is not a trivial matter and, absent a compelling public interest, would inherently constitute a grave intrusion on a person's right to personal and informational privacy"[6]:

> . . . While no specific provision of either *Act* modifies s. 487.051(1)(a) or (2) of the *Code*, it is clear that Parliament intended their shared principles to be respected whenever young persons are brought within the Canadian system of criminal justice. . . . In particular, Parliament has taken care to ensure that the consequences of conviction for young persons are imposed in a manner that advances the objectives of youth criminal justice legislation. This legislative policy is apparent in both Acts. To disregard it is to frustrate Parliament's will.[7]

R. v. C. D.[8] involved two Alberta youths. The first had pleaded guilty to possession of a weapon, arson, and breach of a recognizance. The second had pleaded guilty to dangerous driving, possession of stolen property, and theft under $5,000.

Both youths were sentenced to deferred custody and supervision — a new non-custodial sentence under the YCJA, which can, however, result in custody upon breach of community supervision. The sentence was appealed on the grounds that s. 39 (1)(a) of the YCJA, "A youth justice court shall not commit a young person to custody" unless "the young person has committed a violent offence." On appeal, the higher court upheld the sentences, ruling that, in each case, the offences were violent within the meaning of the YCJA: an action is violent if it causes bodily harm, is intended to cause bodily harm, or if it is reasonably foreseeable that it may cause bodily harm. An appeal was launched on both decisions on the grounds that none of the charges could be considered violent offences for the purpose of imposing custodial sentences on youth. The Supreme Court allowed the appeals, finding that both the original trial judge and the Court of Appeal had overextended the definition of "violent offence":

> Although the definition of "serious violent offence" is relatively straightforward, even if a young person's actions would appear to satisfy it — i.e., even if a young person causes or attempts to cause serious bodily harm in the course of committing an offence — it does not automatically follow that he or she has committed a "serious violent offence" . . . and the youth justice court to which the application is made is required to hold a hearing before it makes its decision. . . . Much is involved in deciding whether an offence is a "serious violent offence" because the consequences of such a designation are quite severe.[9]

These decisions illustrate the interdependency of legal interpretations of the *Criminal Code* and the *Youth Criminal Justice Act* in proceedings against youth.

Mental Disorder Provisions

The *Criminal Code* contains provisions to determine whether a person is unfit to stand trial (UST) or not criminally responsible on account of a mental disorder (NCR). By virtue of s. 141 of the YCJA, these apply to proceedings under the YCJA. A court may order an assessment of a person's mental condition if it needs to determine whether the accused is unfit to stand trial, was suffering from a mental disorder at the time of the offence, or was suffering mental instability at the time of the offence (*Code* s. 672.11). The court may also require an assessment to determine the appropriate disposition to be made where a verdict of not criminally responsible or unfit to stand trial has been rendered, or whether an order should be made to detain the accused in a treatment facility, if convicted (*Code* s. 672.11).

The *Youth Criminal Justice Act* provides a broader authority than did the *Young Offenders Act*[10] both in ordering assessments and in determining the qualifications of a person who may be called on to provide them. According to the YCJA (s. 34(1)), "A youth justice court may, at any stage of proceedings against a young person, by order require that the young person be assessed by a qualified person who is required to report the results in writing to the court," provided there are reasonable grounds to believe that the young person may be suffering from a physical or mental illness or disorder, a psychological disorder, an emotional disturbance, a learning disability or a mental disability, and the consent of the accused and the prosecutor has been obtained. Assessments may be done by a medical doctor, psychiatrist, psychologist or whoever is designated by the lieutenant governor in council of a province as qualified to provide them (s. 34(14)).

Section 16 of the *Criminal Code* defines the legal test for criminal responsibility:

(1) No person is criminally responsible for an act committed or an omission made while suffering from a mental disorder that rendered the person incapable of appreciating the nature and quality of the act or omission, or of knowing that it was wrong.

(2) Every person is presumed to not suffer from a mental disorder so as to be exempt from criminal responsibility by virtue of subsection (1), until the contrary is proved on the balance of probabilities.

(3) The burden of proof that an accused was suffering from a mental disorder so as to be exempt from criminal responsibility is on the party that raises the issue.

Not criminally responsible on account of a mental disorder is, according to s. 672.1 of the *Code*, "a verdict that the accused committed the act or made the omission that formed the basis of the offence with which the accused is charged but is not criminally responsible on account of a mental disorder."

There are two sections of the *Code* that are relevant to fitness issues. Section 606(1) provides procedural protections that should apply to matters that are set for plea in youth court. The court may accept a "plea of guilty only if it is satisfied that the accused (a) is making the plea voluntarily; and (b) understands (i) that the plea is an admission of the essential elements of the offence, (ii) the nature and consequences of the plea, and (iii) that the court is not bound by any agreement made between the accused and the prosecutor." (s. 606 (1.1)) The onus would be on the defence or the judge to raise questions of fitness to plead.

Section 2 of the *Code* deals specifically with the legal test for unfit to stand trial (UST). UST means "unable on account of mental disorder to conduct a defence at any stage of the proceedings before a verdict is rendered or to instruct counsel to do so, and, in particular, unable on account of a mental disorder to: (a) understand the nature or object of proceedings, (b) understand possible consequences of proceedings, or (c) communicate with counsel."

If, on assessment, the accused is found fit to stand trial, the proceedings continue as if the issue had not arisen (*Code* s. 672.28). If the accused is found unfit to stand trial, the proceedings are set aside, and an inquiry must be held every two years until the accused is either acquitted or found fit to stand trial; the Crown must establish a *prima facie* case every two years (*Code* s. 672.33). For young persons, however, such an inquiry must be held every year (*YCJA* s. 141(10)).

Substantive changes to the mental disorder provisions of the *Code* (Part XX.1) have resulted in significant changes to determinations of NCR and UST. The changes came about as a result of the Supreme Court's 2004 decision in *R. v. Demers*,[11] which found that sections 672.33, 672.54, and 672.81(1) of the *Code* infringed the *Canadian Charter of Rights and Freedoms*. Section 7 of the *Charter* provides that "everyone has the right to life, liberty and security of the person and the right not to be deprived thereof except in accordance with the principles of fundamental justice."

In *R. v. Demers*, an appeal was launched on behalf of the accused, an intellectually handicapped adult who was found unfit to stand trial on charges of sexual assault and had remained in the review board process for six years.[12] According to the *Code*, an accused person who has been found unfit to stand trial remains in the system until he or she either becomes fit to stand trial or the Crown fails to establish a *prima facie* case. In finding these sections invalid, the Supreme Court of Canada said ". . . [the Criminal Code] fails to deal fairly with the permanently unfit accused who are not a significant threat to public safety. Society's interest in bringing accused persons to trial cannot be accomplished, nor can society's interest in treating the accused fairly. The regime fails to provide for an end to the prosecution."[13]

The Court gave the federal government until June 30, 2005 to amend the mental disorder provisions of the *Code* with respect to the alternatives provided for persons judged unfit to stand trial or not criminally responsible. In response, Bill C-10 was passed in the House of Commons in February 2005 and was given royal assent in May of that year. While not all the amendments are in force as of the writing of this book, those that are have resulted in significant changes for those found unfit to stand trial or not criminally responsible.

To appreciate the significance of *R. v. Demers*, it is useful to examine two cases that have subsequently grappled with these issues.

R. v. D. (W. A. L.) (1)[14] involved two youths, twins, who had been found unfit to stand trial. Two years later, they were found still unfit. Then 17 years old, they had each been diagnosed with fetal alcohol spectrum disorders (FASD) at six months. "They are not likely to be found fit to stand trial in the foreseeable future," wrote the trial judge, Sheila Whelan. "They have acquired secondary disabilities and have been charged with numerous criminal offences for which they have appeared before the Youth Justice Court on an ongoing basis for over four years."[15]

On determining them once again unfit to stand trial, Judge Whelan addressed the issue of what the court should do with respect to restorability issues — whether or not the twins could be restored to fitness. Eventually they were given a discharge for one year, with conditions which took into consideration the need to protect the public, the mental condition of the accused, and their reintegration into society. As Judge Whelan noted, "Part of the difficulty preventing effective planning" for the youths in question "lay in a failure to understand the impact of FASD on their functioning and their status in the justice system as persons who have been found unfit to stand trial."[16] Judge Whelan clearly set out the difficulty experienced in discerning who is responsible for supervision and treatment of these youths. Youth who are found to be permanently unfit to stand trial, whether because of FASD or another cause, clearly require a multisystemic intervention and long-term supports in the community.

R. v. B. (D.)[17] also involved a youth with FASD and significant cognitive impairment. The youth's Section 7 rights were involved because he stood charged with a criminal offence, though he was found unfit to stand trial and would never become fit. His status in the system, which Judge Mary Ellen Turpel-Lafond described as a "legal limbo," placed both his liberty and his security in jeopardy. Technically, the youth could remain under the review board indefinitely. In this respect, Judge Turpel-Lafond wrote, he "receives different treatment in comparison to others in the regime because he does not join the mainstream of mental disordered persons who can be treated, become fit, and stand trial. Neither is he a dangerous person or a risk to public safety."[18]

In reference to the Crown's having to present a *prima facie* case against the accused every two years (the charges were laid before the enactment of the *YCJA* which made this a requirement every year), Judge Turpel-Lafond noted that "the threshold for such a case is low, even lower than the standard required at the preliminary inquiry stage of a criminal trial process. Evidence can be submitted by way of affidavit or admitted as hearsay by necessity. Hence, the possibility of these matters disappearing is remote. . . ."[19]

Judge Turpel-Lafond noted that the case

raises the principles of fundamental justice in relation to the requirement of reasonably clear laws. In this regard, the jurisprudence has accepted that overbreadth and vagueness in criminal law will offend principles of fundamental justice. A criminal law can be unconstitutionally vague if it does not set an intelligible standard for its citizens and officials who must enforce it. The obverse of vagueness is overbreadth. Overbroad law in the court realm arises when a law is so broad that it catches a class of persons or conduct which should not be captured within its ambit, based on the purposes of such laws.[20]

In her decision, Judge Turpel-Lafond followed R. v. *Demers* and ordered that the youth found permanently unfit to stand trial in this case and no danger to society should be given an absolute discharge, a disposition that had previously applied only to persons who were found not criminally responsible on account of a mental disability.

As the Supreme Court ruled in R. v. *Demers*:

> Insofar as the aim of Part XX.1 is concerned with the treatment and supervision of *temporarily* unfit accused and the protection of the public during the accused's limited period of unfitness, its ultimate aim is to try the accused once he or she becomes fit. . . . Under the existing scheme, an accused who is *permanently* unfit will forever be within the grip of the state's machinery for criminal justice. . . . His or her continued detention or conditional liberty cannot be justified by progress toward a trial."[21]

The Supreme Court, however, did not recommend an absolute discharge for persons found permanently unfit to stand trial. It recommended "a stay should be granted to permanently unfit accused who do not pose a significant threat to the safety of the public, in order to prevent their indefinite subjection to criminal proceedings. In deciding whether or not to grant a stay, courts will have to consider such factors as the nature of the accusation, the time since the offence, later conduct, initial and current medical evaluations, whether the accused is taking medication required to eliminate the risk, as well as all other relevant information and circumstances of the accused."[22]

The resulting amendments to the Code (s. 672.54), which apply to youthful offenders as well as adults, enable a Court or Review Board to order (1) an absolute discharge for cases with a verdict of NCR; (2) a conditional discharge for an accused found either UST or NCR; or (3) commitment to an institution for either UST or NCR. Pursuant to s. 672.851, a Court may grant a stay of proceedings for the permanently unfit.

Key Aspects of Youth Justice Legislation

The Preamble to the *Youth Criminal Justice Act* provides a philosophical orientation for the *Act* itself. Recognizing that Canada is a party to the *United Nations Convention on the Rights of the Child*, and that youth are guaranteed certain rights and freedoms under the *Charter* and the *Bill of Rights*, it states, in part:

- members of society share a responsibility to address the developmental challenges and the needs of young persons and to guide them into adulthood;

- communities, families, parents and others concerned with the development of young persons should, through multi-disciplinary approaches, take reasonable steps to prevent youth crime by addressing its underlying causes to respond to the needs of young persons, and to provide guidance and support to those at risk of committing crimes;
- Canadian society should have a youth criminal justice system than commands respect, takes into account the interests of victims, fosters responsibility and ensures accountability through meaningful consequences and effective rehabilitation and reintegration, and that reserves its most serious interventions for the most serious crimes and reduces the over-reliance on incarceration for non-violent young persons.

The Preamble provides a strong message of restraint,[23] and foreshadows some of the key themes of the YCJA. The message of restraint was important to legislators in part because of the May 2001 *Report to the Department of Justice Canada* prepared by Dr. Anthony Doob. Based on a survey of youth court judges across Canada, Doob concluded that "one of the major concerns about the operation of the youth justice system . . . was the view that there were too many cases coming to youth court in Canada that could better be dealt with outside of the formal court system. . . ."[24]

Significantly, the Preamble states that youth crime is not simply a matter of law, but concerns the entire community. In fact, as the YCJA states in s. 4(a), "extrajudicial measures are often the most appropriate and effective way to address youth crime," and should be designed to:

(a) provide an effective and timely response to offending behaviour outside the bounds of judicial measures;
(b) encourage young persons to acknowledge and repair the harm caused to the victim and the community;
(c) encourage families of young persons — including extended families where appropriate — and the community to become involved in the design and implementation of those measures;
(d) provide an opportunity for victims to participate in decisions related to the measures and to receive reparation; and
(e) respect the rights and freedoms of young persons and be proportionate to the seriousness of the offence. (s. 5)

The message of the *Youth Criminal Justice Act* is that out-of-court responses are the expected way of dealing with less serious offences. As one observer remarked, "This is not a matter of leniency in the exercise of discretion or giving the young person 'a break'." Parliament has said that this is simply the appropriate action to take under the Act."[25]

Of course, there have been differences among provinces in how these out-of-court measures are to be conceived and applied. Concerns that the YCJA would intervene unnecessarily in some jurisdictions that had established protocols for diverting youth from the courts weighed against the likelihood that over-reliance on the courts in other jurisdictions could not be effectively abated without a legislated mandate to do so. The fact remains, extrajudicial measures are not optional or discretionary. Section 6(1) of the YCJA requires police officers to consider first such measures as warnings, cautions, and referrals before initiating any judicial proceedings.

There are two forms of extrajudicial measures. The first involves police interventions such as those mentioned above, while the second (s. 10) involves extrajudicial sanctions if warnings, cautions, or referrals are not appropriate. These might include victim/offender mediation, family or group conferencing, restitution, and community service. As under the former legislation, extrajudicial sanctions may be considered only for youth who commit non-violent offences. However, under the YCJA, youth with a prior criminal record or record of extrajudicial measures may still be eligible for extrajudicial sanctions.

The Preamble underscores the interdependence of the youth justice system and the Canadian *Constitution*, reminding us that youth who break the law are vulnerable by virtue of their status as young persons. Actions against them will inevitably come under the scrutiny of the advocacy system, and laws dealing with them will be tested against the *Constitution*.

The Preamble sets the stage for the Declaration of Principle, which defines the intent and purpose of the youth criminal justice system. It is intended, first, to "prevent crime by addressing the circumstances underlying a young person's offending behaviour"; second, to "rehabilitate young persons who commit offences and reintegrate them into society"; and third, to "ensure that a young person is subject to meaningful consequences for his or her offence."

The Declaration of Principle affirms that the youth criminal justice system must be separate from that for adults, and reiterates the principle that special considerations apply when the system decides to proceed against a young person. Respect for societal values and reparation to victims and the community are emphasized, as are the rights of the accused, including "the right to be heard in the course of and to participate in the processes . . . that lead to decisions that affect them." The rights and obligations of the parents and the extended family of the accused are also emphasized "within the limits of fair and proportionate accountability." Whereas the Preamble provides the mission statement underlying the *Youth Criminal Justice Act*, the Declaration of Principle provides the interpretive guide for legislation, particularly in regard to sentencing. The YCJA requires, for example, that every custodial sentence must be followed by a period of supervision in the community; release of the youth after two-thirds of the sentence has been served in custody is mandatory. The last third of the sentence is to be served in the community, unless the youth presents a risk of committing a serious violent offence.

The sentencing provisions (Part 4 of the YCJA) are consistent with the Declaration of Principle in that they appear to strive for a balance between accountability, proportionality, rehabilitation, and reintegration (s. 38(2)). They are structured around four major themes: (1) sentences shall be proportionate to the seriousness of the offence as well as the degree of the responsibility that the young person had in committing the offence; (2) sanctions should not be more severe than those for adults convicted of a similar offence; (3) sanctions other than custody should be exhausted before considering a custodial sanction; and (4) parity of sentencing within regions should be encouraged.

Section 38(3) provides that the mitigating factors the judge should take into account include the youth's degree of participation in the offence, the harm done by the offence and whether it was intentional or reasonably foreseeable, the amount of time in detainment prior to conviction, and the youth's previous convictions, if any. Section 39(9) of the YCJA requires judges to provide reasons for a custodial sentence. Sentencing must consider the "least restrictive" alternative in determining a fair and proportionate sentence, and judges must consider all other options before sentencing a youth to confinement or imprisonment. Custodial sentences should be reserved for the most serious or repeated violent offences, and the judge should not "use custody as a substitute for appropriate child protection, mental health, or other social measures" (s. 39(5)). The YCJA also lists guidelines for determining the availability of a responsible person to provide care for the youth, and provides the court with jurisdiction to remove or place the youth in the care of a responsible person (s.31). A judge can refer the youth for child welfare assessment at any time during the proceedings (s. 35).

Judges must examine the particular circumstances of the accused, including his or her status as an Aboriginal youth and other factors that may indicate the need for special considerations or requirements.[26] Sentencing options for offences other than presumptive offences are also subject to jurisdictional decisions about whether they will be offered.[27] They include a number of new alternatives to custody that are consistent with Parliament's intent to reduce the system's unfortunate reliance on incarceration for non-violent offenders. Non-custodial sentences range from a reprimand by the judge to intensive support and supervision order, to deferred custody and supervision (s. 42(2)).

Probation is the cornerstone of sentencing in the *Youth Criminal Justice Act*. The conditions specified in a supervision order govern the behaviour of the youth being supervised in the community. Conditions for a sentencing order include mandatory conditions (i.e., keeping the peace and being of good behaviour; appearing before the court when required), and one or more of the following (summarized from s. 55(2)):

1. reporting requirements;
2. notification of change of address, employment, education, or training;
3. remaining within a territorial jurisdiction;
4. efforts to obtain and maintain employment;
5. attending school, training, or recreation programs;
6. specifying with whom the youth should reside;
7. specifying the youth's place of residence;
8. compliance with additional conditions to support a case plan; and
9. prohibition against weapons, ammunition, and explosives.

The aim is to find the conditions that are most likely to rehabilitate the youth and reintegrate him or her into the community. In relation to the *Young Offenders Act*, the *Youth Criminal Justice Act* includes no substantive changes to the issue of breaches of probation (s. 102); however, there are extensive guidelines on custody and supervision. Neither did maximum sentences change under the YCJA. A youth still cannot receive a probation period of more than two years for a single offence (s.42(2)(k)), and if the youth is convicted of more than one offence at different times, s. 42(15) provides "the continuous combined duration of those youth sentences shall not exceed three years, except if one of the offences is first-degree murder or second-degree murder." The continuous combined sentence for first-degree murder may not exceed ten years; for second-degree murder, it may not exceed seven years.

The mandate of youth custody or supervision is essentially twofold (Part 5 of the YCJA): the protection of society and the reintegration of the youth into the community. Custody and supervision are both aimed at providing safe, fair, and humane supervision of young offenders, with an emphasis on providing access to appropriate programs to encourage rehabilitation and reintegration. In sentencing a young offender, the courts are mandated to impose the least restrictive measures appropriate, to recognize that youth in custody have the same rights as other young people, to involve the family and other relevant parties as much as possible, to ensure that all decisions are transparent to the parties involved and are made in a fair and timely manner, and to ensure that youth serving an adult sentence in an adult facility are held separate and apart from adult detainees.

Again in relation to the *Young Offenders Act*, there are no changes in the levels of custody under the YCJA — there is open and closed custody — but the YCJA offers substantial assistance to decision-makers regarding the principles for determining custody, affirming that "the level of custody should allow the best possible match of programs to the young person's needs and behaviour." Additional factors in determining custodial dispositions include the seriousness of the offence, the needs and circumstances of the accused, and the safety of other persons in custody. In addition, custodial sentences should serve the interests of society, and should consider the likelihood that the youth will escape from the facility.

The review process (s. 87) for young persons who are already serving sentences is based on principles that potentially provide procedural safeguards for the youth. For example, a youth can apply for a review in cases where he or she feels the level of custody or restraint is not appropriate, and the review cannot result in an increase in the degree of restraint. Sentences not involving custody can also be amended to reflect changing circumstances; the order can be confirmed, revoked, or varied, but the review process should not result in variations of the original order that are more "onerous than the order being reviewed" (s. 52(3)(4)).

Reintegration leaves (s. 91) — which allow a youth to leave a custodial facility for a period no longer than 30 days for compassionate or medical reasons, or reasons consistent with his or her case plan — also allow for some flexibility. Applications for specific days and hours, for example, allow young persons in custody to attend school, keep appointments, or take advantage of training or employment opportunities.

One of the more dramatic additions to youth justice legislation that came into force[28] with the *Youth Criminal Justice Act* is the Intensive Rehabilitative Custody and Supervision order (IRCS) (s. 42(7)). Essentially, an IRCS order is a treatment sentence for serious violent offenders who have a mental disorder. It can potentially apply to youth who have been found guilty of a presumptive offence. It is available if the following criteria are met: the youth has committed a presumptive offence and other serious violent offences; the offender has a mental illness or disorder, psychological disorder, or an emotional disturbance; the youth has a plan of treatment and intensive supervision; and the provincial director[29] agrees with the recommended plan. This provision sets a precedent, affirming the importance of the youth justice system in mandating adequate supervision and rehabilitation programs for youth who commit serious offences.

A key concern about IRCS will be determining who is eligible for this sentence. Many youth are potentially excluded from the IRCS provisions based on how mental disorder will be defined. Will young people with Fetal Alcohol Spectrum Disorders (e.g., pFAS), or disruptive behaviour disorders (e.g., ADHD) be eligible? There are substantial impediments in the legal process to a youth actually receiving this sentence, and the provision may rarely, in fact, be used. The resources that must be concentrated on the few youth who meet the criteria must be considered. Will allowing broader access to this option result in more stable and accessible services for offenders who have mental disabilities? Will it promote the development of more stable and accessible services in the community for serious offenders who have mental disabilities? How will the youth's amenability to treatment be assessed? And once the youth is deemed amenable to treatment, what will the treatment entail? Will the youth consent to it? If so, what will be the nature of that consent? Can the youth's consent be truly voluntary under such circumstances?

Conferences

Conferences can be a key factor in making decisions regarding appropriate measures for youth and ongoing support and planning. Under s. 19 of the *YCJA*, "a youth justice court judge, the provincial director, a police officer, a justice of the peace, a prosecutor, or a youth worker may convene or cause to be convened a conference for the purpose of making a decision required to be made under this Act." A conference's mandate is, among other things, to "give advice on extrajudicial measures, conditions for judicial interim release," and "sentence, including the review of sentences, and reintegration plans." Further, "the Attorney General or any other minister designated by the lieutenant governor in council of a province may establish rules for the convening and conducting of conferences."

Conferences were sanctioned under the *Young Offenders Act*, but statutes neither defined nor explained their function, so they were not consistent, and their success or failure often depended on the advocacy of the people involved with the accused. Under the *YCJA*, conferences provide social workers and mental health professionals with a vital tool in their advocacy for young offenders, enabling them to contribute to pre-trial and sentencing decisions. The developmental needs and risk factors associated with a young person's previous and possible future offences can be examined in a conference setting, as well as issues related to self-harm, risk management in the community, conditions of probation or release, and treatment or rehabilitation.

Conferences can provide support to families, ensuring that appropriate generational boundaries are respected and reinforced. They also provide an opportunity for youth to observe the conduct of the adults in their lives, and are therefore encouraged to behave maturely and to participate in a process of mature problem solving. Conferences can also provide a means of increasing community, victim, and stakeholder involvement in the delivery of youth justice. They can be used for giving advice on extrajudicial measures, conditions of bail, sentencing, reviews, and reintegration plans.

Court-Ordered Reports

Assessments provided by mental health professionals can help explain a youth's behaviour in a way that facilitates a constructive understanding of the accused and the implications for intervention. They may also address legal issues such as fitness to stand trial or not criminally responsible.

There are four types of reports that may be used by the court that call on the expertise of social workers and other mental health professionals: medical, psychological, child welfare, and pre-sentence reports. Medical (including psychiatric) and psychological reports may be ordered under section 34 of the *YCJA* at any time during the judicial process, and section 35 provides that a judge may "at any stage of proceedings against a young person, refer the young person to a child welfare agency for assessment to determine whether the young person is in need of child welfare services." This provision alerts the court to the nature of child welfare issues, and encourages the notion that identified problems should be dealt with, where appropriate, by systems other than the justice system. Section 40 of the YCJA provides an outline for the content areas a pre-sentence report should cover. Reviews (s.94) or applications for continuation of custody sentences (s. 98) may also require an update to a pre-sentence report to assist with decision-making.

Adult Sentences for Young Offenders

The types of offences that could result in a young person being considered for an adult sentence under the *Youth Criminal Justice Act* has been broadened from murder, attempted murder, manslaughter, and aggravated sexual offences listed in the *Young Offenders Act* to include patterns of serious, repeat violent offences. The definition of "presumptive offence" is the key to the youth's liability for an adult sentence. Under the YCJA, the Crown can apply for access to adult sentences when a person over the age of 14 but not older than 16 has committed a presumptive offence. (Provinces have the discretion to set the age at 14 years or higher, but not higher than 16) (s. 61).

Two criticisms of the *Young Offenders Act* involved the long transfer hearings prior to the youth's trial and the absence of clear procedural protections for youth during these hearings and the subsequent trial in adult court.[30] Another objection was that the youth could potentially be "raised to adult court" before he or she had been found guilty of an offence in youth court. Under the YCJA, youth can only be liable to an adult sentence after they have been found guilty of the offence. The provisions for youth who stand charged with a presumptive offence are complicated and are set out in ss. 61 to 81. The Crown, the Attorney General, Defence counsel, or youth themselves, upon their own election, can apply for an adult sentence (s. 67(2)).

The proceedings can all occur within youth court. If an adult sentence is considered for a young offender, a placement hearing (s. 76) is held to determine where the youth will serve the sentence — a youth facility, a provincial correctional centre, or a federal penitentiary — based in part on the length of the sentence and age of the accused at the time of sentencing. If the offender is under 18 at the time of sentencing it is presumed that the sentence will be served in a youth facility.

Constitutionality of the *YCJA*

When the *Youth Criminal Justice Act* came into force in April 2003, the Attorney General of Quebec challenged the constitutionality of numerous provisions of the YCJA in the Quebec Court of Appeal. Although *Quebec (Minister of Justice)* v. *Canada (Minister of Justice*[31]*)* — hereafter, *Que. v. Can.* — dealt with a number of aspects of the YCJA, this discussion will focus on the constitutionality of the Declaration of Principle, the constitutionality of the presumption of adult sentences for certain offences, and the constitutionality of a presumptive rule that the identity of young persons could be revealed when charged with presumptive offences.

The Attorney General of Quebec claimed that, in the YCJA, proportionality trumped all other principles of sentencing and potentially undermined the others. As a signatory to the *International Convention on the Rights of the Child* and the *International Covenant on Civil and Political Rights*, it was argued, Parliament was ignoring its treaty obligations and infringing the rights of youth as enshrined in the *Canadian Charter of Rights and Freedoms*. The Court did not agree.[32] Neither did it support the challenge that the Declaration of Principle of the YCJA was unconstitutional, ruling that the inclusion of proportionality in the YCJA as a sentencing principle did not create grounds for discrimination, for it does not override the general principles set out in sections 3 and 4 of the YCJA, which focus on rehabilitation and reintegration into the community.

A substantive change under the YCJA is the imposition of an adult sentence for presumptive offences and a broadened definition of what constitutes a presumptive offence. The Attorney General of Quebec asked the Court of Appeal if the presumption of an adult sentence for particular offences infringed Section 7 of the *Charter*. The Court's decision, this time, was that the challenge was warranted. The legislation clearly indicates that "the sentence normally applied in cases of presumptive offences is considered to be the sentence that adults found guilty of the same crimes receive. In doing so, the legislator sends the public a clear message, that, generally, young persons are dangerous criminals if they commit certain types of crimes after the age of 14. . . ."[33]

Any young person found guilty of a presumptive offence risks the stigmatization of an adult sentence unless he or she can "prove such factors as the seriousness of the offence, the circumstances of the offence, his or her age, maturity and character, the absence of a record and previous convictions, and any other relevant element that can guide the court in determining whether the adult sentence normally applied is appropriate."[34]

Considering the purpose of the YCJA and the vulnerability of the young persons it must deal with, the Court considered this an excessive burden which violated an accused youth's right to liberty and psychological security and was contrary to the fundamental principles of justice. It is the prosecutor who assumes the burden of proving beyond a reasonable doubt that there were circumstances in the commission of an offence sufficient to warrant an adult sentence. Hence, the Court ruled, "section 72(2) of the YCJA violates the rights guaranteed by section 7 of the *Charter*."[35]

The Attorney General of Quebec also challenged the constitutionality of publishing the identity of youth when charged with a presumptive offence under the YCJA. Once again the Appeal Court supported the challenge:

> As we have seen, fundamental justice requires a fair balance between the rights of a young person and the protection of society. However, the violation of the young person's psychological security stemming from that breach of the principle of confidentiality completely disregards the nature and scope of the protections given the young person under the criminal justice system as a whole.[36]

The court goes on to say that, in some cases, the public safety may justify the lifting of a publication ban, but confidentiality is a critical component in fostering the rehabilitation of a young person, and the burden of claiming it as a legal right should not fall to the accused.

Conclusions

Changes in the law with the advent of the *Youth Criminal Justice Act* and subsequent amendments to the mental disorder provisions of the *Criminal Code* are illustrative of the dynamic nature of criminal law in Canada. The complexity of law cannot be understood in its whole through knowledge of its parts. Criminal law and youth justice legislation operate symbiotically to direct and control the youth justice system. The goals of youth justice legislation are many, but its major objectives are reducing the use of court and incarceration for young offenders. The YCJA emphasizes restraint, accountability, proportionality, and discretion, particularly among decision makers. It encourages the use of extrajudicial measures, especially among non-violent first offenders, and recognizes conferences as potentially useful means of making better decisions.

After 100 years of experience with youth justice legislation, we are a long way from a harmonized youth justice strategy in Canada. *Quebec (Minister of Justice) v. Canada (Minister of Justice)* highlights some of the concerns Quebec has with respect to the regional characteristics and prerogatives of provincial jurisdictions. As the Court observed:

> Legislation designed to prevent crime is within the power of the federal government. While the Constitution allows and encourages cooperation

between the federal and provincial governments in criminal matters, it does not require it. While the provisions may impact on child protection, they do not appear to be a federal ploy to legislate in a provincial field of jurisdiction. The provisions are, in pith and substance, criminal legislation.[37]

Still, we can mitigate some of the blunt force of the criminal law through a better understanding of the competencies of youth and the roles of those who work with youth, both in the courtroom and behind the scenes.

CHAPTER TWO

Good Reasons for a Separate System

You call us the future, but we are also the present.
— Children's forum, 2002

The premise of having a youth justice system separate from the adult system is that adolescents have fundamentally different needs and capacities. Having a specialized system for youth is based on sound empirical evidence from a number of fields. This chapter reviews some of this research and the implications for how we view and respond to youthful offending in our society.

A Period of Change and Risk

The great and rapid change characteristic of adolescence is equal to that of early childhood: change is always happening in some area of the young person's functioning. There is no static point, no endpoint of relative stability. Change is constant.[1] Adolescence is a period of biological, cognitive, and social transition. The empirical evidence is clear: although the first few years of a child's life are crucial for the development of many functions, growth and change continue throughout childhood, and many functions of the brain continue to develop well into adolescence and adulthood. Behavioural and cognitive changes occurring throughout a person's life span are related to maturational processes in the brain, and the timing of these processes is different for different people, especially if those people are adolescents.[2]

Vision and other sensory systems develop early in life and then are elaborated and integrated with other functions. The frontal cortex and connections between parts of the brain develop much later than sensory systems and continue to develop during childhood and adolescence. Mental development continues to be influenced by growth in the frontal lobes through age sixteen or so. The emotional limbic system governing the regulation of social and emotional functioning is not fully developed until puberty. The acquisition of language develops until age ten or so, but the continual elaboration and refinement of language skills continues throughout the lifespan.[3]

The consequences of findings such as this need to be understood if we are to appreciate fully the importance of a separate justice system for youth. Variations in the process mean that answers to such questions as "What are the competencies of an adolescent?" and "What are reasonable expectations for an adolescent?" vary widely. Two 12-year-olds are likely to be as different from each other as they are from a third 12-year-old, and all three are likely to be different — in their capacities, characteristics, and maturity levels — from a 14-year-old.

The range between 12 and 18 years is generally considered the adolescent span, but there are gray zones at either end. Some researchers consider up to age 25 as late adolescence because of variations among individuals.[4] Age is therefore not a reliable marker of maturity in adolescents. It is widely accepted that females generally mature more quickly than males, but here again, variations exist.

One way to conceptualize the course of adolescence is to examine the variations that occur during puberty, the period in which chemical and physical changes in the body occur to enable sexual reproduction:

Accompanying the dramatic changes in growth at the beginning of adolescence is the most substantial surge of differentiation between the two sexes since the fetal period. How fast adolescents move through puberty varies as widely as when they start. For example, it may take girls as few as 1.5 years or as many as 5 years to complete puberty. Suppose we were studying a single class of boys and girls in elementary school. If we recorded when the first student began puberty and followed the group until the last student finished puberty, chances are we would have followed the group for a full 10 years.[5]

Because of the enormity and rapidity of change during adolescence, the period is one of both critical opportunity and developmental risk. Some researchers refer to it as the second window of opportunity and risk — the first being early childhood.[6] The neurological, cognitive, and psychosocial developments of adolescence indicate a readiness to learn and experience things in a way that was not possible earlier.[7] Like children, though, adolescents still require appropriate opportunities and stimulation to develop to the best of their abilities.

Adolescence is a time of increased personal risk. Although the young person's mental acuity is expanding, it is happening at a time when his or her psychological and biological vulnerability is greatly heightened. This is owing not only to the magnitude and rapidity of their development, but also to the timing of biological and social triggers that may place their health at risk. [8]

Adolescents, by virtue of being adolescents, are stretching their emotional, intellectual, and physical capacities and participating in an increasingly competitive and complex array of activities. They are prone to sports injuries, for example, because of their growing independence and desire to take part in unsupervised activities, including extreme sports. Adolescents are vulnerable to mental and social problems, as well. The period has long been associated with the onset of depression, eating disorders, substance abuse and dependence, risky sexual behaviour, antisocial and delinquent activity, and school absenteeism. [9] All these variables place the adolescent's physical and mental health at risk, and some are more vulnerable than others. Youth with pre-existing cognitive disabilities or disruptive behaviour disorders are more susceptible to mental health problems and may develop secondary disabilities. As a group, they tend to have a greater propensity for engaging in high-risk behaviours.

Competencies in Youth

Among adults, there is a wide variation in physical, psychological, and social maturity, and there seems to be no last or closing stage to a person's ability to learn. But research has shown that learning in adults is largely predictable and remains relatively stable over time. Having benefited from experience and opportunity, and having developed the critical ability to reflect on a course of action, adults tend to consolidate their competencies over time and across situations.

Among adolescents, in contrast, variation in competencies is much less predictable and far less stable. A young person who has developed an ability in one context may fail to apply it in another. Newly acquired skills are unstable; they require practice and consolidation before they are established in a young person's repertoire. The inconsistent expression of developing skills among young people is a normal phenomenon. Their ability to handle stress, particularly, is related to their responses to situations that require decision-making.

Adolescents are influenced by stress and emotion to a much greater degree than adults. [10] As a result, they are more susceptible to the influence of others, and their ability to act independently is less developed. [11] To an adolescent, pressure from others is far more significant than it would appear from an adult perspective. [12]

Sensitive to peer pressure and the opinions of others, adolescents are likely to be greatly influenced by group persuasion and subtle pressure to conform. They spend more time in groups than adults, and are more prone to emotional arousal. They tend to make riskier decisions when they are in groups. Once again, to an adult, such peer pressure may appear minimal, but to an adolescent it can be overwhelming.

Adolescence and Stress

It is evident from both research and clinical practice that adolescents differ substantially from adults in their perception of stressful events and in the number of stressful events they are likely to encounter on a given day. There are many sources of adolescent stress: young people must respond to hormonal and other developmental changes in their bodies over which they have no control; they must adjust to changing socio-environmental contexts and expectations; they face peer pressure daily, and at the same time must cope with increasing personal independence.[13] Stresses, especially perceived stresses, will interfere with a young person's capacity to use the abilities they have recently acquired, resulting in a much greater likelihood that their behaviour will be influenced by emotional arousal and perceived stress.[14]

Preliminary evidence suggests that adolescents, when compared to children and adults, show elevated cardiac activity when faced with stress. Young persons with apparently normal decision-making capacities may exhibit much poorer cognitive performance under circumstances involving stress that, for adults, would be considered normal.[15]

The prevalence of depression in adolescents, in fact, may be related to the increase in the number of stressful events they experience during this period. Negative events and emotions are experienced more intensely during adolescence than in other developmental periods. During early adolescence, for example, females perceive events as more stressful than at any other age, even in comparison to males of the same age.[16]

Whereas preadolescents tend to experience negative events in relation to family matters and their immediate surroundings, adolescents are more likely to experience negative events among their peers. Older adolescents may experience academic issues as particularly stressful. Parental conflicts are more common in younger adolescents, while mood disruptions tend to appear in mid-adolescence, and risky behaviours emerge later.[17]

The number of changes occurring either simultaneously or in rapid sequence during adolescence is associated with an escalation in problem behaviour, a decrease in academic achievement or motivation, and diminished involvement in extramural activities. Among female adolescents, a decrease in self esteem may also be evident.[18] Perceived levels of stress are more strongly associated with alcohol and drug abuse in adolescents than among adults.[19]

Early or late changes associated with puberty add additional pressure, with behavioural and emotional problems manifesting in a gender-specific manner. Among girls, early maturation is associated with emotional or behavioural problems, including emotionality, depression, and an increase in risk-taking behaviours. Early maturing boys may also exhibit risk-taking behaviours, but they are usually associated with involvement in athletics, increased popularity, and confidence.[20]

The degree to which adolescents are preoccupied with their changing bodies affects each individual differently. Some merely observe themselves with interest and curiosity; others find their preoccupations interfering with their schoolwork and their role in the community. As a rule, though, adolescents have greater difficulty coping with physical and hormonal changes than adults, and a preoccupation with their symptoms can affect their ability to adapt to a range of situations and activities.[21]

Normal weight gain during adolescence, for example, can result in a poor self-image, a fear of attending physical education classes, and eating disorders.[22] Skin problems can lead to self-consciousness and withdrawal. Headaches and abdominal discomfort, while painful, may also lead to poor nutrition and difficulty in concentrating. Delayed or precocious puberty can lead to feelings of intense self-consciousness, anxiety, and isolation, while a perceived physical unattractiveness can lead to inappropriate self-criticism, even self-loathing, and the youth may find inappropriate compensation in high-risk behaviours.

Mood Disorders

The incidence of mental disabilities such as depression and schizophrenia multiply as children enter adolescence. The rates for such disorders are similar in adults, but when we examine studies about the affective states of adolescents compared to adults, it is clear that there are far more mood-related disturbances among adolescents.[23] Thus, while the same number of adolescents and adults may be diagnosed with an anxiety or a mood disorder, the number of adolescents who report feeling miserable, depressed, and having sleep problems is much higher. Adolescents also tend to present with greater emotional volatility, resulting in more intense feelings of anxiety, self-consciousness, and euphoria.[24]

Rapid and extreme mood swings are more common among adolescents than adults. Adolescents therefore tend to be more impulsive and less able to regulate their behaviour, leading to risk-taking or sensation-seeking experiences. Some researchers have hypothesized that adolescents have a propensity to anhedonia — the loss of pleasure in activities that are normally enjoyable — and this leads to risk-taking behaviours.[25] Compared to both children and adults, adolescents have a greater propensity to experience, and to expect to experience, positive situations and events as less pleasurable.[26] One study found that, between late childhood and early adolescence, the number of reported feelings of "very happy" drops by 50 per cent.[27]

Compared to college students and adults, adolescents tend to be less optimistic about the outcome of a given situation or event.[28] They don't trust the future, and they derive less satisfaction from events and situations that have moderate to low incentive values. This may be why some have a higher propensity for risk taking and sensation seeking; they're trying to "fill in the gap" left by disappointed expectations. Some researchers refer to it as a "reward deficiency," leading adolescents to seek higher levels of novelty and stimulation.[29] Normal teenage rebellion occurs as a result of youth seeking out experiences that reflect different values and preferences in comparison to adults, but it can lead to interests and behaviours that are inherently risky, such as using illicit drugs.

Planning, Judging, and Decision-Making

The adolescent brain is undergoing regressive and progressive changes, leading to a greater capacity for abstract reasoning.[30] Again, there is a wide variation in the development of abstract reasoning and planning abilities in youth. Higher order capacities — those required for complicated tasks involving long-term planning, rational judgement, and decision-making — are considerably less developed in adolescents than in adults, and may remain so into late adolescence.[31] Many adolescents show consistent abstract reasoning when dealing with the physical world, but such reasoning tends to be delayed when applied to the interpersonal domain. This can affect their capacity for decision-making well into late adolescence and sometimes even adulthood.

Adolescents tend to have difficulty imagining events that have not yet occurred. This may stem from their tendency to place more weight on the short-term consequences of their decisions. Because they have less experience than adults, they perceive the risks and benefits of making certain choices differently. A short-term reward may seem more relevant to them than long-term consequences.[32]

Adolescents assess risks differently than adults. Risk-taking is generally associated with negative outcomes, but, on the positive side, taking risks does allow the youth to experiment with adult behaviours and privileges, encourages normal developmental outcomes such as personal independence, and promotes the acquisition of skills the youth will need in the adult world. Some authors propose, in fact, that adolescent risk-taking is both normative and adaptive. It has been linked to gains in self-esteem, suggesting that approval from one's peers is consequent upon taking certain risks.[33] Indeed, active risk-taking may be a means of developmental experimentation building on a youth's experience and resourcefulness, and thus enhancing confidence and self-esteem. Reactive risk-taking, on the other hand, in response to a situation that is perceived to be unfair or unpleasurable, may be more negative. Some adolescents take risks not for the adrenaline rush but to relieve dysphoria or to cope with stress.[34]

Given that adolescents place less weight on risk than reward, it comes as no surprise that they display a disproportionate amount of risk-taking, even reckless, behaviour than adults. Studies indicate that half of all adolescents may drive a vehicle while under the influence of alcohol, engage in unprotected sexual relations, use illegal drugs, or commit minor criminal acts. It is no coincidence that mortality rates increase dramatically from early to late adolescence, with homicide, suicide, and accidents accounting for more than 85 per cent of all adolescent deaths.[35]

Substance Abuse and Addiction

Youth are more likely to try illicit substances than adults, and are more likely to become addicted to them. They differ from adults in their responses to a variety of stimuli, ranging from novel activities to drugs and alcohol.[36] Novelty and sensation seeking are highly correlated with drug and alcohol use in both adults and adolescents, but the mechanisms of dependence seem to be different. Adolescents become dependent on drugs and alcohol more rapidly, and studies indicate that physical addiction appears to play a strong role in the stability of cigarette use in young people from early to mid-adolescence.[37]

Adolescents are also at greater risk of addiction from illicit drugs.[38] From first exposure to dependence for alcohol, cannabis, and street drugs, adolescents have been shown to become addicted more quickly than those who start using drugs as adults, and the finding appears to be slightly stronger for adolescent males.[39]

Adolescents differ from adults in their response and sensitivity to a variety of illicit and prescription drugs. Some of these responses have been linked to the changes in body composition and organ function associated with the adolescent growth spurt, as well as hormonal changes that could alter drug metabolism and excretion rates.[40] The differences in response may be further related to the neural system of adolescents, who may exhibit reduced sensitivity to certain drugs and thus promote their more frequent use. As a group, then, they are much more vulnerable to a wide range of mental health problems relating to substance abuse.

Substance abuse is highly correlated with antisocial behaviour, interpersonal violence, and criminal offending during adolescence.[41] Clinical and anecdotal evidence suggests that many youth undergoing court-ordered assessments are dependent on one or several substances, often nicotine and one other drug of choice. One-third regularly use various pills, street drugs, and inhalants.

Implications of a Developmental Perspective

The capacity of a young person to participate in criminal justice proceedings with consent and awareness depends on certain mental capacities, including the ability to think in abstract terms about issues such as rights and freedom, distinguish relevant from irrelevant information, evaluate options, make informed choices, judge situations, and self-monitor what they understand and how they react. There are large differences in the decision-making capacities of adolescents of different ages. Younger ones, for example, will tend to focus on short-term consequences, and this will have a deleterious effect on their ability to weigh their options rationally, as they would if they were more mature. Younger adolescents and those with mental disabilities have been shown to be less competent decision-makers than adults in a variety of legal settings.[42]

The overwhelming evidence of developmental differences between young persons and adults underscores the importance of adopting a developmental perspective with regard to the youth justice system. Youth develop at different rates, with unique patterns of spurts, delays, and temporary regressions, and there are huge differences among individuals in their capacity to participate with full awareness in the systematic and progressive stages of the justice system. There are large differences, too, among youth in their response to sanctions, mandated services, or conditions of probation.

The Truth about Consequences

When the youth justice system becomes ambivalent about its objectives, its guiding principles become diluted. There is great danger in minimizing the differences between adolescents and adults. It is incumbent upon the system and the people who serve it to consider how young people's development can be hindered or encouraged by the blunt processes of the law. Adults making decisions for young people must call on their own maturity and experience to evaluate the consequences of criminal sanctions on the developing personality. They must also evaluate the consequences of criminal sanctions on the youth's ability to take advantage of social, educational, and work-related opportunities in the community. Adults may view the process as a formative experience — character building — and this fallacy is supported by anecdotal reports about youth who rise to the occasion, overcoming the shame and reconstructing their lives in a manner such that their brush with the law appears as no more than a blip on the screen of their lives.

In reality, many youth suffer permanent social and emotional consequences as a result of their involvement with the criminal justice system. They are stigmatized; they feel debased; they feel the progressive steps of the process as individual assaults on their self-image. Some encounters with the law create blocks or "snares"[43] in the adolescent psyche, effectively arresting young people's development or restricting their opportunities to attend schools of their choice. They may be separated from their family or community, and they often lose their friends.

The typical pattern involves a lowering in confidence and motivation, depression, the loss of optimism, and anger, turning to self-medication and sensation seeking. Such youth seek out, in turn, like-minded peers, and frequently act out self-fulfilling prophecies: "They think I'm bad, so now I'll show them!" They drop out of school. They are unemployed. They fail to set goals, or they set unrealistic goals. They can become disaffected about all aspects of their lives.[44]

Of course, there is the school of logical consequences. "They've brought this on themselves," adults will say. "What else could they have expected?"[45] But many so-called logical consequences, such as criminal sanctions, go far beyond logic when the crime is considered. Furthermore, there may be indifference about the fact that many youth suffer "natural consequences" of their criminal justice involvement (e.g. failing a grade), consequences that can often have life-altering repercussions (e.g., school drop out).

Conclusions

Most crimes go undetected. Young people and adults alike engage in much more criminal activity than is ever reflected in the statistics. Few youth, in fact, make it through adolescence without breaking the law at least once. Given that much youthful offending is transitory and virtually normative, society should try to ensure that those who do get caught are not subsequently stigmatized and emotionally scarred by their experience with the youth justice system. One way to ensure this is to keep them separated from adult criminals.

CHAPTER THREE

Even More Reasons for a Separate System

Although there are different terms and individuals have preferences for which ones to use, the important thing to remember is that we are talking about *people*.

— Karin Melberg Schwier and Dave Hingsburger
Sexuality: Your Sons and Daughters with Intellectual Disabilities

Youth with mental disabilities are over-represented in the Canadian justice system relative to their numbers in the general population. This is true not only in Canada, but in the United States, the United Kingdom, and Australia.[1]

Youth with mental disabilities are likely to have difficulties in one or more areas of their day-to-day functioning. Common, and often overlapping, disabilities experienced by young offenders include language and memory deficits, social and behavioural deficits, planning deficits, attention deficits, visual-spatial and motor deficits, an inability to regulate their emotions, and academic deficits, including illiteracy. When they come into conflict with the law, they inevitably face demands that challenge their functional capacities. This means, in effect, that they face challenges over and above those faced by the average, non-disabled young person in conflict with the law.

Being a lawyer or a psychologist requires particular abilities, depending on the demands of the situation. A lawyer's courtroom eloquence is quite different from the reassuring confidence necessary when interviewing a client. A psychologist, similarly, employs quite different skills when completing a court-ordered assessment than when providing therapy to a client. Young people involved with the justice system must also employ different skill sets in different situations. The difference is that they have not been trained for it, and generally have no previous experience of it. When there is a mismatch between the demands of the justice system and a youth's functional capacities to meet them, there is the potential for biased treatment. When there is a significant discrepancy between a youth's competencies and the expectations of the system, there is a chance that the youth will be misunderstood or that his or her competence will be overestimated.

In clinical practice, many young offenders with mental disabilities present with stressful or traumatic life experiences and unhealthy lifestyles. These, in turn, place them in danger of further criminal activity and the development of more serious mental health issues. Unfortunately, there is no mechanism or philosophy in the justice, health, or education systems to guide the professional in deciding how to intervene or what to focus on. The interplay between physical and mental health, between victimization experiences and mental capacity is neither widely understood nor appreciated. Misunderstandings about the nature of mental disabilities and how they affect young people's functioning often result in situations in which intellectual disabilities are likely to be overlooked when youth are labeled as "young offenders." In Canadian society, mental disabilities are still associated with significant stigma. This lack of acceptance spills over into the youth justice system.

Conceptualizing Mental Disabilities

Imagine mental disabilities as occupying adjoining but functionally related compartments in the human psyche. There are no physical or observable boundaries between them, and the divisions are somewhat arbitrary, but the image can assist us in coming to some kind of conceptual clarity.[2]

Mental disorders are those which involve alterations of mood, thinking, and behaviour, such as disruptive behaviour disorders, anxiety disorders, and mood disorders.

Disorders of psychological development are characterized by impairment or delay in the development of specific functions — language, non-verbal reasoning, memory, fine motor skills — or overall pervasive delays such as intellectual disabilities, autism, and speech and language disorders.

Mental health problems are indicative of an altered functioning of the central nervous system that causes distress to a person, but they may be not interfering with their day-to-day functioning and quality of life to the same extent that mental disabilities do. Most people have experienced mental health problems at one time or another, although we may not have labeled them as such. They generally manifest themselves as temporary changes resulting from specific stressors such as relationship problems, work related stress, the death of a loved one, or financial difficulties. Such changes are normal; they are simply the indicators of the normal ups and downs of a person's mental health.

It is normal for adolescents to experience stress related to school transitions, increased expectations, performance anxiety, divorce and other losses, and new and complex relationships. The majority of young people pass through them, experiencing episodes of brief but temporary mental instability. Most young people do not develop mental health disorders. Many have supportive families, teachers, or friends that help them through these difficult times, usually without the intervention of mental health services.

Similar comparisons can be made between normal variations in psychological functioning and disorders of psychological development. Everyone has experienced transitory problems with psychological functions: poor memory, loss of concentration. Most psychological functions can be disrupted by emotionally charged events. The stresses of daily living, a changing or inadequate diet, and fatigue all contribute, to a greater or lesser degree, to the disruption of normal mental processes. Their effect is often minor, but they are still distressing. That young people are more susceptible to momentary lapses in psychological functioning is simply a feature of their development. They may be forgetful or disorganized in certain circumstances, or when they are under certain types of stress, but such lapses are not usually chronic, and their impact is not usually permanent. However, when there is a significant discrepancy between a youth's capabilities and the expectations placed on him or her, and when the discrepancy is more than temporary, we begin to suspect that there may be a disorder of psychological development.

When normal fluctuations of mental health and psychological functioning become chronic or extreme, when they begin to interfere significantly with a young person's performance in more than one functional area, there is reason to be concerned about a possible disability. A useful way of defining disability is as follows:

> Disability typically refers to how physical or mental limitations are manifest within a specific social or environmental context. Thus, a disability can be thought of as the outcome of an interaction between impairments, or functional limitations, and behavioural/performance expectations of socially defined roles. An individual who is impaired/limited in his or her ability in one environment may not be limited when elements of that environment are changed.[3]

A young person with a reading disability may not appear disabled when playing soccer, but will appear highly disabled when required to read a passage from a book. The difference is that playing soccer is not a necessary life skill, but a reading disability will affect many other areas of the youth's functioning, especially when it comes to such things as applying for a job or taking a history class.

The difficulties a young person faces as a result of a disability may range from mild to moderate to severe. Some disabilities, such as autism, are pervasive over time and across situations, while others, such as a reading disability, are more circumscribed. Still, a young person newly diagnosed with a particular disability may have been suffering from it for years. The emergence of a disability relatively later in life is more a discovery than a diagnosis, driven by the demands of a particular environment on that person's capabilities and vulnerabilities. A young person's disability may well have lain dormant until he or she experienced sufficient stress to trigger it.

Mental disabilities are assumed to be caused by the interplay of biological, psychological, developmental, social, and cultural factors, but the precise causes of most mental disabilities remain unknown. Fortunately, it is not necessary to know the precise cause of a mental disability in order to intervene effectively.

It is important to note that mental health disorders, mental health problems, and disorders of psychological development may coexist with one another in the same individual. One disorder may be primary, the other secondary, and medical diagnoses may exist in tandem with psychological or psychiatric diagnoses; an young person with FASD, for example, may have a concurrent mood disorder. A young person with a physical disability may also struggle with co-occurring physical illnesses and mental disabilities; a young person with asthma, for example, may also be suffering from a generalized anxiety disorder.

Often, the difficulties associated with a mental disability are "invisible." With an obvious physical or intellectual disability — a crippled limb, say, or Down Syndrome — the problems the youth is facing are transparent. A person who cannot walk is clearly identified as having a physical disability; he or she encounters numerous and obvious barriers in navigating the day-to-day world, and society responds by attempting to create a wheelchair-friendly environment, replacing stairs with ramps in public buildings, or sheltered workshops where the intellectually handicapped can perform meaningful work and provide valuable services to the community. Clearly, the extent to which a disability interferes with a person's daily life is critical in determining the level of intervention or support society may need to provide.

Multiple Pathways Leading to Mental Disabilities

Physical and mental health have a profound influence on one another. Anxiety, for instance, can stimulate negative changes in endocrine and immune functioning, which, in turn, increase a person's susceptibility to a range of physical illnesses. Behaviour, too, is largely motivated by mental health;[4] a depressed person or a drug addict is much more likely to smoke than a person who does not suffer these problems.[5] Some researchers propose that smoking plays a role in the development of depression in adolescents.[6] Others report that regular smoking may start earlier in male adolescents who suffer from attention deficit disorder.[7] Neurochemical mechanisms may play a role in the relationship between mental health and smoking. Nicotine may precipitate an increase in the release of dopamine in parts of the brain that are related to depression and other mental health disorders.

Although most people understand that the things they do affect their health, few appreciate how their social experiences can have the same effect. A person's vulnerability to mental disabilities is a combination of pre-existing genetic, biological, and temperamental factors, as well as a wide range of social, emotional, and physical factors. Mental disabilities can be triggered by a traumatic event —witnessing a violent act or experiencing the death of a parent — or by chronic social stressors such as poverty, marginalization, and victimization. The degree of disability or impairment often depends on the severity or the persistence of the stressor, a person's coping skills, and whether support and intervention are provided in a timely and adequate manner.[8]

At Risk for Secondary Disabilities

Many people with mental disabilities are at risk for developing secondary disabilities because a mental disability itself is a chronic stressor. Young people with mental disabilities may develop distorted thinking about themselves, have difficulty adjusting to changing circumstances, and develop clinical depression or anxiety disorders. The mixture of primary and secondary disabilities can prove toxic, infecting every aspect of a young person's life. Health Canada underscores the importance of early identification and intervention:

> The onset of most mental illnesses occurs during adolescence and young adulthood. These affect educational achievement, occupational or career opportunities and successes, and the formation and nature of personal relationships. The greater the number of episodes of illness that an individual experiences, the greater the degree of lasting disability. Receiving and complying with effective treatment and having the security of strong social supports, adequate income, housing and educational opportunities are essential elements in minimizing the impact of mental illness.[9]

Researchers and clinicians alike have emphasized the importance of early diagnosis, as many youth who come into contact with the justice system suffer from mental disabilities that should have been identified much earlier, preventing the development of secondary problems. For example, the importance of timely diagnosis is underscored by the developers of Health Canada guidelines for the diagnosis of Fetal Alcohol Spectrum Disorders (FASD):

> An early diagnosis is essential to allow access to intervention and resources that may mitigate the development of subsequent "secondary disabilities"

(e.g., unemployment, mental health problems, disrupted school experience) among affected people. Furthermore, an early diagnosis will also allow appropriate intervention, counseling and treatment for the mother and may prevent the birth of affected children in the future. It may also prompt caregivers to seek diagnosis and support for previously undiagnosed siblings. . . . misclassification leads to inappropriate patient care, increased risk of secondary disabilities, missed opportunities for prevention and inaccurate estimates of incidence and prevalence.[10]

The psychological consequences of a mental disability may appear as low self-esteem, self-preoccupation, immaturity, or depression. The educational consequences may present as underachievement or failure, illiteracy, and truancy. The social consequences may manifest themselves in the distortion of social cues, difficulty in controlling or modulating the emotions, poor impulse control, low frustration tolerance, and an increase in social conflict and inappropriate aggression. All these consequences can extend into late adolescence and beyond, resulting in an adulthood of chronic underachievement, marginal employment, and unsatisfying and conflictual personal relationships.

Victimization

Research has shown that many thousands of children develop serious mental health problems as a result of violent victimization.[11] Not surprisingly, sexually victimized youth run a substantially higher lifetime risk for psychiatric disorders,[12] and experience much higher levels of post-traumatic stress disorder and depression.[13] Twenty-five years ago it was reported that 20 to 30 per cent of preadolescent Canadians had been sexually abused; current estimates are at least as high.[14] Using a conservative definition of sexual abuse as "unwanted sexual assault involving physical contact," the prevalence of sexual abuse before the age of 16 among Canadian girls is about seven per cent; for boys, five per cent. If it is true, as the research suggests, that fewer than 10 per cent of children who have been sexually abused ever tell about it, the actual incidence of violent sexual victimization is much higher.[15] Youth with such histories are likely to develop mental health problems as well as come into conflict with the law.[16]

Symptoms related to victimization include low self-esteem, difficulty forming close relationships or trusting others, feelings of chronic vulnerability and anxiety, self-deprecation, perfectionism, poor social and assertiveness skills, and poor motivation. Victimization experiences can retard or inhibit developmental processes that are critical for psychological adjustment, including such things as emotional regulation and impulse control.[17] Such children and adolescents may develop strategies for managing themselves and hence "survive" the experiences, but the maintenance of these strategies over time may be detrimental to a healthier, long-term adjustment. There is evidence, for example, that maltreated girls have "difficulty accurately appraising the causes and consequences of emotionally arousing situations, fail to respond to emotional displays by others in a culturally appropriate manner, and maintain lower levels of awareness of their own emotional experience, all of which may compromise them in traversing various relationships."[18] And it is not only direct maltreatment but other types of violence that place youth at risk for social and emotional difficulties.[19] Indirect victimization can include exposure to family violence or to rumours being spread at school; both have been shown to have the same effects on children as direct abuse. Domestic violence can result in any number of negative outcomes among children, and has been clinically associated with depression, self-harm, post-traumatic stress, and psychosomatic complaints.[20]

Similarly, peer violence, "either as a participant or witness, exerts a powerful shadow over adolescents,"[21] and has been shown to produce post-traumatic symptoms similar to those found in bullied children and adolescents.

Victimization at different stages can have different effects on the victim. Young children victimized by their care-givers may develop insecure attachments and employ dissociation as a chronic defence mechanism. Sexual abuse can hasten the onset of puberty. Children's beliefs about what may happen to them mediate their experiences of victimization, but how they makes sense of their experiences will change over time; disruptive behaviour in school may take the form of self-blame or depression at a later stage. Environmental factors such as support and access to appropriate resources — or the lack of them — can have a profound influence on the impact of the experience and the youth's recovery from it.[22]

Children with disabilities are twice as likely to become the victims of physical abuse than children without disabilities.[23]

Mental Disabilities and Delinquency

As we have seen, young persons who have become involved with the justice system are much more likely to have personal histories that include some form of victimization than their peers in the general population, suggesting that youth with mental and legal problems are often victims themselves. Indeed, there is evidence that youth who have been the victims of repeated maltreatment may be at greater risk of continued victimization,[24] and that a youth's victimization experiences can lead to disabling mental health problems.[25] The affects of trauma or prolonged stress on the developing brain are well known. Frightening events are thought to be related to elevated cortisol levels in the brain, which may lead to poor impulse control in victimized children.[26] There is empirical evidence to show that children's cortisol levels are related to the severity and the persistence of the abuse.[27]

Often youth who attract the attention of the police do so during a time in their lives that is fraught with other stressful events.[28] The risky behaviours associated with a criminal lifestyle may trigger certain mental health problems, particularly if they are highly charged or traumatic, such as witnessing a stabbing or being involved in a high-speed car chase. Youth have reported that their deteriorating coping ability and consequent development of mental health problems coincided with having witnessed some violent act as a feature of their high-risk lifestyle.[29]

An Australian survey that examined 242 youth in custody, aged 14 to 21, found that over 60 per cent of them had experienced some form of abuse or neglect during childhood.[30] Further, a majority of the young women in the correctional facility were found to have mental health problems directly related to an episode of physical or sexual abuse that had occurred prior to their incarceration. Another study of incarcerated youth found that over 60 per cent of the girls and over 30 per cent of the boys who had committed serious offences had a history of physical abuse, neglect, or parental abandonment.[31]

There is much speculation about why some youth are repeatedly abused. One hypothesis suggests that young people who develop low self-esteem and chronic feelings of vulnerability and powerlessness choose to enter into relationships or situations that may be harmful to them but nonetheless give them a sense of belonging. On the other hand, some may adopt a criminal lifestyle as a means of escaping abusive family or peer relationships; associating with delinquent peers may provide protection from further victimization or compensation for an abusive family environment.[32]

Victimization and Violent Offending

Though traumatic experiences have been linked to antisocial patterns in youth, the mechanisms by which it occurs have been difficult to establish.[33] Understanding the link may help us discover the pathways to serious offending and allow us to intervene earlier. We know that the risk factors for early onset offending and later violent offending are likely to be similar; young offenders of any age are likely to share similar histories of victimization combined with other types of adversity.[34]

Studies examining the link between criminal victimization and criminal offending in samples of youth between the ages of 11 and 17 years suggest that there is a link between violent offending and violent victimization.[35] Many of the youth studied were repeat victims of violent crimes, but not all went on to commit violent offences.

The link between sexual victimization and sexual offending has been difficult to establish, and the results have been inconsistent.[36] Several researchers suggest that experiencing physical violence may lead to perpetrating it, in turn, and that victims of sexual abuse are more likely to become sex offenders. But not every young person who experiences victimization goes on to commit a violent offence.[37] We know that many adult sex offenders exhibit sexual deviancy and aggressive tendencies during adolescence,[38] but so far the risk factors associated with adolescent sexual aggression have been validated only on a small sample of offenders.[39] Not all studies show a difference between sex offenders and other groups with regard to their history of victimization. Determining causes is always complex, and there are likely multiple risk factors for violent offending.[40]

It could be that the propensity toward criminal behaviour involving crimes against persons generally (as opposed to sexual offences specifically) depends on the type of maltreatment experienced by the individual. But here, too, the results are inconsistent and sometimes unexpected.[41] A 1994 study of Canadian adolescents discovered that less than five per cent of victimization experiences were consistent with one type of maltreatment, but that a combination of physical abuse, neglect, and verbal abuse resulted in the worst consequences for quality of life and a wide range of negative outcomes.[42]

Victimization and Youth Justice

Support from significant others — including parents, friends, and teachers — can mitigate the effects of violent offending by youth who were previously victimized themselves.[43] This has clear implications for youth justice. Victim services in criminal justice programs and allied services for youth can play an important role in halting further victimization, preventing victims from becoming victimizers themselves. Timely interventions will help victims understand the impact the act has had on them personally and also help them develop empathy for other victims.

The patterns of coping youth may develop in self-defence following an experience or experiences of abuse may place them at risk for further episodes of victimization. For example, a young woman who tries to deal with being sexually abused by using drugs is making herself vulnerable to further abuse while under the influence of the drug. Furthermore, the use of an illicit drug associates her with a criminal lifestyle.

The role of delinquent peers is critical in understanding the link between victimization and criminal offending. Time spent in unstructured activities with peers has been shown to be a significant risk factor for violent victimization.[44] Often, the victim and the perpetrator know one another. Peers play a major role in both victimization and offending behaviour.[45]

Youth with histories of victimization who commit serious offences must take responsibility for their behaviour, but they must also deal with their own victimization. With the assistance of a therapist, they can recognize their own victimization as a contributing factor to their antisocial thoughts and behaviours.[46] Youth who have suffered repeated victimization will require extra attention, as the cumulative effects of abuse places them at higher risk for future abuse or becoming abusers themselves.

Youth who have been victims of interfamilial abuse and neglect often require multi-modal interventions to prevent further abuse. They and their care-givers also need to be aware of their susceptibility to future abuse. They need to develop self-confidence, self-esteem, and they need to be taught strategies for protection. This may require that they be placed in a home environment that keeps them safe while they heal from their experiences.

Child service agencies are sometimes blind to the kinds of victimization that youth may experience in their homes, yet they can be quick to lay charges when a young person commits an assault or other violent offence. It is particularly disturbing when a youth is charged with assaulting one of his parents when it is clear that both the youth and the parent were being abusive. The youth may have been witness to longstanding domestic violence and been exposed to abysmal role models, and it sets a dangerous example when the rights of adults are placed above the rights of children in cases of domestic violence. The inappropriate use of the justice system for issues that should to be dealt with by involving other systems — such as mental health and child welfare — can have negative consequences for families as a whole. Parents sometimes are led to believe that their son or daughter will get the services they need if they press charges against them, but this promotes the view that justice is an instrument to be used on social problems and mental health issues that are actually the mandate of other agencies.

A recent and distressing trend in Canada is the increasing ambivalence about the disclosure of abuse because of legal cases in which children admitted to lying. Media coverage has emphasized the pain and anguish of the falsely accused — and, in some cases, the falsely convicted. Some have been vindicated, but the fear remains among foster homes and daycare providers that they may be accused of heinous crimes they have not committed and be swiftly and brutally dealt with by the media and the justice system. One must wonder, too, whether the police have become reticent about investigating reports of child abuse because of the potential backlash. Therapists, certainly, have become more wary of involving themselves in sexual abuse cases. The result seems to be that the old taboos have come full circle, and society seems unwittingly to be telling children to keep their dark and dirty secrets to themselves. Children in need of foster care are being given to families with little information about their histories, leaving care-givers in the dark about possible past abuse and offering little guidance on whether the children should be assessed or treated.

All forms of abuse are bad, but keeping it secret serves no one but the abuser. Schoolchildren and the public need to know the nature of abuse and its consequences. Educational efforts must be designed to counteract fears about false reporting and focus on the importance of open and clear communication between children and their care-givers, and between families and the institutions dealing with them. Turning a blind eye to victimization is not a good crime prevention strategy.

Stereotypes Associated with Mental Disabilities

Words shape perceptions. Labels such as "young offender," "sex offender," "violent offender," "mentally disabled," and "psychopath," among many others, shape our perceptions of youth who are in conflict with the law. Such words have a negative and sometimes deterministic value, so it is important to understand how using them may affect people involved with the youth justice system.

An extensive review of criminological and legal literature suggests that, in the adult correctional system, there has been a history of discrimination against offenders with intellectual disabilities. The literature suggests, in fact, that people with intellectual disabilities were more likely to receive prison sentences for crimes of violence because prosecutors and judges regard them as inherently dangerous.[47]

"A common misconception," according to the American Psychiatric Association, "is that classification of mental disorders classifies people, when actually what are being classified are disorders."[48]

Labels are powerful and should be used with great care, especially in their application to youth. Foster placements may not be available for children who have been described as sneaky, unpredictable, volatile, or impulsive. The characteristics associated with some types of mental disabilities are thought to lead these youth to make up stories to hurt their care-givers, and foster parents are fearful of allegations of abuse. Similarly, youth with diagnoses associated with impulsivity may be seen as prone to violence. Such children are feared and then stigmatized. Liability becomes a major issue for workers and counsellors who are in the position of making decisions for them.

The link between mental illness, victimization, and violence is difficult to dispute, but it is important to understand the specifics of the association before making sweeping judgements or recommending particular courses of action. In the adult literature, a number of studies have established that there is a relationship between severe mental disorders and violence. There is also evidence that violence among persons with severe mental disorders is moderately higher than violence in the general population. However, it is usually people who have severe mental disorders in combination with a substance abuse problem that have violence rates higher than others.[49] The research also stresses that violence and risk for violence must be understood in reference to situations. People with mental disabilities are susceptible to abuse not just in their homes but in the wider context of their lives. Their vulnerability is compounded by the fact that they are often socially isolated, lacking work and purpose, and living in unsafe environments. They are easy prey for predators and criminals, and they are more prone to substance abuse as a result of their impoverishment. Many live in neighbourhoods with high crime rates.

In the adolescent literature, it is much more difficult to accurately predict violence and risk for violence.[50] One study found that, when clinicians predicted that a person would be violent, they were accurate no more than one in three times.[51] Recent reviews are more optimistic, suggesting there has been substantial improvement in the prediction of violence among adolescents. The use of multiple criteria and a focus on short-term predictions are two recent developments, as well as advances in the identification of risk and protective factors. The development of assessment measures has been increasing, and actuarial tools that employ a combination of risk factors are being developed and validated.[52]

As with adults, the association between mental disabilities and violence in youth is mediated by other factors. Youth with mental disabilities may be prone to violence when they are struggling with addictions, placed in situations of conflict, or being abused, but it is difficult to justify the notion that they pose a public safety risk on the basis of their mental disability. The vast majority do not.

Mental Disabilities and Education

There is a theory in the educational system that youth who end up in court are likely to have a history of negative interactions with the school system, resulting in a disengagement from the values and activities of the school. These youth experience little success and, over time, their frustration and negativity increase. Many of them will have cognitive disabilities. Academic failure sets them on a path toward satisfying their needs in alternative venues, usually in the community with like-minded peers. Truancy results in even fewer ties with the values of the school, less supervision by adults, and gravitation toward rebellious and antisocial activities.

Where does this cycle begin?

Some suggest that a disparity between capabilities and expectations develops early. For example, youth with hyperactivity, impulsivity, and attention disorders perform poorly or inconsistently in school. Their interactions with other students and teachers is also inconsistent, and often negative. Over time this pattern repeats itself and intensifies.[53] The youth becomes increasingly marginalized. Negative interactions lead to frequent changes of school, periods of lost education, suspensions, and expulsions. It is an insidious and alienating process, and its chief victims in Canada have been Aboriginal youth, 60 per cent of whom never complete high school.[54] But non-Aboriginal youth are also victims.

Obviously, young people who are disconnected from school no longer have access to the programs offered there. In Canadian society, schools are a crucial community resource; they do far more than meet the academic needs of their students. They also address the physical and mental health needs of students and their families. They are conduits for sharing information and monitoring children's behaviour and functioning, and they provide an environment in which their health can be monitored. Schools strive to be "user friendly," and play a huge role in engaging marginalized or struggling families. In this context, it is well known that parents and children prefer school-based over clinic-based services, because they are less stigmatizing, less frightening, and more accessible.

Youth who become disaffected and disengage from their school, then, also become disconnected from a vital system of supports and supervision. They develop entrenched negative attitudes. They seek acceptance and approval from young people who have had similar experiences. They are hostile to the idea of returning to the system, partly because of repeated failures but also because of an increasing awareness that their academic skills have sunk below an embarrassing level. Parents and other concerned adults must often use huge incentives to lure them back to school. Sometimes, unfortunately, the justice system is seen as one way to force them back; school attendance can be mandated as a condition of probation in the hope that the young person will re-engage with the school.

Disability Rights

There are currently no disability laws that protect the rights of children under school age in Canada. There is no legal mandate to provide services for infants or preschool children with disabilities. Still, prior to the 1970s there were no major federal laws protecting the civil and constitutional rights of children or adults with disabilities. Rights for the disabled began with prohibitions against discrimination on the basis of physical handicaps; by the end of the 1980s, these prohibitions had extended in all Canadian jurisdictions to include mental disabilities.

The Community Living movement accompanied the disability rights movement from the 1970s into the 1980s. Institutional care for persons based solely on a perceived mental disability was seen as inappropriate, unnecessary, and an affront to their rights and dignity. International, federal, and provincial legislation now guarantees the rights of persons with disabilities to appropriate services, accommodation, and equal opportunities in education and employment.

In 1989, Canada became one of the first signatories to the *United Nations Convention on the Rights of the Child*, signifying a national commitment to the rights and freedoms of children, including their right to develop to their fullest potential. In 1994 Canada signed the *Salamanca Statement and Framework for Action on Special Needs Education*, which obliges member nations to make primary education compulsory and free, encourage the development of different types of secondary education, make higher education accessible to all on the basis of capacity, make educational and vocational information and guidance available to all, and to take measures to encourage school attendance and reduce dropout rates.

It looks good on paper, but there is a feeling among human rights advocates that educational systems in Canada may be guilty of passive non-compliance with human rights, disability, and education laws. Canadians have rarely challenged the education system on behalf of young people with disabilities. There has been little attention paid to the education system's compliance with human rights legislation, and the few litigations that have been launched have been largely unproductive. Proving discrimination or intent to discriminate are the key issues in litigating for disability rights, but Canadian judges tend to defer to the education system. "The judicial tendency of deference to educational decision-makers is resilient and perplexing," observed Dr. Ailsa Watkinson, an educator and human rights advocate. "Although educators may be experts in public education, they are not necessarily experts in the rights of students with mental disabilities."[55]

In October 2003, the monitoring body of the *United Nations Committee on the Rights of the Child* challenged Canada on the limited avenues available for advocating for Canadian youth when their rights were being violated:

> The Committee notes that eight Canadian Provinces have an Ombudsman for Children but is concerned that not all of them are adequately empowered to exercise their tasks as fully independent national human rights institutions in accordance with the Paris Principles. Furthermore, the Committee regrets that such an institution at the Federal level has not been established.[56]

Without an ombudsman, the lone advocate faces formidable odds. Navigating the labyrinths of the legal system to resolve a problem can take a great deal of time, money, and energy, and there remains in Canada a profound misunderstanding about the rights of persons with mental disabilities.

Conclusions

Prejudice and discrimination against people with mental disabilities and illnesses are inspired by fears based on stereotypes and misunderstandings about how people with disabilities ought to be treated. The marginalization of people with mental disabilities often begins with prejudice — a thought, feeling, or action based on pre-judgement. When prejudice against a particular group or person becomes entrenched, it creeps into everything we do. When it enters the collective thought stream and daily actions of society, it becomes systemic.

A young person's vulnerability to a mental disability is a combination of preexisting genetic, biological, and temperamental factors, as well as a wide range of social, emotional, and physical factors. Mental disabilities can be triggered by a traumatic event or by chronic social stressors.

The functional impact of a mental disability depends on the severity or persistence of stressors, whether the young person has adequate coping skills, and whether adequate supports and interventions are provided. Early identification of mental health issues is critical for youth who become involved in the criminal justice system. While mental disabilities pose definite challenges to understanding and responding to a youth's behaviour, most young offenders with mental disabilities do not pose a risk to public safety. Thus, we need to be vigilant and sensitive to how the identification of mental disabilities in youth affects the legal process for them, especially when we make short- or long-term predictions about youth based on their mental disability. While we need to encourage an understanding about the functional competencies of these youth, we must be sensitive to the fact that misinterpretations could affect the legal consequences they face.

The way in which offending and victimization may influence one another is an important consideration, as the negative experiences of young people are often set aside because of fears they will develop a victim mentality and not take responsibility for their offences. The challenge facing the justice, health, and education systems is to provide timely treatment and long-term rehabilitative services for these youth in the community. This includes determining how to use the justice system appropriately so that their involvement with the system does not further stigmatize or harm them.

CHAPTER FOUR

The Snowball Effect

... it is important to understand that equal treatment will not always result in equality; in fact, treating everyone in an identical fashion may frequently produce serious inequality.

— J. Epp Buckingham
Human Rights

A young person's vulnerability may be evident long before he or she comes into contact with the law. Pre-existing behaviours associated with delinquency and high-risk lifestyles are the result of a youth's disconnection from his or her support systems. Some professionals argue that it is impossible to distinguish the adverse effects of a young person's contact with the criminal justice system from the ongoing difficulties of living with a mental disability, but in many clinicians' experience, youths' mental states prior to running foul of the law exacerbate their vulnerability when they find themselves up against the blunt instrument of the criminal justice system. Lack of resources and supports cannot but work against them, and, once caught, they have difficulty extracting themselves.

Like a snowball gathering bulk as it rolls down a hill, the system gathers increasing numbers of young offenders with mental disabilities as it proceeds downhill. The snowball effect is an apt metaphor for the cumulative fears and anxieties that manifest themselves when a youth with mental disabilities is held to the same standards and expectations as others. The situation is analogous to demanding that a one-legged person stand up and walk, or that a sightless person read passages from a book. Yet the system routinely expects comparable feats from youth who suffer mental disabilities. Differential processing is both a cause and an effect of the systemic prejudices that exist against youth with disabilities within the justice system.

A systemic bias results when young people with mental disabilities are misunderstood and mistreated, often unintentionally, by procedures and practices that are already difficult for the non-disabled offender.[1] Youth with mental disabilities, for example, are far more likely to get caught committing criminal acts than are their non-disabled peers. Statistically, they are more likely to be arrested, charged, found guilty, and formally processed.[2] They are less likely to be able to take the steps necessary to avoid apprehension and arrest, and less able to construct alibis or deflect blame. Moreover, they are prone to self-incrimination.[3]

Systemic biases tend to pigeonhole youth with disabilities according to common denominators rather than the unique characteristics of each person. Thus, intellectually handicapped youth with intense or prolonged involvement with the justice system are generally subject to greater restrictions and receive more intensive supervision in the community. This differential processing may not appear to be a bad thing, but in reality it increases the chances that the youth will be caught committing further violations, such as breach of probation, resulting in new charges. The youth is thus at risk for harsher sanctions, as he or she will now have a prior record.

The cycle repeats itself, collectively resulting in disproportionately large numbers of mentally disabled youth involved with the youth justice system at any one time. The number of youth involved at later stages of the process — those serving custodial sentences or on probation — reflects the cumulative effect of systemic biases at earlier stages: there are, again, a disproportionate number of youth with mental disabilities on probation and in custodial facilities.[4]

Differential treatment is not necessarily unfair. Police have a discretionary role in dealing with young offenders, and their decisions may be influenced by a number of factors related to their perceptions and interactions with a young person. An arresting officer's perceptions may well lead to a more sensitive approach to the young person's plight, but they can also lead to systemic bias if the officer misinterprets the youth's behaviour. Adolescents with severe and easily recognizable mental disabilities may be swiftly and appropriately diverted from the justice system, but mental disabilities that are not immediately apparent often go undetected. More subtle types of disabilities will have little influence on police officers' decisions.

Youth with impulsive traits and deficiencies in interpersonal skills may present as defiant, manipulative, and uncaring during their contact with police. They lack the social skills necessary to make a favourable impression on the arresting officers,[5] and are therefore more likely to be arrested.[6]

Out-of-Court Measures

The *Youth Criminal Justice Act* requires police officers to consider such measures as warnings, cautions, and referrals before initiating any judicial proceedings. But a good deal of expertise and sensitivity on the part of both the police and the Crown are necessary in the consideration of out-of-court measures for particular offenders. Ideally, arresting officers will have highly developed interpersonal skills as well as a thorough knowledge of community services. In reality, discretionary actions by the police will be determined in large part by what they believe is likely to work in deterring youth crime. Officers who have had experience with a particular youth may be unable to suppress their biases.

The Crown is also subject to various pressures as it deals with information provided by police and submissions from parents and others in the community. If defence counsel are involved early in the process, many difficulties can be dealt with in terms of mitigating possible biases or overlooking important information, but this assumes that youth will exercise their right to have counsel involved at this stage.

In order to be considered for extrajudicial measures, youth must present themselves as willing and able to comply with the expectations of the proposed measures. This assumes a level of sophistication and competence that is well beyond the capacities of many, even among non-disabled youth. They will be expected to understand complex concepts, and pick up social cues and other nonverbal information. They will be expected to provide appropriate responses, attuned to the perspectives of authority figures. They will be expected to weigh the costs and benefits of a particular course of action, to follow long explanations and complex reasoning, and to remain patient during verbally mediated processes. In a situation that is placing impossible demands on them, many look for the quickest way out and agree to things they do not understand. In such circumstances, it is highly likely that youth with mental disabilities will not appear amenable to extrajudicial measures.

The *Youth Criminal Justice Act* states that evidence on which police have taken no further action in respect of an offence should not be used as evidence of prior offending in future court appearances. In practice, however, evidence that a previous offence has been dealt with extrajudicially can still bias decisions made by the Crown or the police. Information about the youth's compliance, amenability to treatment, and motivation based on previous interactions with the system will be available to police and prosecutors, and could easily bias their decisions.

For example, the fact that a youth has offended once and has now re-offended could be construed as resistance to rehabilitation and deterrence. This may suggest, in turn, that the offending behaviour is becoming a pattern. On the other hand, the knowledge that previous offences have been handled by extrajudicial sanctions could be a positive factor in the court's considerations. That the youth had been compliant and amenable in the past would suggest deference to authority and a capacity to behave responsibly.

Under the YCJA, there is potential for a wide range of extrajudicial measures and sanctions that could be beneficial for youth with mental disabilities. In many cases, however, their success depends on the presence of a knowledgeable, unbiased, and supportive person to advocate for the young person's rights, to explain concepts and procedures, and to correct misinterpretations or misunderstanding about the youth's demeanour or capabilities. Efforts by police, lawyers, and parents to inform the youth, to assess the youth's understanding, and assist the youth to act maturely, thoughtfully, and decisively will vary depending on the situation.

Extrajudicial measures would allow youth with suspected mental disabilities to be referred to assessment services that could prevent the youth's further contact with the police. Instead of being charged with an offence, the youth would be referred to a community program or agency to assist him or her in avoiding future criminal behaviour.

Substance abuse offers an apt example. Police may indicate that, if the accused fails to comply with treatment, a charge will be laid. It seems simple enough, but it becomes rapidly complex if the police don't have adequate information to make an informed decision about what kind of referral is appropriate or what type of services are likely to be successful. Further, the youth's family may not agree to the referral. The youth may not, either. The youth, in fact, may be utterly unmotivated to participate in treatment, even if he or she consents to the referral and attends an initial appointment or two. Almost all services will require the consent of the youth and, depending on the capabilities or age of the person in question, the consent of the parents. By the time the youth gets to the appointment, however, he or she may not understand or appreciate the need for it.

Extrajudicial measures require that youth understand the implications of the decisions they are making, but they may end up agreeing to something they do not fully appreciate, or they may refuse co-operation outright, not understanding the implications of being formally charged under the law. Youth with mental disabilities will be prone to behave impulsively and unlikely to appreciate the nature of their decisions. Their behaviour may indicate to police that they do not take the situation seriously; it may present as a complete lack of empathy for the victim, or merely defiance.

Other factors influence the process. Many adolescents with mental disabilities present with disruptive behaviours, and their relationship with their parents may be strained as a result. Police generally treat parents as reliable sources of information about their child's history and current needs, and tend to accept at face value that the youth is exhibiting an escalating pattern of antisocial behaviour without obtaining confirmation from other sources.

Police might be largely ignorant of the type of disability a youth is struggling with. So might the parents. Parents may also be unaware of services that could be provided through the school or mental health services. Some parents don't even know their child has been identified as having a disability and is receiving special services at school.

Because of narrow definitions and mandates, child welfare services are often unwilling to get involved with families unless the parents are the ones abusing their children, so the parents of mentally disabled youth will sometimes seek help from the justice system when they feel they have exhausted their other options. Some parents tell the authorities that they have become afraid of their child, and they fear that other children in the home are at risk. When the youth is formally charged, the parents hope that the authority of the law will make the youth attend treatment sessions and get the services he or she needs. These parents, feeling misunderstood and depleted, come to view criminal sanctions as a respite from long-standing conflicts both with their child and with the various systems that were supposed to support them.

Some parents — at the height of discouragement and frustration, and feeling utterly disempowered — finally set a bottom line with their defiant and oppositional child only when contact with the law pushes them to make a decision. The parents' exhaustion as much as their behaviours and attitudes can have a marked influence on how decision-makers view the adolescent offender and his or her situation. The police might well feel empathy for the parents and want to rescue them from their plight.

Many factors come into play when interpreting a young person's presentation during extrajudicial measures. It is likely, for instance, that the youth is experiencing high levels of emotional arousal that will amplify any tendencies he or she may already have. Youth who are temperamentally impulsive become more so when they have been drinking alcohol. Some youth become passive and uncommunicative when under the influences of illicit drugs. Others become agitated or paranoid. Youth who perceive the situation in a way that causes them to become anxious or fearful may react at an instinctual level and try to escape the situation. They may make impulsive decisions simply to terminate the anxiety. They are vulnerable to police interrogation tactics that may include the promise of leniency and an expedited return home in exchange for co-operation. They may be influenced by immediate rewards and not bother to weigh out the consequences of their decisions. Some may view being charged and put on probation as the easier and simpler option when compared with proposed extrajudicial measures.

Conditions of Release and Probation

Youth with mental disabilities generally have to comply with more conditions during the period of their probation than do their non-disabled counterparts. This is a result of the perception that mentally disabled youth need more supervision, more external controls, and more immediate consequences. On the positive side, such youth benefit from an individualized approach, and court-sanctioned conditions may include assessments and other services that could assist the court in later proceedings and assist the family in accessing services. Involved and supportive parents usually have a good idea of what their child can handle. They may seem overprotective at times, but they can usually predict when a particular condition may lead to failure. Overriding the authority of parents in setting up conditions rarely helps youth with mental disabilities.

Legal professionals and justice workers may not always realize how much parents must do to ensure their child's compliance with court-ordered conditions. The court may not realize how much parents or others working with the youth must structure experiences for their youth so they don't continually fail or make mistakes that have serious consequences. The question of whether the parents have the resources to support the conditions imposed must be taken into account if the youth is to succeed.

Many young people, while remaining dependent on their parents in many ways, experience a strong drive toward independence on entering adolescence. Youth with mental disabilities are no different, and they are not immune to the embarrassment normal youth feel at the insinuation that they are not capable of handling certain things on their own. Youth who are appearing in court with their parents are keenly aware that the courtroom is a public place, and they are sensitive to the fact that judges are asking questions of their parents about what conditions to set or what conditions they think their child can handle. The result is that they feel stupid and embarrassed. Sometimes it cannot be avoided, but it would be preferable if the judge sorted out these issues prior to court, with the help of pre-sentence reports and other assessments, or adjourned briefly to meet with the family about these matters. Youth will save face tremendously if conditions are set carefully and fairly, and they are spared the shame of hearing in court that they are incapable of meeting one condition or another.

Although there is potential here for meaningful intervention, youth with disabilities experience difficulty dealing with more than two or three conditions. Attempts to impose a comprehensive set of conditions should be discouraged in cases where a few, well-framed conditions will suffice. Unrealistic or onerous conditions will have the opposite effect of their intention, setting the youth up for failure and differential processing.

The Adverse Impact of Custody

When young persons with mental disabilities are remanded for short periods, or sentenced to longer periods of custody, they are in danger of developing secondary disabilities and mental health problems.[7] Many find being confined and separated from their families traumatic, the trauma generated by anxiety, fear, and loneliness. Some experience a loss of emotional and behavioural control in reaction to unfamiliar authority figures. Perceiving staff and other youth as threatening, they may develop paranoid thinking and become agitated and tense. Youth who are ill equipped to handle such stress are not able to solve problems well and generally have difficulties with language. They may be afraid to voice their concerns to staff. Staff, in turn, may be unaware of the distress these youth are experiencing, so it comes as a surprise when they lose control, badmouthing staff or striking out at other youth. Such offenders are placed on stricter schedules and watched more closely, and may now be ostracized by other youth. They may be placed in isolation for a time as a consequence of their acting out. This is where the snowball begins to gather momentum.

In a correctional facility, youth with mental disabilities are at greater risk of victimization than their non-disabled peers.[8] They are more likely to be harassed, sexually assaulted, and taken advantage of.[9] Peer groups in such settings are quick to notice signs of weakness, and may try to manipulate the disabled among them for their own agendas.[10] Youth with mental disabilities may go to great lengths to be accepted because of their previous experiences of peer rejection. They are therefore more susceptible to peer pressure and more suggestible to criminal attitudes and behaviours. Having experienced social isolation in school and the community, they tend to feel somewhat grandiose when their peers are paying attention to them.[11]

Some youth with mental disabilities actually manage fairly well in custody. They seem to benefit from the structure and predictability, and they don't seem as upset about being there as they probably should be. It seems almost as if their functional impairments go underground while they are in custody, but once they are released to the community they struggle; difficulties with day-to-day managing resurface, and they quickly come into contact with old and new stressors.[12] They have little idea how to create structure for themselves, and are in danger of attaching themselves to a negative peer group. Some say they wouldn't mind returning to custody, where life was less stressful, safer, and more predictable. Some experience custody staff as caring and consistent, but relationships that may have developed during their time in custody are abruptly terminated when they get out, leaving some with little or no support in their lives.

This is hardly a rationale for keeping them in jail, however.

Conclusions

The snowball effect is a metaphor for the cumulative disadvantage that results when youth with mental disabilities are held to the same expectations as non-disabled youth during their involvement with the justice system. Systemic biases can be mitigated by a better understanding of the impact of developmental issues unique to the adolescent period, as well as a better understanding of the impact of cognitive, behavioural, and emotional difficulties that stem from a mental disability.

CHAPTER FIVE

Examples and Strategies

Beyond motivation, there must also be ability. . . . *Good motivation does not compensate for poor strategies.*

— Michael Yapko
Breaking the Patterns of Depression

Examples

It is relatively easy to characterize the general features of common mental disabilities found in young offenders, but there is no single type of person who conforms to the diagnoses. Every youth is possessed of a unique constellation of characteristics, personality and behavioural features, proclivities, and preferences. Youth who meet the criteria for these mental disabilities are a heterogeneous group. While many may have characteristics related to a particular mental disability, this does not mean that they *are* their disability. As with any method of classifying symptoms, one must be cognizant of the tendency to lose sight of the person behind the label.

Intellectual Disabilities

The label "intellectual disability" applies to a broad range of thinking and learning skills, and generally presents as a significant discrepancy between a youth's chronological age and mental ability relative to peers of the same age. The capacities of a youth with an intellectual disability may be characterized as a type of intellectual immaturity: the youth has the intellectual capacities of a younger child. The comparison is useful in helping parents and teachers gauge appropriate expectations for the child — especially for a younger child, but it is an oversimplification which offers no hint of the full extent of the personality types and capacities found among youth with intellectual disabilities. They are a heterogeneous group who show different patterns of assets and deficits, and they vary greatly in their adaptive coping skills.

There are many prenatal, perinatal, and postnatal factors[1] associated with intellectual disabilities, and they may overlap in youth with multiple disabilities, including physical disabilities, medical disorders, genetic disorders, pervasive developmental disorders, and behavioural disorders. Most children are identified as having intellectual disabilities well before their 18th birthday, although some in the mildly impaired range may not be identified until later adolescence. It is easier to identify intellectual disabilities in children who present in the moderate to profound levels, because their intellectual impairment obviously affects their living skills. It is more difficult to distinguish intellectual disabilities in the mild range because such children can have relatively good daily living and social adaptation skills earlier in their development. Thus, the discrepancy between the individual and his or her age peers does not become apparent until much later.

Many children in the mild range may also remain undiagnosed because there is significant dispersion among their intellectual profiles and functional abilities, and they are able to cope fairly well with supports and strategies that compensate for their slower learning ability. It usually becomes obvious between the ages of 10 to 12 that they will not "catch up," however, and as they get older the gap between their abilities and the abilities of their age peers widens. Expectations and demands increase rapidly as children move into adolescence and adolescents move into early adulthood, accentuating youths' functional impairments related to their intellectual disabilities.

It is not unreasonable to expect youth with mild intellectual disabilities to achieve a grade six reading ability and acquire some of the necessary functional skills for independent living and vocational training. But the fact remains that they have a learning style that places them at risk for a host of adaptive problems as they mature.

There are many secondary disabilities and mental health issues that may develop in youth with intellectual disabilities, but they are extremely difficult to diagnose owing to such things as poor communication skills and avoidance behaviours — features of intellectual disabilities. Because of the difficulties in diagnosis, such secondary disabilities are rarely addressed at an early stage of development.

Research with groups of youth with mild intellectual disabilities suggests their self-concepts may be quite fragile. Some have inordinate difficulty accepting and admitting to their limitations, a feature of their presentation that goes beyond the problem of comprehension.[2] They are in fact capable of developing complex defensive structures as a result of their negative experiences and assaults on their self-esteem.

Youth with intellectual disabilities learn more slowly than others, and so the skills they acquire may be limited. Some complex skills will take many years to acquire, and expectations must be gauged appropriately. Youth with intellectual disabilities generally require repeated learning experiences to solidify new skills, while skills they have acquired at one time or in one setting may be lost if they are not used. They have difficulty transferring or generalizing a skill from one context to another, and may require instruction in each environment in which the skill is supposed to be used.

Youth with intellectual disabilities also suffered deficits in regard to social skills. These may present as problems with self-control or cooperating with others, an inability to assert themselves or take responsibility for their actions, and difficulty demonstrating empathy. Their social skills may be variable, and their performance inconsistent, often depending on the context. They often display a social gaucherie that they are utterly unaware of, annoying or affronting others without the least intention or awareness of it.

Borderline intellectual functioning or the "slow learner" range refers to cognitive abilities that fall a little above the mild intellectual disability range, but still below the low average range.[3] Youth in this category experience difficulties with rates of learning and tasks that require abstract thinking. They represent a grey zone on the spectrum of intellectual functioning, and are often overlooked. It is particularly difficult to diagnose borderline intellectual functioning in children who have co-occurring disruptive behaviour disorders. Many may have a specific learning disability. Compared to children with mild intellectual disabilities, they have much better prognoses in terms of adaptive living and vocational training, particularly if they receive appropriate services and educational supports. They must put extraordinary effort into academic learning, but many are capable of achieving literacy and vocational skills. On the other hand, they are more likely to have undiagnosed social, emotional, and learning problems. Yet they are often aware of their difficulties, and suffer embarrassment and frustration as a result.

Many have a history of being misunderstood, and they can be difficult to assess owing to cultural and other factors that may have affected their acquisition of information, language, and social skills. Their abilities can seem fragmented, incomplete, or inconsistent. They often suffer from low self-esteem and chronic anxiety, and resort to disruptive behaviour to avoid academic tasks. Others withdraw into the social background in an attempt to hide their difficulties, and do not ask for or receive the academic assistance they need. Some simply foreclose on problem solving in academic or otherwise complex situations.

Some youth with borderline intellectual functioning are performing far below expectations as a result of learned helplessness, passivity, and demoralization. They may show acquired learning disabilities or attention deficit symptoms in academic areas because of their ongoing attempts to conceal their difficulties so they will not stand out. Many will drop out of school.

Despite their academic difficulties, many slower learners have specific strengths and interests in areas such as music, drama, art, dance, and sports. The recognition and encouragement of these personal assets can be an important way to help these youth build self-esteem and motivation.

There is evidence to show that youth and young adults who have an intellectual disability have a higher rate of rearrest than individuals who do not have an intellectual disability.[4] In part this may be linked to another line of evidence which shows that youth with intellectual disabilities who come into contact with the justice system may have complex needs including dual diagnoses that require multisystemic and long term supports.[5]

Fetal Alcohol Spectrum Disorder

Prenatal alcohol exposure is one of the most common non-hereditary causes of intellectual disabilities in Canada. FASD is an umbrella term describing the range of effects that can occur in individuals who were exposed to alcohol prenatally, including physical, behavioural, and intellectual disabilities with lifelong implications. According to Health Canada,

> FASD is the result of maternal alcohol consumption during pregnancy and has implications for the affected person, the mother, the family and the community. Since FAS was first described in 1973, it has become apparent that it is complex; affected people exhibit a wide range of expression, from severe growth restriction, intellectual disability, birth defects and characteristic dysmorphic facial features to normal growth, facial features, and intellectual abilities, but with lifelong deficits in several domains of brain functioning.[6]

Until recently, there was no consensus in diagnosing alcohol-related disorders. The guidelines developed by Health Canada in 2005 offer the potential to improve both data collection and the understanding of prevalence rates. Some quarter of a million Canadians suffer the effects of prenatal alcohol exposure, ranging from mild to severe. Nationwide, full-blown Fetal Alcohol Syndrome (FAS) is estimated to occur in one to three of every 1,000 live births, and partial Fetal Alcohol Syndrome (pFAS) in five to 15 of every 1,000 live births, although variations in communities and small samples make it difficult to estimate the prevalence accurately.[7]

FASD-related disabilities can be lifelong.[8] A study published in 1999 reported that over 23 per cent of youth remanded to a forensic psychiatric inpatient assessment unit in Vancouver were found to have alcohol-related diagnoses.[9] In 1996 a Federal-Provincial-Territorial Task Force on Youth Justice voiced many concerns about the prevalence of fetal alcohol spectrum disorders in the youth justice system and the challenges of providing services for these young offenders.[10] For young people with FASD-related disabilities "involvement with the criminal justice system is the final common pathway resulting from complex interactions among adverse developmental, environmental, medical, and psychiatric conditions."[11]

Under the Health Canada guidelines, there are three primary alcohol-related diagnostic terms that fall under the umbrella of Fetal Alcohol Spectrum Disorder (FASD): Fetal Alcohol Syndrome (FAS), Partial Fetal Alcohol Syndrome (pFAS), and Alcohol-Related Neurodevelopmental Disorder (ARND).[12] The diagnosis of these disorders requires collaboration between a physician specifically trained in FASD diagnosis as well as a team of professionals that includes a psychologist, at minimum, and ideally an occupational therapist, a physiotherapist, and a speech-language pathologist. Many other professionals — including social workers, mental health workers, nurses, probation officers, and teachers — may contribute to the diagnostic process, which is complex; for instance, other causes of the child's growth patterns, facial features and neurodevelopmental impairments must be ruled out before an alcohol-related disorder can be ruled in.

The criteria for diagnosing FAS and pFAS are:

(1) evidence of prenatal or postnatal growth impairment in one of three areas (more typical in FAS): birth weight or height, current weight or height, disproportionately low weight-to-height ratio;

(2) simultaneous presentation of three facial anomalies (two for pFAS) at any age (short palpebral fissure length, smooth or flattened philtrum, and thin upper lip);

(3) evidence of impairment at any age in three or more central nervous system domains (hard and soft neurological signs, brain structure, cognition, communication, academic achievement, memory, executive functioning and abstract reasoning, attention deficit/hyperactivity, adaptive behaviour, social skills, and social communication); and

(4) confirmed (both FAS and pFAS) or unconfirmed (for FAS) maternal drinking during pregnancy.[13]

The diagnosis of Alcohol-Related Neurodevelopmental Disorder is based on two criteria: evidence of impairment in three or more central nervous domains (noted above for FAS and pFAS), and confirmed maternal drinking during pregnancy. Many people believe that FAS is a more serious diagnosis than pFAS because of the word "partial" in the diagnostic term. In Saskatchewan, for example, some school divisions do not always recognize pFAS as a designated intellectual disability that should receive special education funding. But Health Canada stresses that both FAS and pFAS can have serious implications for a child's functioning, as "the deficits in brain function may be similar."[14]

Youth with ARND may also have serious functional deficits. There is growing awareness among public, legal, educational, medical, and mental health professionals of the functional impairments that can result in such disorders.[15] Partial FAS and ARND can seem "invisible" and have often been overlooked entirely or their impact has been grossly minimized. But we now know that a number of secondary issues may develop alongside these so-called subtle forms of alcohol-related diagnoses, including school difficulties, mental health problems, frequent foster placements, alcohol and drug abuse, inappropriate sexual behaviour, and incarceration. Many have poor prospects for independent living, and may end up homeless and unemployed.

Protective factors for youth with FASD-related disabilities have been found to be: living in a stable and nurturing home for greater than 70 per cent of their life, diagnosis under six years of age, no history of physical abuse, eligibility for and access to special services, and living with alcohol abuse in their homes for less than 30 per cent of their lives. Youth with FAS have slightly better outcomes than those with pFAS and ARND, perhaps because they are likely to be diagnosed earlier and are thus more likely to have protective factors in place at an earlier age.[16]

School-age and adolescent youth with FAS may experience functional deficits related to memory, judgement, abstract reasoning, and adaptive functioning. They may also show uneven verbal receptive and expressive skills, although the low quality of their verbal skills is frequently masked by high fluency or verbosity. These functional impairments may lead to socially inappropriate behaviour, anger management difficulties, indiscriminate friendliness toward new acquaintances or strangers, fearlessness (often related to impulsiveness), and persistent or repetitive behaviours or thoughts. Youth with alcohol-related diagnoses may also struggle with hyperactivity, heightened sensitivity to sensory stimulation, and a variable attention span. Many also suffer from Attention Deficit/Hyperactivity Disorder (ADHD).

Of course, not all youth with FASD will present with these symptoms; each person will show a unique profile of strengths and difficulties.

Interventions that have proved effective with children and youth with alcohol-related diagnoses include educational programming, vocational services, behavioural interventions, the psychiatric management (including medication) of co-existing mental health problems, a stable home environment, positive role models, and long-term case management.

A number of strategies have been recommended for youth with FASD. Some are similar to those for youth with intellectual or learning disabilities, disruptive behaviour disorders, and autism spectrum disorders, but, once again, their effectiveness will depend on the profile of the youth in question. Some will benefit from medications that target such symptoms as impulsivity, inattentiveness or hyperactivity, mood swings, aggression, depression, and seizures.[17]

There is great heterogeneity in youth who fall under the umbrella of FASD, pointing up the importance of careful diagnosis and sensitive treatment strategies.

Disruptive Behaviour Disorders

Many youth who find themselves involved with the justice system have a history of disruptive behaviours; many will be experiencing one when they come into contact with the law. They include a spectrum of interrelated conditions such as Attention Deficit/Hyperactivity Disorder (ADHD), Oppositional Defiant Disorder (ODD), Conduct Disorder (CD), and a few residual categories. As with most other disorders, they frequently overlap in an individual, and sometimes there seems to be a progression from ADHD to ODD to CD. About 80 per cent of people with ADHD have at least one concurrent disorder. The co-occurrence of ODD in children with ADHD doubles the risk of developing CD.[18]

Conduct associated with a disruptive behaviour disorder may include disobedience, lying, aggressive behaviour, minor theft, truancy during elementary school, and early substance abuse. A quarter of these children are at risk for contact with the youth justice system by the time they are 12.[19]

ADHD can take several forms, but sufferers typically experience difficulty sustaining their attention on a task or event, and frequently interrupt or intrude on others; they may talk excessively, and behave as if they are being driven by a motor. Impaired memory, impaired or nonexistent management abilities, and an inability to organize behaviour across time toward future goals (and the inability to resist distractions in the process) are some of the key difficulties noted in youth with ADHD. They also have difficulty co-ordinating thought, speech, and behaviour in logical sequences, and they often find it impossible to persist at a given activity.

The problem of self-regulation associated with ADHD has an attention component, an inhibitory component, and an organizational component. The attention component relates to focusing or deploying mental resources on a particular task; the inhibitory component refers to the ability to control impulses or delay responding; and the organizational component is the process that guides and directs mental control. A person suffering ADHD will have great difficulty with self-regulation and will likely need external guidance and support to function effectively.[20]

Oppositional Defiant Disorder is characterized by a pattern of negative and hostile behaviour. Youth with ODD lose their temper frequently. They argue with adults, actively defying reasonable rules and requests, and then blame others for their mistakes and misbehaviour. They deliberately annoy people for no apparent reason, and are easily annoyed by others. They are often angry, resentful, spiteful, and vindictive.

Conduct Disorder is manifested in patterns of antisocial behaviour that include aggression toward people and animals, destruction of property, deceitfulness, theft, and serious violations of rules. CD appears to have its antecedents in precocious antisocial manifestations of defiance and patterns of relationships that indicate difficulty appreciating the perspective of others. CD in adolescence frequently brings youth into conflict with the law, and it is sometimes difficult to separate delinquents from those who truly suffer CD. Early onset conduct disorders may indicate a pattern of behaviour that will develop into a continuing criminal lifestyle in adolescence and adulthood.

Aggressive behaviour in ADHD, ODD, and CD can take many forms, but physical aggression, the use of weapons, cruelty to animals, and vandalism are especially high in youth with CD. They, too, have an increased risk of developing a range of secondary disorders such as substance abuse, schizophrenia, mood disorders, obsessive-compulsive disorder, social anxiety, phobias, and panic disorder. CD is associated with self-injury, injury to others, poor school performance, learning disabilities, and early school dropout. CD can arise early, but it is more often seen in older children and adolescents.

Researchers have been trying to discern the core deficit in young people with ADHD, ODD, and CD. Deficits associated with ODD and CD usually focus on compliance issues and antisocial thinking, but most young people with these problems indicate similar deficiencies as those described for ADHD. Behaviours associated with ODD appear to have their roots in developmental processes that are not well understood, but disrupted child and care-giver relationships, as well as coercive parenting practices, often aggravate the initial stages of the disorder. People's reaction to the annoying and often challenging behaviour of ADHD children may result in further negative interactions, as these children seem compelled to push back rather than give in. Over time, they will attempt to control or dominate situations through their negative behaviours.

A key strategy for working with youth with disruptive behaviour disorders is creating external sources of motivation, sometimes referred to as strategies used *at the point of performance*.[21] Talking about what needs to be done at some future time is apt to be a less successful strategy than those that are implemented in a specific context. ADHD has been described as a condition of doing what you know rather than of knowing what to do. Therefore, "evaluating how the individual is performing in meeting daily demands, responsibilities, and other academic, social, occupational, familial obligations will be far more sensitive indicators of ADHD than will evaluation of the individual's knowledge about how to do these things."[22] Treatments for these disorders are usually multimodal and multi-systemic, and may include medication to assist with symptom control and psychosocial treatments. Medications usually focus on reducing symptoms of unfocused attention, impulsivity, over-arousal, and aggression.

Psychosocial treatments that have been shown to be effective include early family and school interventions. Successful behavioural approaches have included social skills and aggression management training, along with developing more positive interactions at home and at school. Providing immediate feedback is likely to be more successful than the promise of future rewards or punishment, as these young people benefit from reinforcement at the point of performance. They also require a fair degree of structure, and need assistance with organization throughout the day. They are less successful in open-ended situations where there is little supervision or structure. Parents of children with disruptive behaviour disorders can benefit from professional support and learning specific parenting techniques, while teachers benefit from assistance in the classroom and open communication between home and school.

Strategies

In clinical practice, three issues stand out when youth with mental disabilities confront the justice system: (1) chronic misunderstanding, (2) reduced remembering, and (3) impulsivity and planning difficulties.[23] When young people experience difficulty in any of these areas, they will have corresponding difficulties navigating the justice system. Youth with intellectual disabilities, fetal alcohol spectrum disorders, and disruptive behaviour disorders may be struggling with one or all three of these issues, in varying degrees.

Chronic Misunderstanding

Youth in court proceedings need to understand the meanings of individual words and the different meanings a word can have in order to follow a conversation. Young people who understand sentences can appreciate the effects of word order, punctuation, and grammar, but they must also grasp the fact that word order and intonation influence the meaning of a sentence. When processing greater amounts of language, they must be able to relate the ideas between sentences and to follow the theme, or narrative, of all the words taken together. This engages not only verbal skills at the sentence and word level, but memory, which is the ability to use prior knowledge in the process of comprehension. It is difficult for youth to comprehend greater volumes of language if they are struggling with phrases or sentences. The result is chronic misunderstanding.

Youth who have difficulties with chronic misunderstanding will have trouble with specific word meanings, or they will be slow in associating them. They may interpret words too literally, or recite them by rote, and in an inaccurate context. They may "tune out" when someone is speaking, exhibiting the classic glazed look as their eyes unfocus, or fix on something other than the speaker. They are unable to paraphrase something that's just been told them, but they rarely ask questions or seek clarification. They will nod their heads to indicate they understand, when in fact they don't. Alternatively, they might appear impatient and rushed, and express dismissive or impulsive disagreement or agreement.

Youth with comprehension deficits at the word level need to be taught word meanings, and will benefit from a simplified vocabulary. It is important to avoid jargon, which they will not understand, and humour or sarcasm, which they may interpret literally. At the sentence level, they will have trouble understanding questions and explanations. At the paragraph level, they will be able to grasp only fragments of what is being said. They may have difficulty with temporal elements of the discourse, and be unable to identify themes or story lines.

There are a number of specific processing problems that may be related to comprehension in youth with atypical brain development, including their *rate of processing* verbal information. When the information moves by too quickly, they are likely to miss the message. They need a slower pace, and will benefit from visual cues, such as pictures or outlines.

Another problem is *small chunk size capacity*. This basically means that they can only deal with a small amount of material at a time. They need shorter sentences, and briefer directions or explanations.

A third problem may involve the *conceptual depth* of the information. Metaphors, analogies, abstract terms, figurative language, and symbolism may be a real challenge. They may not grasp the meaning of words such as remorse, irony, pride, and empathy, or words that don't have an obvious visual or concrete referent. If youth who experience chronic misunderstanding are given visual examples or descriptions of behaviour that illustrate these concepts, they are much more likely to understand them. One young man who was repeatedly told by his workers that he did not show remorse turned out to have no idea what the word meant. Pictures of facial expressions and stories that illustrated the concept helped him grasp the feeling behind the word.

Some youth get caught up in a word or phrase they don't understand and are unable to focus on other parts of the message. Concrete images rather than abstract descriptions can help them focus on the message. "Jail" is more concrete than "custodial facility." Similarly, "You broke the rule about not yelling," will be far more comprehensible than saying, "Your behaviour was noncompliant." A youth who shows no interest in "the outcome of judicial processing" will sit up and take notice when told, "The judge will tell you the sentence."

Another problem often seen in youth with comprehension problems is *inaccurate perceptions about their comprehension*. These youth actually don't know when they don't understand something. Sometimes it is the result of a passive learning style; they skim over things or assume they understand something when they don't. Sometimes they're saving face by not admitting they don't know something. These youth commonly develop personal *barriers to asking for clarification* — whether from anxiety, fear of rejection or put downs, or deference to authority — which may be related to experiences of marginalization owing to cultural factors.

It is important to recognize, too, that some youth have *poor visual recognition*. They do not recognize faces or places; they do not use visual clues effectively. Others have difficulty associating visual and verbal information. In clinical practice, youth often present with incomplete understandings of the court process and their consultations with their lawyers. They often have incomplete understandings of their conditions of release. When asking such youth questions, it is helpful to give concrete reference points rather than abstract questions. "Tell me what happened in court yesterday," is far more likely to elicit a meaningful response than, "What was your experience of being a defendant?" Concepts relating to intangible ideas such as "rights" or "empathy" are difficult for youth with comprehension problems, but some abstractions can be made understandable by getting the youth to visualize a concept — for example, drawing the seating plan of the court and who will be sitting where — or going through a trial run, with the youth role-playing. They will have trouble grasping concepts such as "pre-trial conference" or "plea hearing," but they will do better when a sympathetic lawyer or youth worker walks them through the process.

Reduced Remembering

There is no simple way to understand the brain functions involved in various types of remembering. Memory can be conceptualized as a complex pathway of processes that may be interrupted at any point along the way, leading to reduced remembering. To remember information effectively for later retrieval and to learn new skills or procedures, youth need a number of skills. We cannot possibly cover all of the areas of memory that may be affected in youth with atypical development, however, we will touch on several common difficulties I have seen in justice involved youth with mental disabilities.

Youth who are prone to problems of reduced remembering may lose track of what they are saying or doing, and appear confused and disorganized as a result. They have poor immediate recall of things they have just read or heard or done, and they experience difficulty sustaining a logical development of ideas when writing or speaking. They have a tendency to forget one part of a task while working on another. They may appear anxious or frustrated when performing particular tasks, or have difficulty thinking further about a problem or concept once it has been introduced. They may know both the question and the answer, but be unable to recall one while thinking about the other. Similarly, in mathematical problems, they may have difficulty carrying a number in multiplication while remembering what they are to do next. They can rarely retell or summarize something that was just said.

Problems with active working memory are common among youth with mental disabilities. They seem to have inadequate mental space to store ideas, facts, and procedures while they are working on some other aspect of the idea, the fact, or the procedure. Ideas are held in a temporary way station while they are being manipulated. Youth with difficulties focusing their attention, avoiding distraction, or persisting in an activity may, in fact, be unable to register pertinent information in the first place. Short-term, or immediate, memory may be a prerequisite for active memory. Thus, youth who are inconsistently alert, have difficulty determining what may be important to focus on, or who register only partial or superficial aspects of the information, may exhibit problems remembering.

Youth with reduced remembering sometimes have a problem with *superficial processing of the information they hear or read.* This may stem, partly, from passive learning. One way to help is to encourage them to become more active in strategies for remembering things. For example, highlighting a point in a book is passive, whereas transferring or summarizing a key point on a separate piece of paper is active (and more work). They can be encouraged to reduce their reliance on mental processing by using external aids: urge them to write information down; give them a card with the information on it; get them a day timer. If they then misplace the aids that are supposed to help them, let them write reminders on a card or even the backs of their hands.

Another strategy that helps youth who are trying to grasp sequential information is to externalize the steps to be remembered. Because they do not naturally draw these steps out in their minds, they need to be shown what is important and the order of the sequence. This also helps them focus on the task and not lose their place. A stepwise plan before starting a task or receiving new information can be helpful, as each step can be checked off as they go along. They can then review what they have done, and talk about it. Slowing down the process may also help, as they are less likely to overload and give up on remembering.

Some youth may show difficulties with *inconsistent alertness* or appear *easily distracted.* These problems may be exacerbated by already *weak language processing* abilities. Again, they will benefit from strategies that draw attention to, and simplify, important information: committing it to paper, making lists, and using note reminders.

Some youth may have *weak procedural, sequential, or linear* memory skills and require that instructions be clear and repeated. They need short sentences, and are assisted when they are provided cues, prompts, or visual aids.

Some youth have weak visual-spatial processing skills, and will benefit from approaches that include the explanation of visual-spatial concepts or walk them through an activity or process, such as role playing. They can also be given verbal or written guidelines to supplement visual information.

Some youth have trouble locating precise data in their memory, and perform better when they are given structure. But the structure must be adapted to the situation, lest it result in parroting. In some situations, such as interviewing youth for court reports or investigative police work, the interviewer must make a careful distinction between assisting the youth in expressing him or herself and asking leading questions. Youth with reduced remembering problems are highly suggestible.

Understandably, youth with memory problems experience anxiety and frustration in situations that tax their memory. It is therefore critical to create an atmosphere of calm and patience. They may need more time for some tasks, and may also benefit from spreading the task over several sessions.

Impulsivity and Planning Difficulties

Difficulty with impulsivity (often referred to as response inhibition) and planning has been defined in several ways by different researchers. Often associated with the literature about ADHD, it is generally defined as the inability to withhold a response. The literature on response inhibition overlaps with the literature on self-regulation, self-control, and impulsivity, and for all intents and purposes these terms can be considered interchangeable at the behavioural level. One definition that cuts across different mental disabilities describes impulsivity as "a predisposition toward rapid, unplanned reactions to internal or external stimuli without regard to the negative consequences of these reactions to the impulsive individual or others."[24]

Understanding the deficits associated with impulsivity is critical, as so many problems stem from it, particularly among youth who come into contact with the justice system. Impulsivity appears, at times, to represent one of the core difficulties in a number of conditions associated with atypical development. As the definition suggests, there are several components to impulsivity that need to be understood to grasp the full extent of its functional impact. Three important elements need to be understood in a complete understanding of phenomena related to this difficulty.

First, impulsivity is related to *decreased sensitivity to negative consequences of behaviour*. This aspect of the problem appears to relate to the youth's great difficulty learning from negative consequences in a way that informs future behaviour. Thus, punishment appears to have an inconsequential effect on some offenders; they often persevere in the same impulsive response despite the fact that they have been punished for it in the past. These youth are not able to learn from negative consequences in the same way as other youth.

Second, impulsivity often results in a *rapid and unplanned reaction, often before there is complete processing of information*. This means that youth often react to partial and sometimes distorted information. It also means that youth who are impulsive do not often weigh the consequences of taking a course of action before taking it. Thus, impulsivity is not preceded by planning or conscious judgement, and is fundamentally different from behaviours that result from impaired judgement or compulsive actions.

Third, impulsivity often occurs without an apparent *appreciation of the long-term consequences in tandem with a need for immediate gratification.* Thus, impulsive youth favour the short term over the long, seeking immediate gratification without thought for the long-term consequences of their actions. Similarly, they have difficulty waiting for a delayed — but possibly larger — reward, preferring a smaller one, as long as it is immediate.

One strategy for dealing with impulsivity is to make the longer-term goals explicit and identify the behaviour that creates barriers to it. For example, in clinical practice, one youth wanted to go back to his old school after having been moved following an assault charge. He was close to completing probation, and was doing reasonably well at the new school, but his return to the old school was contingent on his being able to resist getting into an argument with one of his classmates at the new school. When this classmate irritated him, the student tended to throw a book at him. The book-throwing, and the reaction that precipitated it, was highly impulsive. A plan was developed for dealing with this in the classroom. The student developed a signalling system to alert the teacher that he was becoming agitated. The teacher would respond by giving him a 10-minute pass to work on his own in an adjoining room, calming down. To keep the long-term goal in his mind of getting back to his old school, he hung a small sign on his mirror to remind him every morning of his longer-term goal. He used the mantra "think home school," and wrote it on a card he carried with him. This strategy seemed very simple, but it worked.

A problem related to impulsivity is *improper pacing.* These youth favour speed over accuracy, and sometimes a rapid *intellectual tempo* contributes to their impulsive behaviour. They have difficulty slowing down, and often jump to conclusions before thinking things through. The speed of their thinking results in less time for reasoning.

Impulsive youth also have difficulty with *self-monitoring*; they are unable to observe themselves and determine how they are doing at a particular task. Self-monitoring provides a type of internal control over our actions, allowing us to evaluate our performance and make changes based on our evaluation. Many impulsive youth have difficulty with both self-awareness and with taking stock of their performance while they are performing. They may also be insensitive to the cues others are giving them about their behaviour, so they rarely benefit from the feedback of others and rarely adjust their behaviour or performance accordingly. These youth often act as if they are doing just fine, and seem quite unaware of the impression they are making on others or the difficulties they may be having.

Conclusions

Many of the problems associated with systemic biases against youth with mental disabilities can be mitigated by a better understanding of the functional implications of mental disabilities in the context of the youth justice system. It is easy to see that youth who have problems with understanding, remembering, and impulsivity are at risk for legal difficulties as well. Once in the system, they exhibit little knowledge or appreciation of criminal procedures; they don't really understand the nature and purpose of particular proceedings, or the nature and severity of particular charges; and they have difficulty in discerning the role of key participants in the process, including their own.

Youth may struggle with different aspects of the legal process, including the nature of extrajudicial measures, arrest, pleas, court procedures, and their rights as citizens. They may be further compromised by poor self-control, and behave inappropriately in legal situations. They may be socially awkward, unable to pick up social cues or take other people's perspectives. This compromises their ability to relate to people such as police officers, lawyers, social workers, and counsellors who play significant and decisive roles in their present dilemma and their future as well.

These youth do not think in terms of consequences. They have difficulty with abstract concepts and problem-solving. They do not appreciate their personal involvement or responsibility in a given situation, and the significance of the proceedings they are a part of may elude them. They may not appreciate the range and nature of the possible penalties, or of the available legal defences. Some will inevitably be compromised in their ability to advise counsel and make rational decisions as they try to navigate the legal system. They experience difficulties in receiving and processing information and communicating with others, and in recalling information consistently, relevantly, and sequentially.

Their performance may be so inconsistent that it is impossible for people to gauge their abilities — and ultimately, also, their honesty and integrity. They cannot recall with accuracy the arrest process, and sometimes even their crime. They misconstrue information that is presented to them, or they may forget it completely.

Planning and organization skills may be so compromised that these young people are not able to plan a legal strategy at any point during the process. Complex questions that require weighing alternatives and making decisions can defeat them. They may agree to testify in court, unaware that they lack the abilities to do so effectively. Complex, abstract ideas, such as having the right not to incriminate themselves and to use appropriate legal safeguards, are beyond them.

To understand the competencies that youth require in order to navigate the youth justice system, it is necessary to identify the demands and expectations that may be placed on them. The disability paradigm suggested in the introduction to this book allows us to look at young offenders through a different, more optimistic lens. What we have found is that many youth who are involved in the justice system — in particular, youth with mental disabilities — lack the skills necessary to getting out and staying out. When they fail at this daunting task, others are quick to point out that they didn't try hard enough or were simply lacking motivation.

The psychologist Dr. Michael Yapko, quoted at the beginning of this chapter, has some interesting observations about depressed clients that apply to the issues facing many youth who suffer the implications of their mental disabilities when dealing with the law:

> . . . when I ask them *how* they'll go about getting what they want, I discover that they have either no idea or one that won't work. They think that if they just "try" hard enough, they'll succeed. (They've been told, "If at first you don't succeed, try, try again." Okay, I'll accept that, but I'd add "and when you try, try again, do something different!") When I hear them describe *how* they go about trying to do whatever they're trying to do, I almost inevitably discover what I call an "experiential deficit." An experiential deficit is a gap in a person's awareness of a vital skill or a missing step on the path to the goal, an absence that virtually precludes his success. In such instances, it's what you don't know that hurts you and prevents you from succeeding.[25]

Such "experiential deficits" can potentially prejudice young offenders who are developmentally immature or who are compromised by the functional implications of their mental disability.

CHAPTER SIX

Waiving Their Rights

[Procedural protections] must be complied with whether the authorities are dealing with the nervous and the naïve or the street-smart and worldly wise.

— Chief Judge Heino Lilles
Territorial Court of the Yukon

A youth's right to counsel and silence are important protections that are relevant at all stages of the process, beginning with first contact with the police and extending to sentencing. Like adults, youth have the right to avoid self-incrimination and to have legal counsel before and while they make a statement to the police. If they waive their rights to counsel or silence, police must ensure that offenders understand their rights sufficiently to make a knowing, intelligent, and voluntary waiver.[1]

Although the procedures are the same for youth and adults, youth are much more likely to waive their rights to counsel and silence because of their reduced capacity to understand the meaning of rights, their naïvety regarding the adversarial nature of the legal process, their predisposition to answer questions posed by people in authority, and the likelihood that they do not understand the role of counsel.[2] These propensities of adolescents generally are likely to be amplified among youth with mental disabilities.

Adolescents are likely to incriminate themselves because they lack awareness of their rights and freedoms. Without sufficient knowledge to know when to seek guidance or assistance, they may passively accept decisions that are made for them, largely unaware of the consequences.

Adolescents have less knowledge about the legal system than most adults think.[3] Similarly, defence lawyers typically overestimate young people's understanding of the system.[4] If adults, too, are lacking in basic information about the legal system — and they certainly seem to be[5] — can anyone reasonably expect a youth's parents to inform their child about legal matters? Is it any more likely that defence lawyers will offer basic information that they assume their clients already have?

Almost a decade after the *Young Offenders Act* was proclaimed, researchers found that a young person's knowledge about procedures following a criminal charge was highly variable, depending on age, and that what knowledge the youth did have was faulty and inconsistent.[6]

Researchers found no substantial increase, between the ages of 12 and 17, in a youth's ability to understand the right to counsel, although the right to silence was more often understood by older ones. The number of contacts a youth had had with the police appeared to be a mitigating factor — the greater the number understandably corresponding with a better understanding of the rights to counsel and silence.[7] The most difficult role for youth to understand across all ages was the role of defence counsel.

Given their limited knowledge and experience, it is hardly surprising that the majority of young people who come into contact with the law are likely to waive their rights to counsel and silence, even those who are questioned with their parents present. Indeed, few parents explain their children's rights to them, most holding the view that they should encourage them to cooperate with the police when they are questioned.[8] Concerns about youth waiving their rights voluntarily or under the advice of their parents has led many professionals and advocates to question the wisdom of ever allowing a youth to waive the rights to counsel. The state of Wisconsin, alone among North American jurisdictions, does not allow any juvenile to waive the right to counsel, even with parental consent.

The language police use when they interact with young people could be a barrier to youth understanding their rights. Many may not understand what "counsel" means, and most will have no idea how to obtain it. Some may not understand the concept of "rights." In such cases, is it reasonable to assume that the police have properly advised a young person of his or her rights? Do the police have an obligation to explain that the accused has not only rights, but responsibilities as well?

Like adults who are detained or arrested, youth are entitled to know the reason immediately, according to Section 10(a) of the *Charter of Rights and Freedoms*. They must appear before a Justice of the Peace within 24 hours — or as soon as possible if a Justice of the Peace is not available — to determine conditions of release or bail, according to the *Criminal Code*.

Canadian law places the onus on the Crown to establish the voluntary nature of any statement made to police when a youth has waived his or her rights to counsel and silence; judges prefer the waiver to be made in writing, and they emphasize the importance of the accused being given the opportunity to speak with a lawyer, as well as the right to have a parent or other adult present when making a statement. The *Youth Criminal Justice Act* ensures these rights explicitly, and indicates that youth should be given a reasonable opportunity to exercise them at specific points in the criminal justice process. The courts are responsible for ensuring that a young person is represented by counsel independent of his or her parents when there appears to be a conflict of interest between the parents and the youth.

Competencies Required to Waive Rights

Although this area has been less studied than other areas of competency, such as a youth's fitness to stand trial, evidence and common sense both suggest that a valid waiver of rights must meet minimal conditions. Youth must understand the words and phrases used by police to inform them of their rights; they must appreciate the adversarial nature of interrogation; they must understand the nature of the lawyer-client relationship, including its advocacy quality; they must understand the right not to incriminate themselves; they must understand the probable consequences of waiving or not waiving their rights; and they must understand that if they waive their rights to silence and counsel, their statements or confessions can only be admitted as evidence against them in later court proceedings if their waiver is made voluntarily, without duress, and with the full understanding of the implications of doing so.[9]

The adversarial process and the power differential between youth and adults is likely to amplify young people's disadvantage when placed in conflict with the law. The adolescent propensity toward independence is a basic drive of the developmental period which places them at risk for failing to ask appropriate questions or to seek clarification. They may fear being put down or seeming stupid; they may wish to show that they are not dependent on others; or they may deny they need help because of shame or anger. Depending on their age and level of understanding, they may either defer to the adults or refuse to take their advice. Some may be dismissive or impulsive; others may simply distrust adults.

Several researchers have examined the differences in degree among people who yield to suggestions that result in distorted or false confessions.[10] If the validity of a waiver should come under question in court, it is essential to know the circumstances under which the waiver was obtained, including any issues that may have arisen during the process. Courts also recognize that a youth's comprehension at the time of arrest may be different from his or her level of comprehension at the time of the court proceedings.

A young person may have been impaired by circumstances during the process of waiving his or her rights. Such circumstances might include the time of day, the length of time the youth was held and the conditions of detention prior to waiver and questioning, whether the youth was provided food or water, whether the youth was given opportunities to contact an attorney or another supportive person, and the police's demeanour, including urgings, suggestions, persuasive tactics, and forceful or coërcive tactics.[11] Possible intoxication from alcohol or other drugs, fear or anxiety, crying, fatigue, or physical illness are also issues that must be addressed if the validity of a youth's waiver of rights comes into question.

Case law suggests that courts typically associate insufficient understanding of the right to silence, the right to counsel, and the right to avoid self-incrimination with youth who are 13 or under, and those who are functioning intellectually at the borderline or lower range and have poor reading abilities. Research in the United States has shown that the ability to define the words used in police warnings and the ability to explain the meaning of the warnings in their own words are significantly related to cognitive ability, independent of socioeconomic status and cultural background. The U.S. research shows that both youth and adults with mental disabilities are compromised in all areas of competency related to any waivers they may make to their constitutional rights. Cognitive development has been shown to be a particularly strong predictor of difficulty in understanding waivers as well as other legal procedures.[12]

When youth with mental disabilities waive their rights to counsel, there may be problems with obtaining parental consent as a safeguard because many parents may not fully understand their son or daughter's legal situation.[13] They may actually encourage their child to waive his or her rights. Some parents have a poor comprehension of the legal process and may overestimate what they or their children understand. Others may be pursuing their own agenda, wanting to get the system involved so their son or daughter can have access to mental health services.

Young people with mental disabilities have limited ability for abstract thinking. Not only may they misunderstand many questions that are put to them, but they may not indicate their misunderstanding. They may also dwell on the non-salient aspects of a question, interpreting in a concrete manner. For example, one study reported that a youth who had been previously diagnosed with FAS and had a mental age of eight or nine was confused by the statement that he could use the phone when he could see no phone in the room.[14] Individuals with limited abstract thinking abilities may also have difficulty understanding the consequences of giving statements that could later be used in court, for this requires the capacity for forethought and planning and includes the ability to exercise judgement by weighing the consequences of particular actions.

Defiant and impulsive youth are also vulnerable, as they do not understand the impression they are making and fail to consider the long-term consequences of their actions. If they are upset or angry, they may waive their rights in simple defiance. Some might see the humour in the situation and make a poor impression on those who do not. Others might become paralyzed with anxiety and suffer exaggerated fears about telling their parents or involving a lawyer.

Youth who are typically impulsive, such as those with FAS or with ADHD, will have difficulty exercising self-control in adversarial situations involving the police. If they have working memory problems, they may be highly suggestible or have difficulty recalling information accurately. They may confabulate in an attempt to conceal their disabilities, thus calling their honesty and integrity into question. On the other hand, they may be naïve and overly trusting, wanting to please the police.

Admissible Statements and Waivers

Youth may waive their right to counsel and their right to remain silent, but under the *Youth Criminal Justice Act* this must be recorded on video or audiotape, or the waiver must be in writing and contain a statement signed by the young person that he or she has been informed of the right being waived.[15] If "technical irregularities" in the procedure are suspected, according to the YCJA, "the youth justice court may determine that the waiver is valid if it is satisfied that the young person was informed of his or her rights, and voluntarily waived them."[16] In determining the validity of a waiver, mitigating factors must be considered, including the current capacities of the youth in question, information about the procedure used when the waiver was obtained, and the emotional climate at the time of questioning. Statements made under duress may be considered involuntary and may be deemed inadmissible by the court.[17]

In order for the statement to be admitted in law, the Crown has to prove the statement complied with the protections guaranteed under the *Charter* and the YCJA. Previously, under the *Young Offenders Act*, even minor irregularities could be challenged in court and result in the inadmissibility of statements made by youth to police. The YCJA allows the court some discretion in overlooking minor irregularities if police compliance with the statutes has been otherwise correct.

Conclusions

Knowledge of the youth justice system and of the criminal law is limited in youth, and there will be developmental variations in this knowledge over and above those associated with age. Thus, it cannot be assumed that they are able to fully and freely participate, as adults would. Evidence suggests that lawyers may overestimate a young person's knowledge of his or her rights and how the legal system works. Both youth and their parents often overestimate their own knowledge.

Adolescents are also vulnerable because they are at the lower end of the power scale in reference to the people in the system who are dealing with them, and, by and large, they are unlikely to exercise their rights, question the process, express their opinions, or make their concerns known.

These issues will be much more pronounced for youth with mental disabilities.

CHAPTER SEVEN

Competency Assessments in Youth Court

Careful scrutiny of competence evaluation procedures and related forensic evaluation is important because of the potentially serious consequences of competence for defendants and society. Fundamental fairness requires that defendants who truly are disabled in their ability to mount a defence should not be placed in jeopardy.

— Thomas Grisso
Evaluating Competencies

Psychologists and other professionals play an important role in providing assessments to the court when issues of unfit to stand trial (UST) or not criminally responsible on account of a mental disorder (NCR) arise. Assessment orders may be made by the court (s. 672.11) or the Review Board (s. 672.121) and are defined in the Criminal Code (s. 672.1) for both court-ordered assessments and those ordered by the Review Board. Youth are referred to the Review Board after the court has rendered a verdict of NCR or UST. The Review Board is requested by the court to determine a disposition in respect of a young person or make a recommendation that an inquiry be held regarding a stay of proceedings (see Chapter 1).

There is growing awareness in Canadian courts that psychologists have the expertise to provide UST and NCR assessments. As early as 1986, the American Bar Association recognized the expertise of psychologists in their Criminal Justice Mental Health Standards, endorsing "the view that psychologists who are licensed and hold a doctoral degree in clinical or counseling psychology are equivalent in expertise to psychiatrists for the purposes of conducting fitness and criminal responsibility evaluations."[1]

Endorsing the qualifications of psychologists has been slower to develop in Canada, partly because the regulation of the profession in Canada has developed at different rates in different jurisdictions. Provincial legislation sets standards for the scope of practice for psychologists as health professionals and provides the power to establish colleges of psychologists that can develop bylaws regarding such matters as licensing and competence.

Professional psychology in Canada has changed dramatically over the past 10 years, and there is no doubt that, with appropriate training and licensing, competency to diagnose mental disorders and provide forensic assessments are within the domain of practice for many psychologists. The short answer to the question of whether psychologists can precisely and accurately evaluate fitness and criminal responsibility appears to be "yes."[2]

Defining Roles and Preparing Clients

Psychological assessments provide insight into the legal competence of individuals, and must be consistent with the concerns of the law. As one distinguished practitioner has written:

> [A]ssessments should make use of the special expertise of mental health professionals that qualifies them to enlighten legal decision makers. Their disciplines have developed many concepts, theories, and methods that can assist the courts. Yet these must be selected and used in accordance with the structures of the law and its standards for decision-making. Therefore, an assessment model for legal competencies should reflect, not reform, the law's model for addressing legal competencies.[3]

From the mental health professional's perspective, the task must balance two competing demands: one for assessing legally relevant competencies, and one for maintaining the "scientific, empirical and ethical standards of mental health professionals' disciplines."[4] The onus on the mental health professional goes beyond understanding the legal competencies to developing a plan of how to collect data that is reliable and valid for the purpose.

It is judges who decide whether the legal tests have been met for UST or NCR. Psychologists may provide an opinion, if asked, or they may simply provide information that assists the court in making the determination, but they do not decide whether a youth is UST or NCR because these are legal questions. The judge answers the legal questions regarding whether the nature and severity of certain impairments are sufficient that a youth should not be held criminally blameworthy in a verdict of NCR or whether a youth is unable sufficiently to participate in his or her defence to justify a ruling of UST.

Sometimes assessments do provide direct statements of opinion in a court-ordered assessment. In a survey of forensic psychologists and psychiatrists, only 17 to 19 per cent held that offering such an opinion is inappropriate.[5] A few studies have indicated that offering an opinion on the legal question does not significantly affect a judge's verdict,[6] but it remains a personal decision on the part of the psychologist, and it "should be informed by a careful analysis of the ethical, professional and empirical arguments on both sides of the debate."[7]

Lawyers, judges, and psychologists alike must be educated about each other's roles in these matters so that expectations are clear and tensions do not develop to undermine important working relationships. A judge of the Nova Scotia Court of Appeal, writing in *Canadian Psychology*, offered advice to psychologists regarding the relevance and quality of information they should provide:

> What we expect from an expert witness is an opinion as to the significance of, or the inference, which may be drawn from, proved facts in a field in which the expert witness possesses special knowledge and experience beyond that of the triers of fact. The expert is then permitted to give such opinions to assist the jury or trial judge. But where the opinion is one, which falls within the knowledge and experience of the trier of fact, there is no need for expert evidence and an opinion will not be permitted.[8]

Recent amendments to the *Code* suggest that there could be many more requests for assessments from courts and Review Boards, and more than one assessment may be ordered for a particular youth. Thus, it is even more important that the role of psychologists providing assessments to the court is well-defined.

Education is also important with respect to preparing youth and parents, or other significant care-givers, for the assessment process. If they are poorly prepared, they may not understand why the assessment was ordered, and may have unrealistic expectations about the outcome. But this is the role of the defence attorney, not the psychologist. It is the role of the judge to clearly specify the nature of the referral question — i.e., Who asked for the assessment? What were the discussions about in court? What makes people think the youth may be UST? or How may the assessment influence the legal process for the youth?

The Assessment Process

There are unique challenges for psychologists working with adolescents and dealing with the provisions of the law that affect them. The YCJA places considerable demands on psychologists to provide assessments, consultations, and treatment services. As a result, psychologists are developing protocols and policies that are consistent with their ethics and the standards of their profession.

Ethical guidelines for Canadian psychologists working with youth in forensic settings have been slow to develop. A recent book, *Ethics for the Practice of Psychol-*

ogy in Canada,[9] devotes only one short section to ethical issues in the practices of youth forensic psychology. But what it does offer is thought-provoking.

The authors discuss court-ordered assessments under the *Youth Criminal Justice Act*:

> The Youth Justice Court can order a psychological assessment be done with or without the youth's consent and, if necessary, remand the youth for a period of up to thirty days in order to allow the process to be completed. This new *Act* has extensive provisions on the duty of confidentiality, including disclosures made by the youth during the course of a Youth Justice Court-ordered psychological assessment.[10]

The simple statement misses an important fact: the psychologist should not proceed without the youth's informed consent. The authors argue that the YCJA has extensive provisions on the duty of confidentiality, and while it is true that procedural protections are provided — one could argue whether they are "extensive" — there is also a great deal of latitude in sharing information, and this has critical implications for psychologists working with youth.

The YCJA raises a number of issues that will challenge psychologists on how to respond ethically. For example, the provisions of the YCJA have substantially increased the list of people who can have access to a youth's record — the participants at a conference, for example. And many people may attend a conference, including, among others, judges, police officers, justices of the peace, prosecutors, and youth workers, all of whom may also convene a conference to, among other things, give advice on extrajudicial measures, interim release, sentencing and reviews of sentences, and reintegration plans for the young offender (s. 19 YCJA).

Under the YCJA, there is increased opportunity to disclose information to schools and others, as well — to the extent that anyone "engaged in the provision of services to young persons may disclose to any professional or other person engaged in the supervision or care of a young person" information relevant to the young person's mental, physical, and emotional state in order to "ensure compliance by the young person with an authorization . . . or an order of the youth justice court," to "ensure the safety of staff, students or other persons," or "to facilitate the rehabilitation of the young person" (s. 125(6)). When you add them all up, they amount to quite a crowd.

In practice, this means there is much more discretion in the sharing of reports without the youth's or parents' consent based on vague principles labelled "safety concerns" or "rehabilitative concerns." Conferences pose a challenge to confidentiality issues because they form part of a youth's record that can be accessed by so many people. This raises questions about who attends, what is to be shared, and what will go into the youth's record. Determining how to structure the relationship with the youth and other agencies in providing psychological services can be a challenge.

Providing developmentally appropriate informed consent is a key issue that is often overlooked in youth justice settings. Psychologists must determine if informed consent is truly informed, and if voluntary consent is truly voluntary. This leads psychologists to question their obligations regarding explaining the nature and implications of the services they offer. Psychologists must determine their obligations when a youth does not appear to have the capacity to consent to an assessment ordered by the court.

For instance, who is the client? How do psychologists differentiate between their obligations to the youth, the criminal justice agency, and the public at large? Sometimes they must also differentiate between their obligations and advocacy.

Another ethical question involves confidentiality and the limits thereof. What are the psychologist's obligations in reviewing the limits of confidentiality with young offenders prior to providing services? What does the psychologist "need to know," and what do others "need to know"? What obligations do psychologists have to provide information to others who are involved with the youth, decision-makers such as parents, youth workers, and custody staff?

Before agreeing to undertake a court-ordered psychological assessment, a psychologist must first determine if the youth and family in fact know what a psychologist does. Most parents have a general idea, and some may have had prior experience, but many of the clients I see in my practice do not really know what a I do, even though some may have been to a counsellor in the past.

The first thing I tell them is that my job is to provide services to youth who are in trouble with the law. Some youth come to me because the judge has ordered an evaluation or because it is a condition of their probation. But I can only provide services they agree to. I ask them to tell me what they understand about psychology and what psychologists do. Some are fairly sophisticated, since they are in high school and may even be taking a psychology class. Young ones have few ideas. I tell all my clients that a psychologist is trained to look for information about how a person thinks, feels, and behaves, and that my goal is to understand what types of things they think about, what arouses their emotions, and how they usually behave. I also want to learn how they get along with others, and how things are going in their family, at school, with their friends, and in the community.

I tell them that I am trained to find ways to help them deal with the stresses and problems they encounter, and that I will help them look for solutions. They, in turn, will help me understand what they may need to reach their goals and be more satisfied with their life. One of my biggest goals, of course, is to help them stay out of further trouble, and part of my job sometimes is to support young people in sticking to their plans to stay out of trouble.

I usually give examples of the kinds of strategies I have used to help young people find better ways to spend their time, deal with their anger, and reach their goals without breaking the law. I also tell youth and their parents about the actual assessment methods I use, noting that I will talk to them directly, get information from people who know them well (with their consent), and ask them to complete questionnaires and sometimes tests to assess their skills or attitudes.

For consent to be truly informed, youth and parents must have adequate information on which to base their consent. They may be oblivious to these issues unless they are brought to their attention. Most youth caught up in the justice system feel they are not in a position to make choices, and this may be true of their parents as well. They may be concerned about how they appear to others. They may feel that deference to authority indicates they are taking responsibility for their actions. They may have multiple vulnerabilities, including being dependent on adults or, if in custody, under the control of adults. They may have mental disabilities, be educationally disadvantaged, or from a minority group. A youth's vulnerability contributes to a diminished capacity when it comes to providing truly informed and voluntary consent. Obtaining developmentally appropriate consent involves determining the competency of the youth to provide it, and involves breaking down the elements of consent into functional capacities.

Case Study: K.

K. is a 14-year-old youth who stands charged with several counts of being at large on her undertaking, one count of robbery, and one of causing a disturbance by fighting. She was referred to me for an assessment of her fitness to stand trial. I had assessed K. a year previously regarding her mental status and cognitive abilities; lawyers had found during their interviews that K. could apparently not read. In fact, she was reading at about a grade one level. I found she had significant difficulties with age-appropriate thinking and reasoning tasks. In my report I suggested that K. would have great difficulty with academic tasks that rely on verbal skills and long-term memory, but she might have success with tasks that are practical, visual, and structured.

My later assessment of K. regarding her fitness to stand trial was complicated by a number of issues, including whether she could reasonably be expected to understand the purpose of the assessment and therefore consent to it. She was cooperative and pleasant throughout the interview, and appeared properly oriented to person, time, and situation. But she did not understand the purpose of the assessment. I explained it was to assess her ability to understand the charges against her, the functions of various people in the court, her rights, and what might happen to her during and after her court appearance. I was not satisfied that she understood, and when I asked whether she had talked to her lawyer about it, she said she couldn't recall.

I called K.'s mother into the room and discussed the importance of K.'s understanding the purpose of the assessment in order for her to consent to it. K.'s mother did not completely understand the reason for the assessment, particular its implications for the court case. I requested that K. and her mother meet with K.'s lawyer to discuss these issues further. K. became impatient and said, "Let's just get it over with!" Her mother seemed to agree. I explained that, because I could not be satisfied that both mother and daughter understood the purpose of the assessment, I could not proceed. We arranged another appointment and K. and her mother agreed to meet with the lawyer in the meantime.

On the second appointment, K.'s mother had written down "fitness assessment" and was able to define what it meant. She was able to tell me about the consequences of the assessment for the court procedures. K.'s understanding was much more limited. Her mother seemed to have a good idea about the purpose of the assessment as well as the repercussions about a finding of fitness. But K. only really had enough understanding to "assent" to the assessment. I was satisfied that K's mother could consent on her daughter's behalf. K. was not able to read the consent form, so her mother read it to her and we discussed each point before they both signed it.

I proceeded to determine K.'s capacities to participate in the adjudicative process. I did not include her mother during these assessments because I needed to demonstrate that K. herself could be competent without her mother's support. K. demonstrated an understanding of the difference between "guilty" and "not guilty" pleas, but she had great difficulty discussing the implications of pleas as they relate to the court process. She said she knew something about the proceedings as a result of having attended court for her older brother, but she acknowledged difficulty understanding what was happening to her in court. She said that sometimes the court proceedings go too quickly for her to follow.

When asked about the roles of the various people in court, K. had little to say. She said one of the guys in court was the "bad guy," while her lawyer was the "good guy and he wants to keep me out of jail." She also indicated a poor understanding of the role of the judge, but with some discussion she was able to tell me that the judge had told her brother to go to jail. She seemed to think that a sentence necessarily means going to jail, but then later recalled that her brother was on "rules" after he got out of court. She not recall the use of the word "probation." She did not know who gave him these rules, but suggested "probably my parents." When I explained probation to her, she was able to tell me that her brother had "curfew" and "going to school" as rules given by the judge. She reported that at present her judicial interim worker checked up on her because curfew and school attendance are part of her "rules." I told her these were her conditions of interim release. She did not understand "interim" but did understand "release": "It means I get out of jail."

When asked about relying on her lawyer and how to relate to him, K. said she didn't know. She said that she asks her mother to help her with understanding all aspects of the court process, and that she asks her mother if something is important for her to know, otherwise she doesn't concern herself with it. She could not grasp the concept of advising counsel, but deferred to her mother. She said, "When he asks me something, I would say nothing. I get my mom to talk for me. I don't like my lawyer. But, he does good things for me." She did not understand the role of counsel or that she should be advising counsel.

When asked about her charges, K. said I should ask her mother. She had difficulty tracking her charges and was clearly confused about what would be happening in court next time. She could not say what her charges were, but with some prompting she was able to remember them. She seemed to have great difficulty following a discussion regarding her charges. She didn't understand why her lawyer had told her to plead guilty to one offence because she did not do it. She shrugged her shoulders and said it probably wouldn't make any difference now. I encouraged her to say more. She said, "Well, one more charge probably won't make much difference now." The charge she was talking about was robbery, which I suggested was hardly trivial. I later spoke with her mother about K.'s poor understanding of her charges, and found that her mother was similarly confused. Again, I suggested they speak with their lawyer.

I provided the list of charges to K. and we discussed each one. K. was not able to provide a coherent account of any of them. She said she could not remember the events in any detail. Finally she said, in irritation, "I don't want to think about them. They make me in a bad mood."

Overall, K. presented as a youth who may indicate that she understands instructions, expectations, or follows a discussion by either nodding her head or saying she understands when it is clear she does not. Such a strategy is often used by intellectually disabled youth as a way of smoothing over conversations and avoiding embarrassment.

K.'s understanding of the court process was quite rudimentary, based primarily on what she had experienced or what she had heard described by her brother. She was dependent on her mother to walk her through the process. She was unable to recall the substance of her discussions with her lawyer, although she recalled at some point having spoken with him. She said that her mother spoke to her lawyer for her and that typically she did know what the conversations were about. She avoided thinking about them. She also had a poor understanding of her choices and options. She would likely not be able to advise counsel on her own behalf, and clearly did not understand the nature of the plea process, although she had already pled to some of her charges.

Considering her verbal difficulties, intellectual and academic delays, she was unlikely to understand much of what happened in court. She might pretend that she did, but it was clear that following conversation, comprehending abstract, multi-step, and otherwise complex information, was a struggle. Even during the interviews, despite her best intentions, she easily lost track and interest in the conversation. She would likely encounter similar problems in court. I was not even confident that her competencies were restorable. She would always be dependent on her mother or other adults to walk her through the process and to speak for her, yet she will probably be deemed fit to stand trial.

Maturity and Competence to Consent

Common law recognizes the concept of a "mature minor," a young person who is considered competent to provide consent for services. Court precedent suggests a benchmark in which a youth would not likely be considered a mature minor before the age of 15 years and over and of average intelligence, but there are no guidelines on how to interpret this in light of other factors or concerns. If a youth is not a mature minor, then he or she is assumed to be a "minor," and cannot provide informed consent on his or her own behalf; parents or guardians are necessary to provide informed consent.

Courts should exercise extreme caution in assuming competence to consent to forensic services among youth aged 12 to 15. Moderate caution is also warranted for youth 15 and up. Adolescent decision-making capacities are quite different from those of adults. When faced with complex decisions, adolescents often display unsatisfactory coping patterns such as complacency and avoidance, which constrain their consideration of a full range of options. Their personal control and responsibility for making choices is often diminished in the presence of authority figures or people on whom they are dependent. Further, their decisional control may be related to self-esteem or locus of control: youth with lower self esteem or a higher external locus of control — meaning that they feel their actions are determined more by luck, fate, or external circumstances than by personal choice — are less willing to take responsibility for their decisions.

We know that 13 to 15 year olds are likely to accept information without questioning the expertise or credibility of the source, and that adolescents of all ages fluctuate in their preferences because of rapid shifts in mood, perceptions of social pressures, and experimenting with new roles or values. We also know that capacity to appreciate the consequences of one's decisions is more reliably found in older adolescents (above age 15 or 16). All of these issues can be altered significantly by emotional states, contexts, cultural factors, or the presence of mental disabilities.

If the competence to consent is questioned for any youth less than 18 years of age, a parent's or a legal guardian's approval is needed. Biological, adoptive, and foster parents have a legal duty to provide care and support for their minor children and a corresponding legal right to direct and supervise them, although their role is much less clear in the case of mature minors. For youth 16 years and under, if the youth is competent to consent, he or she signs the consent form, and if the parents are in agreement, the psychologist's task is straightforward. But in some situations the role of parents is less clear, and the process of informed consent becomes more complicated.

Following are some situations I have faced and the dilemmas they posed: If the youth attends an appointment with a psychologist without a parent or parents and is a minor under the legal definition of the term, but agrees to the services, should the psychologist terminate the assessment and contact the parents? If the youth is not legally competent and a parent is available and willing to provide consent on the youth's behalf, should the psychologist go ahead with the assessment despite the youth's incompetence to consent? If the youth is not competent to consent and the parent does not agree with the service, or if the parent does not appear competent to consent, should the psychologist refuse services? If an immature minor attends appointment but does not want his or parents involved or does not want the parents to have access to the information from the assessment, should the psychologist refuse services?

When faced with such dilemmas, the psychologist must adhere to certain guidelines, keeping in mind that refusal to consent is handled in the same manner as giving consent; in each case the client must make an informed decision:

1. What is the youth's ability to understand relevant information?
   - Is he/she able to comprehend what he/she is being told about the purpose and nature of the assessment?
   - Is he/she able to comprehend the benefits and risks of the assessment?
   - Can he/she distinguish the various roles of people and procedures in the court?
2. What is the youth's ability to appreciate the relevance of information for his/her own situation?
   - Is he/she able to appreciate the significance of the information for his/her unique situation?
   - Can he/she demonstrate realistic appreciation and application of the information to his/her situation?
3. What is the youth's ability to manipulate information rationally?
   - Is he/she able to process information related to the assessment?
   - Can he/she consider multiple factors, each of which may have different benefits and risks?

- Does the youth become confused as he/she has to work with information he/she can grasp piece-by-piece but not in its entirety?
4. What is the youth's ability to communicate a choice?
  - Can he/she state a preference?
  - Is the youth willing and able to sign the consent and agreement for services forms?

Youth who are not competent to consent, but can assent, still require ongoing management with respect to these issues. Minors who do not want to participate in services that their parents or guardians have consented to on their behalf should be offered choices as to the services that are negotiable. Parents should be informed that the youth is unwilling and the psychologist cannot therefore provide services. Parents should be further advised that the youth may not benefit from services if coërced. Youth and parents alike should be referred back to their lawyer to discuss options.

If an immature minor is unable to provide informed consent but the parent can, and the services are in the youth's best interests, the psychologist should obtain the youth's verbal and written assent. Assent denotes that the youth is agreeing to participate but will still need to agree to procedures throughout the process and still has the opportunity to ask questions and consult with parents about specific procedures. This includes not continuing with the assessment if they are confused or uncomfortable, and providing alternatives to procedures they do not wish to undertake.

Legal Competencies in Youth Court

The determination of unfit to stand trial and not criminally responsible both require an assessment of mental disorder, but it is defined somewhat differently in each case. For determinations of UST, mental disorder must be related to the youth's legal competencies *at the present time*. Legal competency for entering a plea or standing trial requires particular functional abilities and is primarily present-oriented, although assessments inevitably touch on information about the past, such as a youth's understanding of his or her arrest. Fitness to plead and fitness to stand trial assessments are often ordered simultaneously.

The determination of mental disorder in assessments of not criminally responsible is more difficult to define because the legal test refers to the youth's state of mind and behaviour *at the time of the offence*. The determination of NCR is not concerned with current mental disorders, and so requires a different legal test.

(a) Fitness to Plead

The court can only accept a guilty plea if the youth is able to demonstrate his or her understanding of what it means to make a plea. As noted in Chapter 1, s. 606.1.1 of the *Criminal Code* applies to proceedings under the *YCJA*. Essentially this means the young person must understand "the nature and the consequences of the plea," and that "the plea is an admission of the essential elements of the offence." This can be tested in court by asking the youth to articulate his or her understanding, but it will only come about if someone raises the issue. If the youth cannot articulate his or her understanding in court, the plea cannot be accepted. The presence of a mental disorder is relevant to determinations of fitness to plead only if it can be demonstrated to be relevant to the legal test for accepting a plea of guilty. The legal test in the *Code* relates to specific functional competencies.

A useful tool for assessing the specific competencies involved in fitness to plead is the *Fitness Interview Test* (FIT). Interview questions in the FIT are designed to assess the youth's understanding of the following legal issues:

- the nature of the arrest process, including rights when arrested;
- the nature and severity of the current charges (e.g., does the youth know the actual charge?);
- the role of the key participants in the legal process, in particular the adversarial nature of the process;
- possible defences to the charges, which may include an understanding of the consequences of the plea for the court process and the youth's own future;
- the likely outcome in the youth's particular case, that is, the youth's sense of realism; youth who are unrealistic, naïve, or immature may not have the capacity to participate adequately in their defence.[11]

(b) Fitness to Stand Trial — The Limited Cognitive Capacity Test

If the youth has a mental disorder that can be clearly associated with his or her current level of functioning in specific competencies related to the court process, it is obviously relevant to the assessment of UST. Some of the disorders that have been associated with fitness determinations include brain injury, personality disorders, drug and alcohol disorders, delirium tremens, fetal alcohol syndrome, and intellectual disabilities.[12] Some of the symptoms of mental disorders relevant to UST verdicts have included concentration deficits, problems with a person's rate of thinking, delusions or hallucinations, and memory deficits.[13] However, the presence of these symptoms does not necessarily mean the individual has a mental disorder, nor does it automatically mean the individual is unfit to stand trial. Psychological symptoms or the presence of mental disorder may not result in a

UST judgement, even if a person is considered certifiable under Canadian mental health legislation: "Even a person certifiable under mental health legislation may be considered fit to stand trial, though there appears to be a strong relationship between unfitness and certifiability."[14]

The legal test for determining UST in the *Code* was revised in 1992 and has since been refined by various court decisions. *R. v. Taylor*[15], which came shortly after the 1992 revision, has probably had the most impact. Based on the *R. v. Taylor* decision, adequate cognitive capacity for fitness was defined as the capacity of the youth to be able to recount the necessary facts relating to the offence so that a lawyer can mount a proper case. This lowered the threshold substantially for determining UST, suggesting that youth should not be expected to have the capacity to act in their own best interests, which would require analytic abilities.[16] The decision means that the court must determine whether the youth is capable of communicating with counsel.

R. v. S. L. (2004)[17] referred to the limited cognitive capacity test as the central issue in determining UST:

> The issue in the case at bar isn't as to whether or not the accused was capable of understanding the process. It is clear from the evidence that he is not. It is also clear that he appears to suffer from a limited cognitive capacity. I am also satisfied that it is clear from the case law that in some instances a limited cognitive capacity can be as a result of a disease of mind.[18]

The youth stood charged with aggravated assault. The matter was set for plea, but during the proceedings it became evident that S. L. was having difficulty in recognizing the judge, his own lawyer, and other people on the courtroom. An assessment for fitness to stand trial was ordered, but because the psychiatrist only saw the youth for a short interview, he felt he could not provide a diagnosis of a mental disorder, and he could not, on the basis of his assessment, determine the likely causes of the young person's apparent lack of fitness. Despite the inconclusive testimony of the psychiatrist, the judge found the accused unfit to stand trial:

> It defies logic and common sense to hold that a limited cognitive disability would be anything other than a disease of the mind as that term has been interpreted in the legal context. The evidence of Dr. Skinner does however clear the threshold and satisfy the court on a balance of probabilities that the accused is unfit to stand trial by reason of a mental disorder, such mental disorder being a limited cognitive ability which renders him unable to understand the nature or the object of the proceedings or understand the possible consequences of the proceedings.[19]

R. v. S. L. illustrates another important point with respect to UST determinations. The way in which youth are advised by their lawyers, or the way in which lawyers are advised by their clients, may determine whether the issue is raised in court. Often it will not be discussed, because of the repercussions for dispositional alternatives, the slowing down of the court process, and the possible stigma associated with it. S. L. was charged with aggravated assault and faced considerable consequences. His lawyer may have explained the possible dispositional alternatives and legal strategies. Perhaps the lawyer and S. L. weighed the lesser of two evils — on the one hand a custodial sentence versus indefinite involvement with the Review Board should he be deemed unrestorably unfit to stand trial. Because of the amendments to the *Code* in 2005, there may be more options available where youth (and adults) are found permanently UST than those faced by S.L.

There may also be other considerations that outweigh the importance of pursuing issues of fitness. This is noted by the presiding judge in *R. v. Taylor*, who discussed the factors that may result in the court passing over fitness issues in order to expedite the legal process:

> [O]ne must remain cognizant of the rationale for the fitness rules in the first place. In order to ensure that the process of determining guilt is as accurate as possible, that the accused can participate in the proceedings or assist counsel in his/her defence, that the dignity of the trial process is maintained, and that, if necessary, the determination of a fit sentence is made possible, the accused must have sufficient mental fitness to participate in the proceedings in a meaningful way. At the same time, one must consider that principles of fundamental justice require that a trial come to a final determination without undue delay. The adoption of too high a threshold for fitness will result in an increased number of cases in which the accused will be found unfit to stand trial even though the accused is capable of understanding the process and anxious for it to come to completion.[20]

By "too high a threshold," the judge apparently meant that the broadening of the criteria of who could be presumed unfit to stand trial must be sufficiently high to catch those who are truly unfit, but not so high as to catch those borderline cases or cases that are not. Nonetheless, *R. v. S. L.* illustrates that many youth will be presumed fit to stand trial when in fact they are not because the threshold for determining fitness in youth court is assumed too low; without an understanding by the defence of the legal test for UST, fitness may be presumed, or — probably more often — the issue will simply not be raised.

Do mental health professionals have an obligation to alert the court to issue of fitness — for instance, following a psychological assessment that is not specifically focused on UST? Psychologists themselves may have a poor understanding of the legal competencies required for fitness, and therefore not raise the issue. When not specifically asked to comment on fitness, psychologists may not do the necessary assessment.

The *Fitness Interview Test* (FIT) provides interview questions to examine six legal competencies that youth need in order to be able to communicate with counsel and participate in their defence. Questions about their relationship with their lawyer, including the ability to relate facts and whether or not they are able to trust their lawyer, are needed to determine the first area of competency. Next, can the youth understand the legal process and co-operate in planning a strategy? These questions relate to the youth's ability to engage in his or her defence. The FIT also provides questions to evaluate the offender's awareness of the need to protect themselves in the conduct of their defence. Another area that requires examination is the offender's capacity to challenge prosecution witnesses and recognize inconsistencies or exaggerations in testimony. Another area assessed by the FIT is the capacity to testify relevantly. The focus is on the ability to maintain composure and stay on track when testifying. Finally, it is important to determine if the youth understands the basic rules in the courtroom and expectations for their behaviour during all aspects of the proceedings.

Case Study: M.

M. was a 16-year-old youth who was referred to me for an assessment of fitness to stand trial. His overall cognitive ability fell in the borderline range of intellectual functioning in comparison to his age peers. He demonstrated a number of weak cognitive skills, particularly in his general knowledge and vocabulary; his verbal skills were at the level of an eight or nine year old. In terms of non-verbal skills, he had inordinate difficulty with simple visual tracking and scanning, which affected his ability to comprehend and learn new information. These skills were somewhat better than his verbal skills, but still indicated that he required more time to complete some tasks and that he struggled with mental flexibility, concentration, and multi-tasking.

On the positive side, M. indicated average abilities to recognize familiar objects, to detect essential from non-essential visual details, and to analyze whole-to-part relationships in spatial configurations. His visual motor coordination was adequate. Thus, he would clearly benefit from visual feedback and would be alert to details in visual information, suggesting that using visual cues might enhance his learning. His basic academic skills in reading, spelling, and mathematics fell in the grade three to four levels. Additional tests provided estimates of his word fluency, his auditory short-term recall for contextual information, his story generation ability, his ability to give directions, and his ability to explain steps in sequential tasks. Taken together, his oral language abilities (listening and expressive abilities) were at the level of a nine or ten year old, and consistent with his verbal abilities seen in cognitive testing.

M.'s functioning in the custody setting could be described as "improving slowly." He demonstrated initial difficulties in following through on simple plans and adhering to simple rules. Of most concern were his clinical symptoms. He reported feeling sad and overwhelmed by being separated from his family. He had difficulty sleeping. On assessment he scored in the clinical range for mild depression, moderate sleep disorder, and severe posttraumatic stress disorder. Follow up on these symptoms indicated that he had been a witness to a violent incident that critically injured his older sister. He reported that the police had interviewed him a few days previously. He reported PTSD-like symptoms, including intrusive and distressing recollections of the event, which was a stabbing. He also reported a feeling of detachment from others since the event. He reported irritability and increased difficulty concentrating.

M. demonstrated an understanding of the difference between guilty and not guilty pleas. He was able to identify which charges he had pled guilty to. He reported that he had spoken with his lawyer and that he had a basic understanding of his rights. His lawyer thought that he understood his pleas and the distinction between them. He tried to take part in discussions with his lawyer, but noted that he was easily overloaded by information conveyed verbally. His lawyer reported that sometimes M. appeared to tune out relevant information or appeared unresponsive during consultations. He did not appear to grasp his own role in advising counsel. Thus, he was a passive rather than an active recipient of the information; he was dependent on counsel to instruct him if he was to have any input into the process.

M. clearly struggled with formulating his verbal responses. As a result, he could easily be misinterpreted, or could incriminate himself by providing tangential details or straying from the topic. He became distressed when relating information about his charges, and quickly became frustrated when asked to explain himself more fully. Given that the legal process tends to proceed at a rapid pace and involves the processing of vast amounts of verbal information, M. might easily suffer information overload and lose his self-control. Without preplanning, teaching, repetition, and support, he would have difficulty understanding what is going on in court. Thus, his ability to participate fully and freely would be questionable at best. It would be critical that a supportive adult provide emotional support during the process. In addition to the charges he was facing, M. was dealing with a number of emotional stresses, adding to his difficulty in processing complex information.

M. was a 16-year-old functioning more like a 9- or 10-year-old. Given the seriousness of the multiple charges he was facing, he was in serious jeopardy should he not be able to participate fully and freely in matters that could greatly affect his future.

The psychological assessment indicated that, while M. was able to understand some aspects of the legal process, others were clearly difficult for him to grasp without clarification and explanation. Even then, it is not apparent that he would appreciate the meaning of the information given to him or the consequences for him personally. To ensure his understanding and participation in the process, he clearly required that the court process be paced and structured, otherwise he may simply tune out.

(c) Restoring Legal Competencies

Youth such as M. will require ongoing assistance to rehearse possible scenarios related to his legal defence so that problems during the conduct of the case in the courtroom can be anticipated. Examples of such problems may include M's understanding of the process, his ability to participate fully, and his ability to behave appropriately. Does M. meet the legal test for fitness to stand trial? Perhaps he does, particularly if his lawyer has counselled him adequately and is sensitive to his particular weaknesses and needs. A period of competency restoration might improve his ability to appreciate the nature and substance of the proceedings. However, even time to mature and the use of specific interventions to improve his legal capacities and mental health still might not bring him up to a level at which he can participate fully and freely.

Competence restoration may simply be a matter of teaching the youth information about legal proceedings, or it may involve treatment if the youth's deficits stem from a treatable disorder. However, there is generally no formal way that competency can be restored in such situations. It is maturity and time that restores fitness — even though, in some cases, fitness never existed in the first place.

There is little literature on competency restoration in Canada. However, in the United States, Florida appears to have an impressive system for restoring competency in youth and has collected systematic research on the subject.[21] Of 361 youth who were determined to be incompetent in Florida between May 1997 and August 2000, for example, 30 per cent were mentally ill and 40 per cent suffered from mental illness as well as an intellectual disability. About two-thirds of the total sample were eventually restored to competency and returned to court. Eight per cent of youth with mental illness and 34 per cent of youth with mental illness and an intellectual disability were determined to be unrestorably incompetent. The average time spent in restoration treatment was five to six months.

Assessing Criminal Responsibility in Youth

Criminal responsibility is not an issue of legal competencies *per se* but, rather, refers to the youth's state of mind during the commission of the offence. If the debate on mental disorder as a "disease of mind" was onerous in cases of UST, it is even more complicated in the case of NCR. *R. v. Cooper* (1979) set a precedent for definitions of the term:

> The term "disease of the mind" embraces any illness, disorder or abnormal condition, which impairs the human mind and its functioning, excluding, however, self-induced states caused by alcohol or drugs, as well as transitory mental states such as hysteria or concussion. Thus, personality disorders may constitute diseases of the mind. The word "appreciates" imports a requirement beyond mere knowledge of the physical quality of the act and requires a capacity to apprehend the nature of the act and its consequences. Any mental disorder could qualify as a "disease of the mind" even if the mental disorder itself was poorly understood or defined. For example, mental retardation is recognized as a mental disorder and has been used in defences for not criminally responsible, even though technically a disease of the mind does not have to be irreversible to be so defined. [22]

While previous law in Canada pertaining to NCR referred to "insanity" rather than "mental disorder," insanity tended to refer mainly to delusional states at the time of the commission of the offence. Under the current legal test, if the person had a mental disorder at the time of the offence, it could occur with or without delusions. Thus, delusions are no longer a limiting factor in the legal test for mental disorder in NCR.

The legal test for NCR is provided in s. 16 of the *Code*: "[T]he mental disorder must have rendered them incapable (1) of appreciating the nature and quality of the act or omission or (2) of knowing that an act or omission is wrong." In other words, the person must have indicated alterations in thinking, emotions, and behaviour to the point that it rendered him or her incapable of appreciating the nature and quality of the act (or omission) or from knowing what he or she was doing was wrong. An individual who can be proved to meet these criteria (on the balance of probabilities) may receive a verdict of not criminally responsible.

It is a question of law as to whether a particular mental disorder resulted in sufficient involuntary action to warrant a determination of NCR. For instance, *R. v. R. F.* (2002) established that the offender was suffering from a disorder under the FASD umbrella, meeting the first part of the legal test. The youth's mental disorder (FAS) caused the inability of the youth, at the time of the offence, to appreciate the nature and quality of the offence and of knowing that the offence was wrong, which is the second legal test. [23]

Determining the nature of the alterations to the youth's thinking, emotions, or behaviour during the offence is a complex matter, requiring a determination that the youth's state of "altered" mental functioning at the time of the offence somehow prevented the youth from knowing what he or she was doing. These conditions cannot be transient conditions, or conditions that result from external factors such as intoxication or drug use, or conditions related to everyday stresses, even extreme disappointments. Even dissociative states associated with a psychotic break or post-traumatic stress do not always meet the test for NCR, although a condition such as delirium tremens may.

The law presumes at all times that persons act voluntarily and are thus criminally responsible for actions that break the law. The defence must prove that the act was reasonably involuntary (i.e., on a balance of probabilities). This requires evidence about the youth's state of mind at the time of the offence and must be corroborated by all other available evidence, including expert opinion. For youth with long-standing mental disorders, and certainly for those with a well-known mental disorder or more severe expressions of mental disorder, it may be easier to determine mental state at the time of the offence, for it may be well known to parents, teachers, and law enforcement officials how the mental disorder has affected functioning and may have resulted in delinquency in the past.

Determining mental state at the time of the offence encompasses a number of interrelated capacities related to judgement or decision-making. Some of the questions that may be considered during the assessment include:

- Was involuntariness caused by a psychological blow and/or did this blow interact in some way with the mental disorder?
- Was the involuntariness a feature of the mental disorder that had, before the offence, presented as a recurring danger to the public?
- Is the involuntariness a current feature of the mental disorder?
- Did external events such as alcohol consumption or drug use interact with the mental disorder to cause involuntariness during the offence?
- Can we discern a difference between the youth's ability to appreciate the physical or real life consequences of the act or the broader "wrongness" of the act, even if there was mental capacity at the time of the offence to know that the act was breaking the law?
- Did the mental disorder affect the decision-making capacities of the youth to decide rationally whether to commit the crime or not?
- Where it was evident that the mental disorder affected the person's mental capacity, did it distort the youth's thinking in believing that the wrongful act was right and justifiable?

Based on the legal test for NCR in Canadian law, some factors could be excluded as irrelevant. For example, mental disorders that relate to a lack of appropriate feeling for the victim or a lack of remorse or guilt may not be relevant (features which are sometimes seen in personality disorders). Current appreciation of the act as justifiable and right, or current mental disorder or delusions, are not relevant to the question of NCR.

The challenge is "how to articulate the logic involved in clinical inferences related to the legal question" of NCR.[24] The appraisal of volitional capacity or lack thereof is probably the most ambiguous concept associated with NCR. Voluntary action during an offence seems to imply a choice — and, thus, intention. Did the youth have the capacity to behave in some other manner at the time of the offence? Some have called this the "policeman at the elbow" test; that is, would the defendant have committed the act even if there had been a police officer standing nearby?[25] But how do we evaluate this notion? It is difficult to make the distinction between the irresistible impulse, the unresisted impulse, and the resistible impulse.[26]

Section 672.34 of the *Criminal Code* requires that NCR must be addressed after the court's finding that the youth committed the act or omission. For the mental health professional, a concern arises during the assessment process of potentially incriminating information gained directly from the defendant about the act with which he or she is charged. The assessment involves enquiring into the youth's actions, thoughts, and emotions at the time of the alleged offence as part of gathering information about the defendant's mental state, and the assessor must disclose that information in the written report when describing the basis for an inference, yet that information might incriminate the youth and bias the judge, resulting in a more onerous disposition or sentence. Although such information should not be used to incriminate the youth — and there are protections provided in the *Youth Criminal Justice Act* (s. 40(10) and s. 147) — there is always the possibility that it will anyway.

Conceptualizing how the legal standards for criminal responsibility apply in the youth justice setting provides challenges both to legal professionals and those who are asked to provide assessments. It is a formidable task to sort out the developmental immaturity we would expect in any adolescent, and then overlay it with an adult legal standard for determining criminal responsibility. There are no psychological tools specifically designed to assess criminal responsibility in youth, and thus, extensions of the adult tools are applied, raising the question of whether we can adequately assess NCR in youth, particularly those under the age of 16.

Practical difficulties in assessments of NCR stem from trying to transport youth back to the psychological moment of the crime, particularly if they have memory deficits or were under the influence of drugs or alcohol. Some youth may be highly suggestible in response to the interviewer's questions and, when combined with the tendency of many youth to be wary of the process or to be manipulative, malingering — exaggerating or feigning illness in order to escape present consequences — is a real issue. Sometimes tangential information emerges, such as an offender's apparent lack of remorse, and while this information is important for treatment purposes, it is not relevant to the immediate question of criminal responsibility. The assessor, too, could become biased as a result of the youth's presentation or information. Separating out the youth's apparent disregard, naivety, or antisocial stance during assessments is also difficult if the youth appears not to care what is happening to him or her. Thus, it may be difficult to establish whether to take the youth's statements at face value.

In fact, sometimes psychologists have (well-founded) fears that youth may manipulate or malinger during the assessment if the legal questions involving criminal responsibility are made more transparent to them. On the other hand, many youth are defensive about their offences and may deny having committed them at all.

Assessment Process for NCR

Definitions of what constitutes criminal responsibility in adolescents and determining when they meet the legal standard for NCR are likely to be problematic. More often than not, adolescents will be presumed to be criminally responsible, leading to the distinct possibility that they will not benefit from the NCR provisions in the *Criminal Code* in the same way adults might. On the other hand, youth advocates in these situations may not see the value of raising the possibility of NCR because of the perceived jeopardy youth face when a verdict of not criminally responsible is handed down, as noted in Chapter 1. Some of the recent amendments to the *Code* may provide more options for youth who receive this verdict, but there are still significant legal complexities involved in these determinations.

The most commonly used assessment tool in adult criminal responsibility hearings is the *Rogers Criminal Responsibility Assessment Scales* (R-CRAS) developed in the United States. Another one, less commonly used in Canada, is the *Mental State at the Time of the Offence Screening Evaluation* (MSE), also developed for adults. Both instruments are based on the legal standard for the insanity defence in US law, and both outline interviewer goals for an evaluation but do not specify the actual questions to be asked.[27] Thus, they provide a conceptual tool that can be used to guide the assessment of NCR in youth. For example, the R-CRAS identifies "specific cognitive and/or volitional elements for each of the major insanity standards"[28] based on the American Law Institute standards. The first is *organicity*, and refers to the presence of an organic mental disorder (i.e., an intellectual disability). The second is a *major psychiatric disorder* (i.e., schizophrenia). Together, the presence of an organic mental disorder and a major psychiatric disorder constitutes "mental disease or defect." The third construct is loss of *cognitive control,* which is defined as the loss of the ability to recognize, at the time of the crime, that the conduct was criminal. The fourth construct is loss of *behavioural control,* which is defined as loss of the ability to choose and to withhold important behaviours. The examiner must also rule out malingering during the process.

The assessment of NCR in the Canadian context can apply the conceptual models of the R-CRAS and MSE. Essentially the assessment involves three components. The first is demonstrating that the youth had a mental disorder at the time of the offence. The second is demonstrating that the mental disorder affected the youth's cognitive abilities at the time of the offence to the extent that his or her ability to accurately perceive reality and make rational and reasonable inferences was seriously impaired. The third is demonstrating that the mental disorder affected the youth's volitional ability to the extent that his or her behaviour was beyond voluntary control. The assessor must also address the following questions:

- Is the youth's self-report reliable?
- What is the youth's mental state at the time of the assessment?
- What is the youth's account of the offence and behaviour after the offence occurred?
- What information is relevant from extrinsic sources such as family, witnesses, reports, Crown disclosure, transcripts, and police reports, including the youth's response to being arrested?

The first component of the NCR evaluation involves determining organicity or psychopathology and may be assessed by information regarding the level of intoxication at the time of the crime, the withdrawal from intoxication or medications, the use of medication, evidence of brain impairment, or an organic process (such as psychosis) or intellectual disability. The assessor must demonstrate that the organic process was related to the commission or omission of the crime. Evidence of psychopathology may include a number of symptoms at the time of the offence, including bizarre behaviour, the level of anxiety, amnesia about the crime, delusions, hallucinations, a depressed mood, an elevated or expansive mood, the level of verbal incoherence or thought disorder, and the intensity and appropriateness of affect (feeling or emotion). These may be self-reported or other-reported.

Cognitive control is assessed by examining evidence of planning and preparation, awareness of the criminality of the behaviour, the focus of the crime (e.g., selective vs. random), and the level of activity in the commission of the crime. Behavioural control is assessed by examining evidence regarding responsible social behaviour during the week prior to the crime, youth-reported self-control, the examiner's estimate of the youth's self-control at the time of the offence, the relation of loss of control to psychosis, the evidence of impaired judgement, impaired behaviour, and impaired reality testing, and an awareness of the wrongfulness of the act. The process is complex and involves a great deal of inferential judgement on the part of the examiner. Two case examples follow.

Case Study: N.

N. stands charged with one count of robbery using a firearm and one count of possession of a handgun. These are N.'s first offences. He is referred for an assessment of criminal responsibility. The offence occurred about six weeks ago. N. is 16 years old and attending a functional academics classroom. He has been previously diagnosed with a mild intellectual disability and generalized anxiety disorder. He was taking medication for the anxiety disorder prior to the offence, but stopped about two weeks before. His parents report that his physician had been tapering him off the medication at their request to see if he could manage without it. He is currently back on the medication.

N.'s family situation has been marked by a number of changes, conflict, and losses. He lives with his mother and his stepfather. His biological father moved to another province when he was an infant and his contact has been sporadic over the years, including many broken promises and missed visits. Two days before the current offence, his biological father showed up and wanted to take N. to a restaurant for a meal. The visit deteriorated when the father started criticizing N. about his appearance and his poor eating habits. The visit ended in an argument. N. left the restaurant and walked a considerable distance home. The next day his father called and asked if he could make it up to him. N. was wary, but, at his mother's urging, he agreed to go to movie with his father the following evening. N. waited until 9:30 that evening and his father did not show up or call. N. became tearful during his recounting of the situation.

According to N. and collateral sources, N. had significant difficulties adjusting to his mother's marriage to his stepfather. His stepfather has a volatile temper. His mother reports that, over the past few months, there has been significant and ongoing strife between her and N.'s stepfather in how to manage N.'s growing independence. His mother reports that her husband has been emotionally abusive toward N. calling him stupid and lazy. N. has been confused about his place in the family and has been doubting his parents' affection for him. Increasingly, N. reports that he has been feeling angry and alienated from his parents, leading him to turn to drugs for relief and deviant peers as a way to feel he belonged somewhere and to get back at his stepfather. N. has a half-brother who is the son of his mother and his stepfather. He reports that his half brother is "good at everything I'm bad at. He is smart, good looking and everyone likes him." N. has struggled throughout his school years both academically and socially. He has never been accepted by his peers and has few friends.

N. has a short but significant history of drug abuse. About six months ago he started using marijuana on a daily basis. He was also snorting crushed tablets of Ritalin. Up to the day of his arrest, he was smoking about five joints a day and using various pills. About one month ago, he was hospitalized voluntarily following an incident in which he became threatening toward his mother following an altercation over family issues. He was delusional and had racing thoughts. The psychiatrist diagnosed him with a substance-induced psychosis and placed him on an antipsychotic medication. N. was discharged two days later, the hospital stay to be followed by a visit to his family physician.

N. was diagnosed at age 14 with generalized anxiety disorder and placed on medication, to which he responded well. After his parents became aware of the extent of the substance abuse that led to the current hospitalization, however, they became wary about the use of medication for him. When N. and his parents saw the family physician for follow-up, N. had already discontinued the antipsychotic medication prescribed by the psychiatrist during his hospitalization. N. and his parents suggested to the family physician that N. no longer needed the medication for his long-standing anxiety disorder. N.'s parents reported their belief that their son was relying on drugs to solve his problems. After the appointment, N. decided to stop his medication cold turkey.

As part of the evaluation N.'s mother and teachers were interviewed and note that N. was increasingly hanging out with a negative peer group. N. appeared gullible and an easy target. He was easily upset by teasing, and was noticed trying to please other youths. N. has long-standing difficulties with judgement in social situations and does not seem to foresee that a course of action will get him into trouble. For example, he was caught by the school janitor breaking into the computer lab after school one day with another youth to view some pornography sites. The other boy said it was N.'s idea, which both the teacher and mother doubt. There is no evidence of thought disorder during the days before or after the offence, although anxiety was evident.

N. is currently on medication for anxiety, but states that the two weeks prior to the offence he experienced sinking feelings, wandering thoughts (obsessive ruminations, perhaps), worries, and panicky feelings. As a result, he started using more marijuana and other pills to cope. The marijuana actually made him feel more panicky at times, and even paranoid.

On the evening of the offences, N. had been waiting for his father to pick him up. When he did not arrive, N. felt upset and panicky. He called some of his friends and they told him to come over and party with them. They told him to meet them at the corner store in the neighbourhood. He left without telling his parents. The boys were waiting for him and they told him, "Let's see you be crazy, wild, and cool tonight." N. thought they were joking. The boys said, "Let's rob this store to get money to buy beer." N. didn't want to but was afraid to say anything. He felt panicky and sick to his stomach, but didn't want to let on. His friends said only one of them was going in the store and they picked him. They pulled out a pellet gun one of the boys had stolen from his father and put it in N.'s hand, saying, "Scare the poor girl and she'll give you the money." His friends put a mask on his face, taunting him: "Come on, show us how cool you are."

N. reports that he was shaky and feeling dizzy. He can't remember how he got into the store, but he recalls the look on the clerk's face when he came in. He could not speak. He dropped the gun by mistake and turned to run out of the store. The boys were already running, too. N. ran all the way home. The next day he was arrested for armed robbery and possession of a weapon. The whole episode was on security camera.

Will N. meet the legal test for NCR? My assessment indicated that he had a long-standing mental disorder (intellectual disability and anxiety disorder). His anxiety disorder was not being properly treated at the time of the offence, adding to the cognitive impairment already evident as a result of the intellectual disability. The stress that N. was experiencing with respect to the disappointment of his father's rejection may have contributed to his instability on the evening he committed the offence, but would not necessarily be sufficient for the test of NCR. But more than this, I believe the pressure to be part of the group and the group's tactics with him overloaded him to such an extent that he was no longer acting on free will. But "peer pressure" would not likely meet the legal test for NCR.

I would argue that N.'s cognitive and volitional abilities were compromised as a result of the combined effect of his intellectual disability and anxiety disorder. His mental disorder affected his cognitive abilities at the time of the offence to the extent that his ability to accurately perceive reality and to make rational and reasonable inferences based upon it was seriously impaired. In addition, his mental disorder affected his volitional ability to the extent that he did not have control over his behaviour. I would suggest that N.'s state of mind at the time of the offence was such that he was not able to fully appreciate that what he was doing was wrong.

Case Study: J.

J. stands charged with one count of mischief. She is a 15-year-old who was diagnosed with FAS when she was six. She has borderline intellectual functioning and severe hyperactivity and impulsivity. She has been on medication for two years and there has been some improvement in her behaviour, but she is sometimes resistant to taking it and her foster parents are not always sure when she is. Her teacher reports that she is functioning at about a grade two level in her academic skills. She is described as immature and not well liked. She is easily upset and will run from the school when she feels slighted.

J. has been a full-time ward since she was about seven and has lived in several foster placements, but has some stability in the current placement and has been there for about two years. J. has been a concern in her community for the past two years, as she has become more defiant toward her foster parents, wanting to stay out late, and has started drinking and smoking. Her foster parents are concerned because she is so impulsive and has such poor judgement, and seems easy prey for peers who try to get her to do things for them. Over the past year she has grown considerably taller and has developed a full figure for her age. Her appearance is more like an 18-year-old than a 15-year-old. She has also insisted on wearing clothes that her foster parents find sexually suggestive. They are worried that she will be sexually victimized (their worst fear is that she will become pregnant) because she is lacking in judgement and is unable to protect herself.

J. is charged with having willfully damaged a trailer that was abandoned in the woods near her home. She was attending a birthday party at a cabin in the woods with mostly older males. They had picked her up on the highway where she was walking in the early evening. The young men and two young women encouraged her to come along and party with them. She agreed and was offered alcohol in the car. She was already feeling tipsy when she got to the party. She drank heavily and smoked marijuana. At one point a young man from the party suggested they go for a ride in his truck. She agreed. They arrived at the abandoned trailer and decided to go in because it had started raining. She says she doesn't understand why the young man wanted to go with her. When they got in the trailer the young man got on the bed. She sat on the couch and was unsure what to do. Eventually the young man passed out and J. was left on the couch and didn't know what she should do. She reports: "I got bored all of a sudden, I got the man's lighter out of his pocket and started playing with it." She played with the lighter and burned some pieces of cloth she found. One of these dropped onto the couch and started it on fire. She froze in shock, as she was not able to wake the young man or put the fire out. She reports that she did not "mean to burn the trailer down." She said she was confused that other people in the community were mad at her for burning it down, because she had not meant to burn it down. She said, "It's not bad what I did because I didn't mean to burn it down and it wasn't that bad because it was an abandoned trailer." Fortunately, the man was roused by the smoke and jumped out of the trailer in time. J. said, "I forgot the man was there." When asked about her thinking at the time, she said, "I wasn't thinking anything. I just thought about getting home because I knew my parents were probably wondering where I was?"

Will J. meet the criteria for a determination for NCR? Although more details of this case are needed to determine criminal responsibility, I would argue that J.'s mental disorder — FAS and severe ADHD — seriously impaired her judgement during this offence. Her use of alcohol and other drugs increased her cognitive impairment and aggravated the symptoms of ADHD. I would suggest that that J.'s state of mind during the offence was such that she was not able to fully appreciate the consequences of her actions or that what she was doing was wrong.

Conclusions

More often than not, youth with significant mental disabilities and functional impairments will be found fit to plead, stand trial, and criminally responsible — even if they are identified and properly assessed during the court process. In part, this arises because there is not always a direct match between the legal tests and the assessment findings. The threshold for determining UST and NCR is ultimately a legal question. Yet some youth who are found legally fit to plead and stand trial will still have great difficulty participating fully and freely in the processes that affect them. This could lead to systemic bias toward youth with mental disabilities, particularly if their parents and their legal defence do not grasp the significance of their disabilities for their functioning. We can mitigate some of these problems by having a better understanding of the competencies of youth that are involved in fitness issues and criminal responsibility, and how they may be at odds with the demands and expectations of the youth justice system. We could improve the manner in which we deal with young offenders with mental disabilities during the different stages of court proceedings. Psychologists and other mental health professionals can assist the court in determining issues of UST and NCR. Under the recent amendments to the *Code* regarding procedural issues and dispositional alternatives, there may be greater demands for competency assessments to assist the court in making UST and NCR determinations.

CHAPTER EIGHT

Perspectives on Criminal Intent

You can choose a ready guide in some celestial voice;
If you choose not to decide, you still have made a choice;
You can choose from phantom fears and kindness that can kill;
I will choose a path that's clear. I will choose free will.

— RUSH
"Free Will"

Intent is a key component of criminal culpability. The law presumes that people act voluntarily, so when they are found guilty of committing a crime, they are criminally responsible. The criminal actions of youth, however, tell us less about the character of youth than they do about their mental capacities and the situational components of their behaviour. In most cases, the criminal actions of adults reflect a different set of capacities; their actions are much more determined by character.[1] This is not to say that adult crime is not motivated or supported by situational factors, but it does mean that adults usually have greater volitional control.

Despite these differences, both youth and adult sentencing statutes are based on the notion that all persons are fully culpable for their actions. A separate justice system for youth is based on assumptions about the fundamental differences between adults and adolescents, but the diminished capacities of youth do not mean that a particular adolescent cannot be criminally responsible.[2]

In adults, the presence of mental disorder or a mental disturbance (as defined by law) at the time of committing an offence can mitigate the proof of specific intent for a crime, resulting in less severe charges — i.e., a murder charge can be reduced to manslaughter. Youth justice principles also stress proportional sentencing based on a number of factors, including the planfulness and the degree of responsibility for the offence. Factors related to criminal intent are thus central to issues of proportionality and accountability in both youth and adult justice systems.

Criminal Intent and Moral Conscience

A young person's moral understanding is not as relevant to understanding youthful offending as some may think. The assumption that youth who are able to resist criminal behaviour (or who are smart enough not to get caught) have a higher state of moral reasoning than those who are not is problematic, for it amounts to saying that youth who resist criminal behaviour go through a logical moral reasoning process, such as: "Let me see, the reason this is morally wrong is because it will hurt the victim. There could be short-term and long-term consequences to the victim and to myself and my family. I am clearly intruding on this person's property and they will likely feel violated by my actions. What was I thinking?"

Assuming that youth go through any kind of rational or thoughtful process when they "decide" to commit a crime is a stretch of the imagination. It is also fallacious to assume that all youth who engage in criminal behaviour lack a moral conscience. Even when a young person may not have appreciated the fact that he or she broke the law, they almost always understand that what they did was wrong. Children as young as six or seven can understand when something is wrong or bad, even though they may be unable to articulate it.

Adolescents understand when their behaviour is morally wrong, in spite of the fact that they are often unable to explain why or give entirely unsatisfying explanations about the reasons for their behaviour. They have hedonistic, concrete explanations for why their behaviour was wrong — "It seemed fun at the time" — and sometimes they don't want to think about how their behaviour was wrong or accept the fact that it hurt the victim. But they know. They are often angry at being found out, and try to avoid the painful consequences of accepting responsibility for their actions, and defence mechanisms cover their embarrassment or shame.

Rarely do adolescents acknowledge that the action they took was right. Even youth who deny their offence — and some persist with tenacity — will understand and even acknowledge that "if it did happen" it would be wrong. It is rare for adolescents to have a total lack of moral conscience. From an adult's point of view, however, adolescents often seem seriously lacking in the ability to offer satisfying explanations about why their behaviour was morally wrong.

There is no aberrant trait or character flaw, such as lack of moral conscience or psychopathic tendencies, in most youth who commit crimes. Most of them lack the intellectual or emotional equipment to have psychopathic personality traits. Most youth who commit offences do so because of their psychosocial immaturity.

It is much more likely that adults who perpetrate criminal offences have deficiencies of moral conscience, and it is possible that a small number of them have psychopathic personality traits. The suppression of moral conscience during a criminal act is a highly specialized condition of the mind that results from a combination of character traits, mental health, experience with criminal offending, and expectations of personal gain. These adult offenders are desensitized to any interference of the emotions, and are adept at neutralizing thoughts and feelings that might de-rationalize their criminal actions.

Youth who engage in similar rationalizations and neutralizations have qualitatively different cognitive processes. Their decisions about criminal behaviour are much more likely to be the product of psychosocial immaturity, as opposed to a character flaw, and they are much more prone to act on external triggers and situational factors. They may operate on a foreshortened time perspective, grasping at immediate personal benefits and discounting the short- and long-term costs. Most youthful offending is the product of immature self-control and a tendency toward intemperate behaviour. When faced with a choice, they have a tendency to choose antisocial alternatives as opposed to socially acceptable ones. This is merely a reflection of their value system and preferences.[3] As they develop, most adolescents cease their criminal behaviour.[4]

To Charge or Not to Charge

Given that most youthful offending is likely to be the product of immaturity, how do we determine whether a young person should be charged? When a youth breaks the law, we can charge them, but should we? There are very good reasons for not charging them, and for keeping them out of the justice system altogether, as the consequences of being charged with a criminal offence in Canada even for youth are hardly trivial.

The legal system sometimes has no choice but to bring charges, as the offence may be serious and the evidence so outstanding that the process takes on a life of its own. When the issue is in the hands of the police or the crown prosecutor, it is they who are making the decisions. But often when parents, teachers, mental health professionals, and others are dealing with youth, we are in a position to ask if we should get the justice system involved. How do we distinguish what we can do from what we should do? Deciding what to do is not just a matter of law, but of morality.

As we are taught as children, choices are the basis of the democratic principles that guide our social systems and laws. We learn early that social control is, or at least should be, only partly externally driven; we don't do things just because we are told to or because we fear punishment. We teach our children that society works best when social control is internal. We abide by our laws because we respect others, want to minimize harm to others, and take responsibility for our own actions.

We believe, as a society, that these principles provide children with the moral basis for their greater independence during the transition to adolescence and then adulthood. They begin to internalize the many messages we give them about the right thing to do under many different circumstances. We encourage them to see the moral value of coping in a way that is within the boundaries of the law.

When young people make mistakes, we continue to try to find ways to teach them. Most times we could charge them, but we don't. Other times we do charge them, and then wonder if we should have. For example, if you are a store owner who catches a 12-year-old boy throwing a rock into your front window, should you charge him? You believe the offence was minor, and that charging the youth might cause harm to him. He lives in a good neighbourhood and you have seen him with his parents in the store many times. You feel it is enough of a consequence to have been caught. You tell the youth that you won't tell his parents, but he cannot come into the store for two months, and if it happens again you may have to take a different approach.

In two other shops that night in the same city, two other 12-year-olds are charged for the same offence. These shop owners believe they need to crack down on crime in the neighbourhood, and think that charging the youth will give them a short, sharp shock to deter them from doing it again. They also feel angry at the parents (and many other parents in the community) for letting their children stay out past 10 p.m., and believe they should be forced to take a tougher line with their kids. They believe that the humiliation and effort it will take the parents to deal with the issue, together with the swift punishment of the youth, will act as a deterrent for the future.

Obviously the actions of the three storeowners were related to their belief systems about what works to deter youth crime and what they feel they should do in the best interests of the youth and the community. Which of them is doing the right thing?

Crimes hurt people, and charging people who commit crimes should be a logical consequence for the harm they do. Most of us know when something is not right about the way we are treated, but children and the disabled have the weakest voices in expressing it, and need the stronger voices of adults to protect them. We are a legalistic society. We know our rights and we are told we should stand up for them. If we witness a mother in a grocery store checkout spanking her two-year-old while cursing volubly, we are stung by the display of violence. If we say something to the mother, she takes it out on the child. If we call for the store manager to speak with the woman, she leaves the store in a temper. Now we are faced with a dilemma: should we report this mother to the authorities? We could, but in the end we decide not to. What is our reasoning for this?

Similarly, we know the house up the street is a haven for drug addicts. We suspect they are selling as people come and go all day. We could call the authorities and leave a tip with the police, but we don't. What is our reasoning for this?

There are many times that we feel wronged or hurt by others but do nothing. Sometimes we are so badly treated that we feel outrage. Sometimes we see others treated badly and we are equally outraged. Past injustices haunt us: abusive foster parent, residential schools that separated us from family and culture, peers who harassed us. Or we are disabled. We are teased and bullied as children, and mortified by our inability to keep up. As adults, we are denied access to jobs and opportunities, and forced to put up with situations that are considered "good enough" by others. These insights may be fleeting for some people with disabilities, particularly those with cognitive impairments, but they know at some level of awareness that they are marginalized and mistreated. But this awareness does not lead to action. Who can we charge for these offences?

The reason we don't often use legal action or report to authorities the injustices we see around us is that we believe that the psychological and social consequences would be too great. In the decisional balance, the costs appear to outweigh the rewards. But what if we were to find out that, if we were to pursue a legal route in a particular case, we would likely experience unanticipated rewards that made the effort worthwhile? Human nature being what it is, we would be much more likely to pursue the legal route. It is human nature to avoid pain and make decisions that are likely to reward us in some way.

Of course, it is one thing to imagine how we might respond to criminal behaviour in a theoretical sense, and quite another when we are personally confronted with a situation. People's attitudes often change when they become a victim of a youth crime or when the police charge their son or daughter.

Community youth workers and custody staff are faced with daily issues in managing difficult and defiant youth. They are responsible for ensuring that any actions they take balance the needs of the youth with concerns of public safety. Youth who are non-compliant place those who are responsible for their supervision in a difficult position: if they ignore the behaviour and someone gets hurt, they must answer to the fact that they did not act when they first became aware of the issue. On the other hand, if community and custody workers were to take legal action on every breach or misstep, the youth court system would be unable to keep up with the demands made on it.

The Incapacitation Strategy

Although the *Youth Criminal Justice Act* emphasizes that the system should not over-rely on criminal sanctions for minor cases and should reduce their reliance on custody, breaches have the opposite effect. Breaches — acts or omissions that are inconsistent with, or breach the terms of, a disposition or court-ordered sanctions — have the effect of criminalizing minor offences, and can lead to incarceration. A youth whose initial offence may have been quite minor finds him or herself, when released to the community, continually breaching the conditions of probation. Now there is seen to be an escalation in the youth's criminal behaviour, and he or she is seen to be showing defiance toward the sanctions imposed by the court. If the youth again commits a minor offence, the pattern will be seen to be escalating, representing a blatant disregard for authority and a failure to be rehabilitated by previous sanctions. The incapacitation strategy — detaining the offender in prison, effectively rendering him or her incapable of re-offending — is appealing because it is simple, authoritative, and potentially swift, but there is little empirical support for the assertion that incapacitation actually works to reduce further offending, or that it keeps communities safer.

Statistical data show that incapacitation may have been used as a sentencing principle with some regularity under the *Young Offenders Act*. According to the Department of Justice, in 1998-99 the number one minor offence that received the highest proportion of custody sentences was Failure to Comply with a Disposition. Forty-seven percent of the youth who were found guilty of this offence received a custody sentence — a total of 4,979 youth.[5]

The fact that they were being incarcerated for system-generated charges[6] supports the theory that an incapacitation strategy was being used as the argument for incarcerating them. The findings also indicate that the likelihood of youth receiving a custodial disposition increased depending on the youth's previous record. This supports the assertion that the incapacitation strategy was invoked for repeat offenders, even though the offences were minor and would not have warranted custody in the first place.

The belief that breaches or custody deter youth from further offending is also behind the philosophy of using short, sharp, shocks, such as keeping youth overnight in police cells or detaining them in remand facilities until they appear in court. Some advocates of this approach see detainment as a logical consequence, or immediate punishment. Others believe that custody administers a threat to young people who are thinking about breaking the law. Thus, short, sharp, shocks are a form of general deterrence. Even if the youth are eventually found not guilty and the charges dropped, advocates of the short, sharp, shocks theory still consider the experience to have been somewhat salutary for the young person.

As a possible deterrent, the practice assumes two consequences: first, that before young people think of committing an offence they actually consider that custody could be a consequence; and second, that when they do think of committing an offence, they will remember how terrible their experience in custody was. It rarely happens. Kids may tell you they hate custody because their every move is being watched, but they are rarely scared of it. Many parents are more scared of custody than their kids are. They see it as highly offensive, and think that realizing this would make young people think twice about committing an offence. It doesn't happen. Youth are actually less deterred by custody once they have been in custody, because they know it's just not as bad as adults would have them believe. The fact is, youth rarely think about any of these things when they commit an offence.

,quire a specialized justice system that is cognizant of their developmen-
,urity relative to adults, why does the legislation include provisions for
aduı . ntencing? The obvious answer is that some crimes committed by youth
warrant an adult sentence. If the objectives of the youth criminal justice system
are to address the underlying circumstances of youth's offending with a view to ensuring that he or she does not re-offend, then perhaps, under some circumstances,
an adult sentence would serve the needs of the youth and ultimately do a better
job of protecting the public. It is not really that difficult to provide a rationale for
imposing an adult sentence on some youth.

Why, then, can't we do a better job of providing a rationale for a youth sentence, even in cases in which the crime is very serious and the youth clearly needs
a sentence that will address their needs and also protect the public? There is danger in setting precedents based on the proposition that the adult system does a better job than the youth system in rehabilitating serious offenders, for it could result
in more adult sentences for youth and a corresponding failure in the youth justice
system to develop appropriate resources for youth. Focusing on the seriousness of
the crime to the detriment of the young person's developmental needs could lead
to the erosion of a specialized justice system for youth in Canada. If left unchal-
lenged, the use of adult sentences for youth may increasingly criminalize youthful
offending, to the point that a separate system is no longer justified.

There are substantial risks in criminalizing youthful offending.[7] One criminolo-
gist suggests that the inclusion of adult sentences in the *Youth Criminal Justice Act*
may be a form of appeasement to public pressures to make the law tougher on
serious crime while at the same time preserving the main thrust of the legislation
for youth:

> There is an unprincipled ancillary advantage associated with a sentencing
> framework that permits the transfer of some cases to adult court or the im-
> position of an adult sentence in youth court. By so doing, the system shows
> that it is "taking serious cases seriously," and thereby responds to critics
> who argue that sentences are too lenient. By allowing more severe "adult"
> punishments for a small number of cases, the system is able to retain highly
> mitigated punishments for the vast majority of cases sentenced in youth
> court. . . . Certainly, the adult sentence provisions in the YCJA respond to
> the public and professional criticism that the *Young Offenders Act* failed to
> deal adequately with the most serious cases of youth violence.[8]

By advocating that adult sentences should be used for youth who have committed
serious crimes, we may be making an error of attribution: we may be assuming that

youth who commit more serious crimes are youth who are more criminally minded. Their criminal actions are now associated with a character trait. This may lead us to think that criminally minded youth think more like adults than adolescents, and should therefore be given adult sentences.

The seriousness of the crime should never be a test of a young person's maturity of judgement or capacity. How does a youth become less a youth and more an adult by committing a serious crime?[9] Youth have diminished culpability as a result of their immaturity, particularly their diminished capacity for judgement, whatever their crimes. In the case of more serious crimes that result in long-lasting effects on victims and families, the young person's diminished judgement is all the more transparent — and there is all the more reason to offer meaningful sentences to ensure that they are influenced to participate in interventions and are held accountable for their actions by the community and the law.

A further point is critical. The process of rehabilitating and reintegrating youth who have committed serious offences is much more complicated than it is for youth who have committed minor offences. Youth are more likely to appreciate the consequences of their actions when they have committed a less serious crime, in which neither people nor property have been irretrievably damaged. In the case of major crimes, such as sexual offences or crimes of violence, they are not likely to appreciate the consequences with the same ease.

The consequences of serious crimes are multiple and complex, and have to do with appreciating the perspective of others, understanding abstract concepts such as the psychological effects of the crime on the victim, appreciating the short- and long-term effects of their actions, and the implications for their own psychological development of their victimization of another person. All evidence to date indicates that it is much more effective to provide offence-specific services for these youth in a youth-focused environment than to assume they will benefit from programming designed for adults. The National Task Force on Juvenile Sexual Offending noted that assumptions that older youths who have committed sexual offences should receive adult sentences should not be made lightly: "Concerns which dictate caution in doing so include lesser availability of treatment in many adult systems and the lack of a true peer group. . . . However, communities should develop juvenile correctional treatment programs for even the most serious offenders."[10]

The nature of the rehabilitation issues involved in violent offences perpetrated against persons is such that youth must both be held accountable and encouraged to take personal responsibility for their behaviour. It is therefore critical that they are charged and found guilty for their offences, and that their treatment is mandated by the court. This process should be a learning opportunity for the youth, who must come to understand the victim's rights and the harm that has been done. The youth must come to understand why we have laws that protect people from this type of abuse and the harm that results from it. The youth must also be challenged on his or her defences, such as the minimization or the denial of their offences. Families must be challenged on the same points, and youth must come to develop empathy for the victim. The National Task Force observed:

> Victim empathy is a trait which most offenders do not initially possess adequately to inhibit abusive behaviour and is a primary goal in treatment. Direct participation in the prosecution process is helpful to the offender. The youth hears the behaviour described as illegal, unacceptable, and having an impact on the victim. Prosecution also provides a strong and critical means for insuring the juvenile's cooperation with treatment and control through court orders. . . . Changing sexually abusive behaviours usually requires creation of a level of personal discomfort. . . . The court's orders mandate that the offender persevere through the discomfort and work of treatment.[11]

Youth who are not held accountable will not persevere through this difficult process. It is critical that they receive treatment in a supportive yet firm framework. We know that many adult sex offenders started offending during adolescence, and are confident that providing developmentally appropriate and offence-specific services to youth could have a decisive impact on interrupting a trajectory of criminality into adulthood.

Implications for Relapse Prevention

Understanding the fundamental differences between young people and adults is also relevant to relapse prevention strategies, so that youth are not set up for failure as a result of criminal sanctions, including court-ordered conditions of probation. Issues of criminal intent and criminal responsibility extend beyond the issue of sentencing to how the youth can be helped with a relapse prevention plan. Youth who have mental disabilities are much more likely to re-offend when the plan designed for them does not take into account some of the issues related to criminal intent. A youth's apparent non-compliance with relapse prevention strategies is poorly understood because expectations may be inappropriate. The question then becomes when or whether such youth should be breached for non-compliance. Their involvement with the justice system is prolonged as a result of breaches, and this can be a source of systemic bias for young offenders with mental disabilities.

Criminal responsibility for an action assumes that the youth's actions were voluntary. Voluntariness — and hence, criminal intent — assumes a level of consequential thinking, including the capacity to form a specific intent given a set of predetermined actions. Volitional capacity can be liberally construed as the ability to inhibit affective or behavioural reactions, to modulate impulses or desires to act, to delay one's responses, or to redirect one's responses toward options that might have less harmful consequences.

One youth I worked with went on a camping trip with the YMCA. This youth suffered from a mild cognitive disability and severe ADHD. The group of boys going on this trip were a mixture of non-disabled and disabled, but many had relatively invisible disabilities, similar to the youth in question. I received a call from his mother, who told me that he had to come home early from camp because of a number of incidents where he "had posed a threat to the safety of the other campers." One incident involved the youth throwing an apparently empty aerosol can into the campfire. The can exploded, narrowly missing one of the campers. When interviewed about the event, the youth reported that he had not intended to hurt anyone. In fact, he had not imagined that throwing the can into the fire could do such harm. All he could remember was the chanting and taunting of another youth who kept telling him how cool it would be to watch the can burn in the fire. We met with the camp counsellor, who corroborated the youth's story about the other youth taunting him, but because they did not know about this youth's mental disability, they believed the youth should or would be able to handle the situation and show good judgement. In fact, one of the goals of the camping experience was to allow youth to grow in their independence and survival skills, so they took a fairly hands-off approach to such incidents unless they got out of hand.

Given this youth's history of impulsive behaviour and his mental disability, it was no surprise that something like this happened. The punishment of being sent home seemed all the more saddening since this youth had never before had the opportunity to attend a camp with mostly "normal kids." We realized then, of course, that we had not planned sufficiently to alert the counsellors to his mental disability and the situations that might bring out the worst in him.

It would be difficult to make the case that this young person intended committing the offence. He could have been charged with mischief for his actions, but fortunately the counsellors thought sending him home was far more appropriate.

Youth with mental disabilities may have greater difficulty with relapse prevention programming because they are compromised in their volitional control over some aspect of their behaviour, and they may have variable responses to the criminal sanctions imposed on them. There are three questions we should be asking when we are working on a relapse prevention plan for youth with mental disabilities:

1. To what extent do they have volitional control over their behaviour?

The first question has to do with the youth's capacity for internal versus external control. It is an assumption of the justice system that we need to hold offenders accountable for their actions,[12] but to what extent can youth be expected to govern them?

Most youth have the capacity for internal control related to a particular offence or a pattern of deviant behaviour. Given that they do have this capacity, their deviant behaviour was not simply a product of external events beyond their control. They made a choice to offend. Given that youth made that choice once, we should expect that, if they re-offend, they will make another choice.

Conditions of probation could be framed within this same logical framework. Youth have been told their conditions of probation, yet they made a choice to ignore them. When they breach once, we assume they have made a choice. This then applies to all further breaches.

For offenders to take responsibility for their actions, they must be able to grasp that they have control over their deviant behaviour. Thus, offenders are challenged about how they talk about and think about their offences. If they misattribute the locus of control to external events beyond their personal control, they are helped to understand that this is not, in fact, the case. A basic premise of correctional treatment, probation, or forensic intervention is that the youth needs to become more aware of this capacity and to use it more effectively.

But what if the youth has a weak capacity for internal control and is actually reactive to external stimuli? Youth whose impulse control functions are intact can be taught to use them more effectively to avoid temptations to re-offend. Youth with impulse control deficits, however, will have more difficulty applying what we teach them in the real world and may need more support and more realistic expectations.

It is important to have a conceptual map in your mind when thinking about relapse prevention for youth with mental disabilities. Succumbing to distractions or irrelevant information may be a key barrier to the youth remaining focused on a particular goal. This same youth, however, may be responsive to external control. Some people have called this providing an "external brain" for the youth by structuring the environment and contingencies in such as way as to maximize the youth's success in complying with a request and completing particular steps in learning a new skill. Youth who do not have the skill set to exercise sufficient personal control in tempting situations will need a different approach to relapse prevention than youth who have.

When youth are expected to follow through on a plan developed for them, there is an expectation that they will be evaluated on their performance; that is, they will need to prove they can do what it is we are expecting of them. This will be harder for youth with mental disabilities, partly because their difficulties in avoiding temptations to re-offend are related to the core deficits associated with their mental disability. Some of these will be lifelong and cannot be remediated during a youth sentence. Thus, we need to ask ourselves to what extent this youth can be expected to improve functioning in the core deficits related to his or her mental disability.

Some core deficits can be improved, but others will continue to affect the youth's performance in many areas. A reintegration plan must therefore include provisions to help the youth with these deficits beyond the duration of his or her sentence.

2. Does the youth have the capacity to appreciate the nature and severity of the offence?

Helping youth take responsibility for their actions in treatment often involves describing the offences in detail. Youth who do not describe their offences fully or truthfully are often seen as being in denial or lacking in empathy toward the victim.

Again, the process is more complicated for youth with mental disabilities. Does the youth suffer memory impairments to the extent that his or her account of the offence is distorted or only partly true? Does this mean the youth is resistant, or intentionally lying, or distorting facts? Is this youth more susceptible to pressure tactics or anxiety? How do we discern whether this youth is being noncompliant with the process or the nature of his or her difficulties is getting in the way? Will youth be able to remember the plans we are expecting him or her to follow?

The answers to these and other questions have implications for the interventions we undertake.

3. What is the youth's capacity for planning and organization?

The first two questions have implications for the third. Youth with specific deficiencies in executive functions such as planning, goal setting, and organizing — and particularly when these difficulties coexist with impulsivity or memory problems — may have inordinate problems with core aspects of correctional programming, probation, and forensic interventions. They may be compromised in their ability to self-monitor, to understand sequences of thoughts, feelings, and events. They may agree to strategies to manage their temptations to re-offend without having the capacity to apply them.

Even youth who may be compliant and demonstrate awareness that a particular plan would be important may not be able to implement it. Some may be able to tell you what they are supposed to do, but their ability to act on the knowledge is compromised. When they are required to follow through on something, but lack the capacity to do so, they are being set up for failure. Expectations need to be gauged appropriately.

Conclusions

We need to examine our beliefs about the causes of youthful offending in a general sense, otherwise we will tend to attribute the causes to character flaws that may lead to criminalizing behaviour that is actually not as criminally motivated as we may suppose. On the other hand, charging youth and providing youth-focused services for youth found guilty of serious offences is important. There is a risk of slippage in the overall thrust of our principles of youth justice in criminalizing normatively deviant adolescent behaviour and in assuming that serious crime necessarily warrants an adult sentence. While this does not happen with great regularity, it could lead to a shrinking, not an expansion, of the resources necessary to adequately rehabilitate youth who commit serious offences. The nature of criminal intent is fundamentally different for youth than it is for adults, and assumptions about criminal intent for youth with mental disabilities must be evaluated against their functional capacities. Youth with mental disabilities may be much more compromised than the average offender in relapse prevention efforts. This can lead to systemic biases toward these young offenders and prolong their involvement with the youth justice system. We need to examine our practices so we are not setting them up for failure.

CHAPTER NINE

Risk-Need Assessment of Young Offenders

Risk assessment is a double-edged sword. It can be used to justify the application of severe sanctions or to moderate extreme penalties. It is easy to "sell" a risk assessment when the instrument claims to identify the dangerous and justifies the imprisonment of those individuals. However, identification of the violent recidivist is not infallible. We are not at the point where we can achieve a level of prediction that is free from error. . . . I sometimes wonder whether risk instruments serve to identify the highly dangerous *a priori* or simply serve to justify decisions already made.

— James Bonta
"Offender Risk Assesment"

The field of forensic mental health in Canada has evolved over the past 20 years owing to an increase in the amount of research that has been invested in understanding both adult and adolescent criminal behaviour. The psychology of criminal conduct (PCC) has had a profound effect on our understanding of youthful offending and now informs many of our practices. The goals of this social psychology is stated by its leading proponents as "seeking ethical, legal, decent, and human ways of introducing human service into the justice context of sanctioning."[1] In reviewing the literature, it is immediately apparent that PCC is more than just a theory; it has evolved into a mindset that informs forensic mental health assessments and treatments with youth, community, and correctional programming, and has permeated our youth justice strategy in Canada.[2]

Key themes of PCC include the importance of focusing on individual trajectories in criminal behaviour, developing individualized approaches, and maintaining reverence toward the complexity of behaviour that defies simplistic or generic approaches. PCC is a particular mindset toward criminal offending that counters criticisms that "nothing works" in offender treatment.[3] The "nothing works" debate has been reframed as the "what works" agenda, focusing on the demonstrated utility of offender treatment based on the research. A philosophical thrust to the "what works" agenda is the rehabilitative ideal — the belief that offenders can change for the better and that practices need to be developed to encourage this change.[4]

The idealism of PCC is tempered by a concurrent focus on practicality. This means finding common principles and empirical data to support the principles so that the delivery of services to young offenders can be more efficient and effective. One of the lines of research involves developing methods of classifying offenders and matching offenders' needs with programs. The technology of risk-need measures has been central to this agenda.[5]

There are a number of ways that risk-need measures may be used in work with young offenders. They may be used as part of pre-sentence reports usually prepared by community youth workers, although jurisdictions across Canada differ in who provides these to the court. They may also be used by forensic mental health professionals, custody workers, and community youth workers for case planning.

The Historical and Philosophical Context

Risk-need assessments for young offenders follow a historical path from its roots in adult correctional practices and research. Risk-need is a social construct developed by criminologists and psychologists to assist in classifying adult offenders in correctional facilities for determining levels of security and the intensity of treatment services. It has also been used for Review Board evaluations and recommendations for release conditions, such as halfway houses and early parole. The majority of these instruments have been spawned from the Level of Service Inventory (LSI) validated on offenders in adult correctional facilities in Ontario.[6] Basically, technologies developed for adults within correctional facilities and adult probation were transplanted to other provinces and to the young offender system throughout Canada.[7]

Early forms of risk assessments in criminal justice (sometimes referred to as first-generation risk assessments) were based on clinical judgements that relied almost exclusively on interview methods with no specific criteria for making decisions about the risk to re-offend and the offender's needs. This method of collecting information was criticized because of the lack of consistent criteria across interviewers, as well as difficulties in using the information to defend certain decisions or recommendations. Second-generation risk assessments attempted to delineate criteria for making decisions by identifying areas that needed to be canvassed; research studying the predictive validity of these criteria began. Third-generation risk assessments refined the task and included forensic needs, on the assumption that the effectiveness of interventions with young people depended on a careful matching of treatment choices with forensic needs.[8] Currently, the field is broadening to include the identification and measurement of a number of characteristics of young people that could affect the success of an intervention. These factors — commonly called responsivity factors — would assist in creating a better match between the youth's characteristics and the type of intervention provided. Some people have stated that this added component represents the fourth generation of risk assessments. Third- and fourth-generation risk assessments make the principle of professional override in risk assessment explicit, validating the role of clinical judgement as part of the process.

Criminal Offending and "What Works"

The brainchild of PCC has been the development of a framework for rehabilitating people involved with the justice system. One of the key goals of PCC has been to validate this framework using an empirical paradigm. The basic assumptions behind it are:

- Higher levels of service should be reserved for higher-risk cases. Intensive service is reserved for higher-risk cases because they respond better to intensive service, while lower-risk cases do as well or better with minimal service. This is called the *risk principle.*
- Targets of service are matched with the needs of offenders. Forensic needs are characteristics of the specific case that are associated with changes in the chances of re-offending.[9] The young offender's needs are not "any old needs."[10] Rather, they are, specifically, a youth's behaviour, characteristics, or patterns of functioning that require intervention to prevent further criminal behaviour. This is the *needs principle.* [11]
- Styles and modes of service are matched to the learning styles and abilities of offenders. This is the *responsivity principle*; a professional offers a style of service that is matched not only to forensic needs but also to those attributes and circumstances of the person that suggest what type of service they are likely to benefit from.[12]
- Professional judgement (referred to as *professional override*) is applied in determining the level of risk and the relevant needs in the final analysis.[13]

Research has increased our knowledge about the personal, situational, and social variables that are likely to be associated with the past criminal offending of groups of individuals.[14] This has helped us understand some of the general characteristics of people who come into contact with the justice system.

Another area of research has begun to delineate some of the personal, situational, and social variables that are thought to predict future criminal offending. This research has also helped us identify factors that might be related to future offending. The importance of this research is immediately apparent because we cannot change the past criminal behaviour of individuals, but we can try to change subsequent criminal offending.

To test some of these hypotheses, a third area of research has focused on manipulating the variables thought to predict future criminal behaviour and then determining whether manipulating these variables may actually affect re-offending. These studies are the most difficult to design because we simply do not know if or when individuals will re-offend. Neither can we control the extraneous variables that might be responsible for a person's desistance from offending. The hope is that these studies will provide information about deliberate interventions that are designed to influence variables that are thought to be linked with offending.[15] If we know what factors we should manipulate – criminogenic needs – we are able to focus our efforts on the most effective variables and not waste resources on targets that have no appreciable influence on criminal offending:

> The practical importance of criminogenic need factors is that they form the immediate goals of treatment. Because we cannot often observe directly an offender's criminal behaviour, we must be satisfied to try to change the aspects of the person and his or her situation that we think are linked to the criminal behaviour. When these needs are successfully targeted in treatment, chances are increased that recidivism will be reduced. [16]

Much of what we know about criminal offending is highly speculative. That is why I emphasize the general characteristics of offenders and recidivists — factors thought to be linked with offending, factors thought to predict future offending, and whether manipulating these variables may actually have an impact on reducing future re-offending.

Best practices for working with young offenders should be derived from a sound evidence base.[17] A number of strategies have been applied to different questions about forensic interventions. Different questions require different methods of data collection and analysis.[18] Misunderstandings about the evidence base for forensic interventions often result from confusion about cause and effect. For example, it is a common error that people fail to separate the characteristics of youth who come into contact with the justice system from factors that are more specifically associated with crime. We know that some risk factors for both mental health difficulties and delinquency may include economic distress or other forms of social disadvantage. The evidence for these associations has been found over time and across cultures. While these are interesting findings, we must remind ourselves that findings of associations between characteristics and outcomes are based on correlational data. A mutual relationship between two factors based on statistical correlation does not imply a cause-and-effect relationship.

The other problem we often face when interpreting causal links has to do with the fact that there are numerous findings of weak causal links or spurious connections in factors thought to cause crime. It is important to be clear about which correlations are weak and which ones are strong when we talk about risk factors for crime. Even if factor A showed a positive correlation to factor B (i.e., youth who live in this neighborhood committed more offences this month), the correlation might be weak. If it was a strong correlation, we would sit up and take notice, but we still would not know why the connection existed.

Weak causal links between factors thought to be responsible for crime has been a big problem for understanding youth crime. A good example is making the assumption that children from families who are economically disadvantaged are more likely to engage in delinquency and crime. This runs the risk of becoming a stereotype, and stereotyping can lead to discrimination. If the research is interpreted incorrectly, it could lead to all kinds of interventions based on faulty reasoning. We would need to examine our findings critically before launching a crime prevention strategy in particular neighbourhoods that are deemed to be disadvantaged. Without an understanding of why this correlation existed, we would be poorly informed about how to intervene.

Most of our evidence base for young offender interventions is founded on the statistical technique of meta-analysis,[19] which relies on empirical data we already have about young offender interventions and is designed to minimize the biases in group designs or qualitative methods of research. In the absence of powerful experimental, multi-wave, or longitudinal designs, meta-analysis has been one of the primary avenues for providing summaries of the evidence base for the "what works" agenda.[20]

In the absence of a validated evidence base, practitioners must combine the evidence base they have with their clinical experience and judgement, and apply good standards of practice. The literature shows that there are at least 14 areas relevant to designing interventions with young offenders. Few practitioners in custodial facilities, community probation, or other justice-related fields would disagree that these targets have face validity.[21] Many professionals in clinical practice have seen the benefits of targeting these 14 areas. The first five of these are considered the "Big Five," as they have the highest correlations with past criminal behaviour and are also considered to be among the best predictors of future offending. They are followed by the "Small Nine" – or complementary – goals for rehabilitation and reintegration:

Big Five Goals for Young Offender Rehabilitation and Reintegration

1. Help the youth change in antisocial/deviant attitudes, thoughts and feelings;
2. Focus on reducing the youth's antisocial peer associations;
3. Focus on reducing chemical dependencies and use;
4. Focus on reducing specific types of antisocial behaviours, such as lying, stealing, and aggression; and
5. Focus on helping the youth gain greater self-control, self-management, and problem solving in day-to-day functioning and in relation to areas related to an offending pattern or criminal lifestyle.

Small Nine Complementary Goals for Offender Rehabilitation and Reintegration

1. Focus on increasing exposure and access to prosocial[22] role models;
2. Focus on healthy use of leisure time, and find concrete and constructive activities to replace unhealthy and non-constructive activities;
3. Help the youth increase prosocial behaviour, such as honesty, responsibility, and respect for others;
4. Assist the youth with safety plans and protection from victimization;
5. Encourage family affection and communication;
6. Encourage family monitoring and supervision;
7. Increase the youth's mental acuity in recognizing and coping with risky situations (situations that could potentially lead to unsafe, antisocial, or offending behaviour);
8. Assist the youth with overcoming personal and circumstantial barriers to accessing appropriate services and making desired lifestyle changes; and
9. Assist the youth with developing plans and constructive steps toward education and vocational goals.

As can be seen, these goals are quite general, and their application to a particular young offender requires an assessment of what a young person needs. We need a clear understanding of what we would like to accomplish by a given intervention for a particular youth. Basically, a needs assessment seeks to answer the question, "What is likely to work for this youth given his or her needs?" The needs assessment provides the basis for determining the goals of intervention, so we need to know how similar the youth is to those who were studied in a particular intervention. Then we are interested in what the literature has to say about youth who have committed particular offences, their characteristics, and what types of interventions work with them. We are also interested in the conditions or contexts in which the interventions are likely to be successful.

The questions we will ask during a needs assessment go beyond an understanding of the characteristics of the youth (i.e., current issues, personal attributes, motivation, current circumstances). We are also interested in other characteristics or issues, such as setting factors (where the intervention will occur), characteristics of the person doing the intervention (age, gender, training, practices), program factors (agency resources, treatment philosophy), process factors (content and process of the intervention), changes expected in the young person in the short term (intermediate outcomes, such as satisfaction or presenting problems), and long-term outcomes (such as more lasting changes in client characteristics and their functioning).[23] Some of the questions we might ask during the needs assessment include:

- What is the nature of the criminal offence?
- What do we know about the antecedents of this type of offence?
- What do we know about the type of interventions that are likely to be successful?[24]
- What do we know about the optimal intensity (i.e., the number of contacts with the youth per week) for this type of intervention?
- What do we know about how best to implement the intervention?[25]
- What do we know about the specific characteristics of the youth that are likely to interfere with or enhance the intervention?
- What do we know about the specific characteristics of the adult implementing the intervention that are likely to interfere with or enhance the intervention?
- How will the issues of continuity, consistency, and aftercare be addressed in setting up this intervention?[26]
- What are the risks, benefits, and side effects for the youth, the family, and the community?[27]

The fit between the purposes of the intervention in addition to the young person's unique characteristics and circumstances are important considerations in determining how best to intervene and support the youth during their involvement with the justice system.

"High, Low, Medium, Slow, Jolly, Pepper"

The concept of risk-need assessments is not unlike this old skipping game. The chant related to how the rope would change in height and speed and swing as you skipped. The goal was to see how well you could manage all the changes without stepping on the rope. Some of us did fine when the rope was low and slow but inevitably failed as the height and speed increased. The risk-needs principle is similar to this chant – our interventions are the height and the speed of the rope. We adjust our interventions according to whether the youth is of high, medium, or low risk to re-offend. Low, medium, and high risk are related to low, medium, and high intensity interventions. Then we watch. Can the youth keep skipping without stepping on the rope?

We are told by the "what works" agenda that low-risk offenders should be left alone because we might make them worse by intervening or supervising them too intensely. But what if the low-risk offender has a number of real-life and self-perceived needs? How do we differentiate between these needs and forensic needs? We are also told that high- and medium-risk both mean we need to intervene, more or less intensely as the case may be. How do we define the difference between high and medium intensity? Until we have a better evidence base regarding these issues, or better definitions of the terms, we should use them judiciously. The focus should be on identifying the nature of the needs and a plan for intervening that balances all three principles — needs, risks, and responsiveness.[28]

The Youth Level of Service/Case Management Inventory

The Youth Level of Service/Case Management Inventory (YLS/CMI) is one of the LSI-based tools that I have used with young offenders, though it has not yet been properly validated in my jurisdiction.[29] Despite this shortcoming, I have found the tool useful in working with young offenders, as it provides a flexible structure for case planning that addresses some of the problems with applying the risk-need framework.

To determine the goals for the case plan, one needs to collect information about the youth from reliable sources. The major domains assessed are: family/parenting, education/employment, peer relations, substance abuse, leisure/recreation, personality, and attitudes/orientation. Information in each area can be based on interviews, psychological tests and behaviour rating scales, school records, criminal records, institutional records, and case conferences.

Case Study: A.

A. is a 15-year-old youth facing assault charges — including one charge of aggravated assault and two involving knives — numerous breaches/failures to comply, and previous charges for which she has been found guilty. She has been known to the court since she was 12. She indicates a pattern of repeat and violent offending, and substance abuse issues. She has generally been unsuccessful at complying with probation orders, but she has been co-operative in custody settings. She had been largely beyond parental control prior to her incarceration, and her living arrangements had been unstable, at times following a transient lifestyle that included chronic drug and alcohol abuse.

Based on A.'s past offending, the seriousness of her current offences, her possession of knives during the commission of the offences, her minimization and rationalization of the offences, her non-compliance with probation orders, her substance abuse, and her difficulty accepting direction and structure, the judge considered her disposition carefully. In the court-ordered report completed prior to sentencing, the psychologist reported that A.'s motivation for change was low, yet she acknowledged her offences and seemed resigned to the consequences. She told the psychologist that she did not believe she had a problem with violence, aggression, or anger. While acknowledging that her substance abuse was clearly related to her offences, she was not clear about her motivation for change in this area. The psychologist observed that A. had a tendency to manipulate others to meet her immediate needs, and suggested that A.'s behaviour might change depending on whom she perceives to be in control.

On the positive side, the psychologist suggested that A. did have potential to succeed academically, as her cognitive skills were intact and she has good basic academic skills. She has also indicated a desire to finish high school and eventually become an elementary school teacher. The psychologist's evaluation suggested that, while A. was articulating some plans for the future, her behavioural patterns and attitudes suggest that she will likely have difficulty following through. She will require a great deal of structure, support, and supervision to avoid falling into a criminal lifestyle. Of main concern were her addictions problems, particularly alcohol and marijuana.

The judge sentenced A. to a period of custody followed by community probation. A few weeks prior to her release back into the community, A.'s community youth worker called a case conference with her custody workers, family, and other people working with her to discuss a case plan for A. The youth worker used the YLS/CMI as a way to organize the case plan and to determine the level of supervision upon release and specific goals for the plan.[30]

Prior and Current Offences/Dispositions
A. has an extensive previous criminal history, including more than three prior findings of guilt (1 point), two or more failures to comply (1 point), prior probation (1 point), prior custody (1 point), and three or more current findings of guilt (1 point). Thus, she receives a score of 5 (high) on this item.

Family Circumstances
Prior to serving the custody portion of her sentence, A. had not been successfully supervised, given her truancy and her difficulty in complying with the

structure provided for her (1 point), and her family had difficulty controlling her behaviour (1 point), despite the fact that her parents had attempted to be consistent in their parenting. It is reported that A. has a poor relationship with her father (1 point), but a good one with her mother. She receives a score of 3 (moderately high) on this item. Her relationship with her mother is a strength in this area.

Education/Employment
A. has exhibited disruptive classroom behaviour (1 point), disruptive behaviour on school property (1 point), problems with peers (1 point), problems with teachers (1 point), truancy (1 point), and was currently unemployed (1 point). However, her achievement levels appear to be commensurate with her abilities. She achieves a score of 6 (high) in this area. Her academic achievement is a strength for her.

Peer Relations
A. has mostly delinquent acquaintances and friends (1 point), though she does have a few positive acquaintances. She scores 1 (low) on this area, and so it is an area of relative strength for her. However, there is a concern about possible ongoing conflict with some of her former peers that may affect her adjustment in the community. In fact, A. is fearful of retaliation because she owes some people money for drugs.

Substance Abuse
A. indicates all types of substance abuse leading up to her current offence, including occasional drug use (1 point), chronic drug use (1 point), substance abuse that interferes with her life (1 point), and substance abuse that is linked to her offences (1 point). She scores 4 (high) in this domain. Although she acknowledges that she had an ongoing problem with substance abuse prior to her incarceration, she does not believe it will be a problem once she is released. Her rationale is that, since she has not used substances while in custody, she will not return to her old habits on release. However, her previous heavy and chronic use means that she is at risk to fall back into this pattern, and so her substance abuse could be a significant factor that may lead to further offending.

Leisure/Recreation
According to staff at the custodial facility, A. had difficulty using her time constructively while in custody, and this is also noted to have been a problem prior to her incarceration (1 point). The information suggests she could be making better use of her time (1 point). She does have interests, including

artistic activities, piano, and sports. Her interests and skills in these areas represent an area of relative strength for her. However, her total score, at 2, is still considered high.

Personality and Behaviour

A. does not appear to have an inflated sense of her own importance, nor does she appear overly self-centred. However, she can be physically aggressive (1 point), and she has a tendency to "lose her cool" when she does not get her own way (1 point). Her attention span seems normal. Based on reports from her custody workers, her frustration tolerance also seems normal, despite her occasional outbursts of anger. She has not physically assaulted anyone while in custody, but she has bad-mouthed staff on one occasion and one of the other inmates on several occasions. In the past three weeks there have been no such incidents.

During her time in custody she has improved in her attitudes and has shown increased ability to take the perspective of others. She has become more co-operative with both staff and programs over time. She expresses adequate guilt feelings about the negative effects of her actions. Her score is 2 (moderately high) in this area.

Attitudes and Orientation

A. does not appear to harbour negative attitudes toward the justice system, but she does indicate procriminal[31] attitudes toward violence, particularly her own physical violence, in that she minimizes it (1 point). She is willing to attend an addictions assessment, but will not agree to addictions counselling. She will also not agree to attend counselling for anger and self control issues (1 point). She is not actively rejecting any services; rather, she appears ambivalent and non-committal. She does not defy authority, as evidenced by her compliance in custody and her current presentation. She does not appear to be a callous person and does shows concern for others. Her score is 2 (moderately high) in this area.

Overall Risk Score and Strengths

A.'s overall risk score on the YLS/CMI is 20, placing her in the moderate range for risk to re-offend (low = 0-8; moderate = 9-22; high = 23-34; very high = 35-42). In consultation with her community youth worker and custody worker, it has been determined that this score is inflated in part because of A.'s past history. Her history is not something she can change. Another source of elevation in her risk score comes from her antisocial thinking, particularly her minimization of her violence and her substance abuse issues. These are areas she can change. We feel A.'s risk to re-offend is probably low to medium, depending on her ability to stay away from negative peers and the possibility she may again resort to substance abuse. A.'s association with some prosocial peers and her good relationship with her mother are strengths for her. Additional strengths include the fact that she has good achievement potential and expresses a desire to complete high school. She also has artistic ability and enjoys sports, having previously played on a soccer team.

Thus, A. has a number of competencies that could serve as protective factors in her reintegration. Her community youth worker notes that, based on the YLS/CMI risk rating of low to medium, she would like to meet with A. several times a week for the first two weeks after release, tapering to twice a week. By the third month (halfway through her community probation) she will be required to meet once a week until the end of probation.

Learning Style and Other Factors

There are a number of other factors to consider in implementing a case plan for A. Her extended family and parents are clearly a support network, but she has been allowed to move around a great deal, following various living arrangements made informally by family members, and has played one family member off against another. She has a conflictual relationship with her father, who is a teacher. She associates an authoritative stance with her father, so we must explore ways that this relationship could become less confrontational and more supportive for her. It is interesting that A. also wants to become a teacher, suggesting that, while she may not feel close to her father at this point, she seems to identify with his value system.

Since A. has been in custody, her parents have separated. Prior to her incarceration, her parents frequently disagreed on how to handle A.; perhaps this will not occur now that they are not living together. Her mother is willing to have A. live with her. However, there are some concerns expressed by both parents and by A. herself that she may find it difficult to adjust to living at home. Her community youth worker is concerned about adequate supervision, given that A.'s mother works full time and that A. did not follow the structure provided by her parents prior to her incarceration. A. suggests that her parents were not "that structured" before, and suggests that the house rules should be in writing so everyone, including her, knows what is expected of her.

Other Needs and Special Considerations

This part of the YLS/CMI examines whether there are particular issues or needs over and above the needs that may be related to A.'s functioning or the functioning of her main supports, parents. The measure provides direction by outlining areas that should be canvassed. The following areas should be considered:

Family and Parents
 Criminal history of a chronic nature
 Emotional distress ✓
 Drug/Alcohol Abuse
 Marital Conflict ✓
 Financial/Accommodation problems
 Uncooperative parents
 Cultural issues
 Abusive Father
 Abusive Mother
 Significant family trauma
 Other ✓

"Other" denotes that the family is currently undergoing a major transition, with parents having separated. Both parents express distress related to this and report that they are both attending personal counselling. They are not sure if reconciliation is possible, but they are keeping the door open. Given the newness of this separation, there is still a possibility that A. will be caught in a triangle between her parents. A.'s father is concerned about his relationship with his daughter and is open to suggestions for improving it. A. has a history of playing family members against each other, so there may be a pattern of over-reliance on extended family to take over when conflict or disagreement with A. is high. The parents will benefit from suggestions on how to manage these times so that extended family are not drawn in, and suggestions as to how the extended family can support A.'s parents' efforts to be clear and consistent.

With respect to A.'s issues noted below, there are a number of special considerations. She is willing to attend an addictions assessment, which is positive. Perhaps if she attends the assessment her thinking may change and increase her motivation to attend again. On the other hand, she is not willing to go to counselling regarding violence issues, and states that she is "over this problem." There is concern because one of her previous offences involved fighting with other youth, and she may be at risk from a third party, given her history of fighting with other youths in the community and the fact that she owes some of them money. By all accounts, she was engaging in a high-risk lifestyle prior to her incarceration, and will likely require a great deal of support to resist slipping into this lifestyle again upon release.

Youth

Mental health problems ✓
Physical disability
Low intelligence/developmental delay
Learning disability
Underachievement
Poor problem-solving skills ✓
Victim of physical/sexual abuse
Victim of neglect
Shy/withdrawn
Peers outside age range
Depressed
Inappropriate sexual activity
Racist/sexist attitudes
Poor social skills ✓
Suicide attempts
Diagnosis of psychosis
Third party threat ✓
History of sexual/physical assault ✓
History of assault on authority figures
History of weapon use ✓
History of fire setting
History of escapes from custody
Protection issues
Adverse living conditions
Engaging in denial ✓
Low self esteem
Other

A.'s youth worker suggests that she would benefit from a schedule of activities, including school and recreational opportunities. They agree on a safety plan should A. be confronted with the peers she is concerned about. The youth worker is not satisfied that A. will not agree to counselling, as it is a condition of probation. Although A. is not willing to attend counselling, she is willing to meet with the school counsellor. Her youth worker still wants A. to address her violence issues with a trained counsellor. An option presents itself unexpectedly later in the case conference, when A. and her mother talk about setting up house rules. A. and her mother will make a list of house rules. These will be presented to the youth worker at the next contact. A.'s mother expresses some concern about whether A. can work on this list without getting into an argument; if this does not work, she will have to reconsider whether she can have A. live with her. A.'s aunt, who is present at the case conference, suggests that perhaps A. and her mother could attend a few family counselling sessions to help them deal with the issue. Mouths drop when A. agrees to this! Her community youth worker states that this type of counselling would meet the condition of her probation.

A. reports that she would like to get a part-time job so she can earn money legitimately. Her father suggests that he could help her prepare her resumé and then take her around to drop them off. A. agrees.

In A.'s case, the YLS/CMI was useful in identifying levels of supervision, risk, and needs in a way that facilitated a constructive and collaborative approach to preparing for A.'s release. There is an option on the measure to specify goals and determine progress, limiting goal setting to three major areas. In A.'s case, these were family/parenting, education/employment, and attitude/orientation. The following plan was developed with her:

A.'s targets for change in the next three months

AREA: family/parenting
NEED: house rules
STRENGTH: relationship with mother
BARRIERS: conflict, defiance
INCENTIVES: live at home; clothing allowance; family counselling (improve relationship with Mom)

AREA: education/employment
NEED: educational and work experience
STRENGTH: good learning and athletic ability; desire for independence; creativity
BARRIERS: poor attendance; substance abuse; poor anger management
INCENTIVES: high school credits; paycheque; time with prosocial peers; father willing to help with resumé and job search (time with Dad)

AREA: attitudes/orientation
NEED: decrease procriminal activities (denial/minimization of violence); move from precontemplative to contemplative stage of change
STRENGTH: agrees to see school counsellor; agrees to addictions assessment; not a callous person; shows concern for others; does not harbour a negative attitude toward authority
BARRIERS: substance abuse; criminal role models; history of violence with peers; third party threats
INCENTIVES: medium supervision by youth worker/regular reporting/ contact; positive relationship with youth worker (challenges distortions/

reinforces taking responsibility); safety plan re: third party threats; reinforcement by family when concern for others shown; completing one more month of probation successfully (Mom takes her out for supper)

Risk-Need Assessments and the *YCJA*

The *YCJA* proclaims that judicial measures should be reserved for the most serious offences. The logic of risk-need assessments actually contradicts one of the main premises of the youth justice strategy: that "young persons are to be held accountable through interventions that are fair and in proportion to the seriousness of the offence."[32] Risk levels obtained from LSI-based measures should therefore not be construed to reflect the seriousness of the youth's offence.

From the perspective of the *YCJA*, the focus is on the present offence and a proportional sentence. The potential of risk-need measures to "predict" future offending is not relevant. The sentence may include conditions that reflect the logical consequences of the offence, but it should not overstep the nature and circumstances of the current offence. Thus, while a judge may believe that a young offender should attend counselling as one of the conditions of probation, it should not be stipulated unless the nature and severity of the offence suggests a logical connection between the offence and the condition.

The terms "high risk," "moderate risk," and "low risk" should be used cautiously, as they relate to the offence, and should not be a judgement on the youth's character. A youth who has shoplifted items valued under $20 may be assessed at a high risk to do so again, but it doesn't mean the youth is a "high-risk offender," nor that the youth should receive a more punitive disposition.

If risk ratings are incorrectly interpreted in terms of "dangerousness" or "anti-social patterns," they may provide a rationale for more punitive sanctions or more restrictive interventions. This is not allowed under the *YCJA*. Similarly, a youth who continually breaches the conditions of probation may receive a classification of high risk to re-offend (that is, high risk to ignore aspects of the probation order). The label may result in more punitive sanctions, perhaps even custody. This, too, is not allowed under the *YCJA*.

The *Youth Criminal Justice Act* is clear about the purposes of the pre-sentence report, and makes no mention of risk assessment. However, according to s. 40(2)(f), the person preparing the report may "include any information that the provincial director considers relevant," so it is left to the discretion of the probation system to provide risk evaluations as part of their predisposition reports. A procedural protection allows the court to withhold parts of a report which may be prejudicial to the young person. However, the court also has the discretion to withhold disclosure of part or all of the pre-sentence report from the youth, the youth's parents, or private prosecutor, if the court believes that "disclosure of the report or part would seriously impair the treatment or recovery of the young person, or would be likely to endanger the life or safety of, or result in serious psychological harm to another person" (s. 33(9)- (11)).

It is unclear how this might play itself out, but the court certainly seems to have a great deal of discretion with respect to information that youth and their parents should have a right to access. In certain cases, people might not be aware of the potential of the risk-assessment to influence the decisions of judges.

Risk-need assessments are not appropriate for decisions made under extrajudicial measures, pre-trial detention, or release from pre-trial detention; using them in these contexts violates a basic principle of youth justice that decisions should be made on the basis of the seriousness of the offence and not on the character and circumstances of the young person. Where such information is deemed important for decision-making, there is discretion in the legislation to call conferences and request child welfare or psychological assessments. Extrajudicial measures, too, should be proportional to the offence, and not more onerous than would have been the case if the youth had been subjected to judicial measures.

Sentencing principles should not be clouded by risk-need assessments, other than to inform the court of the youth's circumstances, degree of responsibility in the current offence, and other mitigating circumstances related to the offence before the court:

> Assessment of risk to re-offend must not be confused with the very valid purpose of this *Act* which is to address the circumstances underlying the young person's offending and criminal behaviour. Nor should it be allowed to influence sentencing decisions because rehabilitation and reintegration are central to sentencing. Based on the foregoing reasoning, I am not prepared to consider the young person's assessed risk to re-offend in arriving at the appropriate sentence. I am concerned about the dangers of misusing the risk assessment and the potential for prejudice to the young person.[33]

Even so, it is not difficult to imagine that lawyers and judges might be influenced by the inclusion of risk-needs assessments in pre-sentence reports.[34] Judges who simply accept the advice of probation officers in handing down sentences to youth are eroding the fundamental purpose of their office, which is to make judgements in a non-prejudicial manner. Probation officers should not be recommending sentencing alternatives, but focusing on the factors contributing to the current offence, the degree of responsibility for the offence, statements of willingness by the youth to repair the harm done, and supports in the youth's life.

A survey of youth court judges across Canada during the period of the *Young Offenders Act* indicated that their decisions to sentence youth to probation were often based on the probation officer connected with the case or on their relationship with a particular probation officer.[35] There may be a tendency among judges to defer to probation officers who come armed with risk-need assessments and recommendations for sentencing, especially if the judge wants to preserve his or her relationship with the probation officer.

Are Practitioners Using Risk-Need Measures Properly?

The assumptions behind risk-need measures do not reflect an intent to harm anyone. Advocates believe that good risk-need indicators can help with case planning for youth, increase efficiency in how young offenders are processed through the system, provide greater consistency in evaluations, and enable youth workers to convey more defensible opinions to the court than would be the case if they were based on clinical judgement alone.[36] As we have seen, they can be used to describe a youth's needs and organize a plan to meet them. Clarity is provided in the goals and roles of everyone involved. The process can be therapeutic and supportive, too, in that it provides a way for the youth and the family to regain some personal control in their lives.

The "what works" agenda sees many benefits in risk-need technology, and a great potential to help young people traverse their probation successfully. But a nation-wide study conducted at the request of the Department of Justice hardly inspired confidence that risk-need measures are being used in the manner they were intended.[37] There was substantial variability across Canada in whether audits were done to check that people were using the measures correctly, and a tendency for practitioners to blend the concepts of risk and need was problematic, as a failure to distinguish which factors are related to risk and which are related to need may result in inflated risk scores for many youth. Criticisms were also made about how practitioners interpreted and understood the scores they obtained, and there appeared to be an inconsistent use of professional judgement in evaluating the outcomes. The researchers also found that the way in which the risk-need measures were used, modified, or interpreted resulted in a potential for gender, racial, or cultural disparity in how they were applied, leading them to question whether the measures were promoting discriminatory practices in some jurisdictions. Finally, there were substantive concerns about the purpose of assessing risks and needs without a parallel emphasis on identifying the resources necessary to meet them.

Some people call the debate over defining needs and risks the "politics of need definition" because there are differing views on which needs are relevant and which are not for a particular individual:

Variables that are significant but not related to recidivism, yet require intervention, are deemed non-criminogenic needs (i.e., poverty, health) and considered at low priority in terms of interventions, except for *humane* consideration. An intervenable need is not an individual's self-perceived need, but rather a characteristic an individual shares with a population that is statistically correlated with recidivism. An intervenable need is defined not only through the availability of resources and structural arrangements that allow for intervention and possible amelioration, but also through statistical knowledge of it as a variable that is predictive of an undesirable and preventable outcome: recidivism.[38]

This is clearly where training and knowledge about the statistical basis for risk-need measures is important for practitioners. Researchers point out that determining what to focus on with young offenders assumes that the important needs are those that are thought to prevent recidivism (as noted earlier, the "Big Five"). But LSI-based risk-need measures do not really have a good evidence base about how these tools can help us with case planning for individual youth, and there are many other outcome variables of interest beside recidivism. In addition, we have limited data about particular needs that are relevant to groups with special requirements, such as youth from different cultural backgrounds or youth with mental disabilities; the risk-need profiles may be very different for these young offenders. We must also remember that the risk-need paradigm was originally developed for adult offenders, and it is assumed to some extent that a downward extension of this paradigm is relevant for adolescents. However, given the difference between adults and adolescents in maturity and capacities, we must question the relevance of this paradigm for adolescents.[39]

Risk-need technology is part of the "what works" agenda, so it is important to be aware that people who conduct research or those who review the research often have a specific agenda. This is one of the criticisms of the research on LSI-based risk-need measures. Critics note that the people doing the validity studies are themselves advocates of the measures, and how the results are interpreted, and what is interpreted, could reflect the biases or agendas of the researchers.

The psychometric reliability of a measure refers to its ability to measure a construct or behaviour with consistency and stability.[40] If I measure a youth's risk-need factors this week, will the outcome be similar if someone else does the same measure on the youth, or if I re-assessed the same youth with the same measure a week or two later? Both answers would be affirmative if the measure has psychometric reliability.

The validity of a measure refers to how well it actually measures what it is supposed to measure. The items on the test must adequately sample the domains we are interested in, and should not contain items that are superfluous to it. One way validity is established is by demonstrating that a measure predicts the future outcomes we are interested in or by showing that it is correlated with other measures that are supposed to measure the same thing.

It is also important to evaluate how each item contributes to the final score. It does not make sense that some items are only loosely correlated with recidivism (if that is what you want to know); each item needs to have predictive validity for the overall domain. Items that are not adequate predictors of risk should not be mixed with items that are important for treatment, otherwise the risk score will become inflated. We need better research to tell us what the central risk-need factors are. We must question whether these factors will reliably predict recidivism, and whether they reliably differentiate between recidivists and non-recidivists.

Items on LSI-based risk measures should also be scrutinized because they may be poor predictors of recidivism for certain age cohorts.[41] For example, the YLS/CMI was developed on young offenders aged of 12 to 15 even though the measure claims to be appropriate for 12- to 17-year-olds. Items relating to family circumstances and parenting may be less important in determining criminal activities for youth aged 16 and 17. Practitioners need to be aware of the age and developmental level of the youth in making determinations about risk-need factors.

Most of the initial validation studies on risk-need measures were done in south-central and northern Ontario, so we cannot make assumptions about whether the samples are representative of youth in other jurisdictions. There is also a problem with using convenience samples (i.e., youth in custody) as opposed to representative samples for developing normative data. The developers of the YSI/CMI intended to establish an initial set of norms in their region with the expectation that other regions would develop their own data. This is important because the scores derived from this measure relate directly to risk classification, which lead, in turn, to supervision levels. Regional differences could reduce the predictive value of the tool if the cut-off scores are incorrect for different regions.

LSI-based risk-need measures have been criticized for their potential to target disadvantages experienced by offenders who may belong to a marginalized group. Some items ask questions about social assistance, the psychiatric history of parents and siblings, and sexual experiences. These types of items suggest a value judgement. They may be relevant for some offenders, but they may have little to do with risk to re-offend. We must be alert to both direct and systemic forms of discrimination that could result from the inappropriate application of risk measures that have not been properly validated for vulnerable groups:

A systematic review of current practices and reports should occur to determine how and if the gender, socio-economic status, and ethno-cultural specific needs of these groups are being considered in the preparation of the PSRs, in the assessments of risk and need by probation officers, and in post-sentences in terms of access to community resources. Specific risk-need assessment tools ought to be examined to determine if the criteria used in the tools to establish levels of risk and need adequately capture the situation of ethno-cultural and Aboriginal youth.[42]

In a nation-wide examination of how practitioners dealt with culturally sensitive items, it was found that some intentionally excluded them.[43] Such practices could lead to inconsistency and ultimately to systemic bias toward some young offenders. Several studies that examined whether the YLS/CMI is able to predict recidivism among female and Aboriginal youth have found some preliminary support,[44] but these findings do not offset the more general criticism of the problem with the way actuarial tools classify females and Aboriginals as higher risk because of their greater needs.[45]

A common problem in risk assessment is making the final and definitive statement. Most of them go something like this: "There is a probability of 70 per cent that this youth will re-offend in a two-year period in the absence of services to address his needs related to his offending."

What is a youth court to make of such a statement? What am I, as a parent or youth worker, to make of it? The equation based on the probabilistic language of risk-need measures goes something like this:

Predicted risk of re-offending = this youth offended before and may re-offend again = he is likely to re-offend = he may offend in the next two years, but we are not sure = right now we don't know who or what kind of offence he may perpetrate = but if he does, the probability is high that we did not provide adequate services fast enough or intensely enough to prevent this inevitability = therefore we should increase his level of supervision now to prevent what we think may happen, given that (a) we don't know what he may do and (b) the likelihood that we don't know what treatment we should give him and (c) the likelihood that we won't give him the treatment he may need to resist further offending = nonetheless, when this youth does re-offend, let it be known that we will raise his risk level one more notch.

In truth, any youth who has offended may offend again. Past behaviour is probably the best predictor of future behaviour. But the level of certainty is poor. We may know that a youth is at high risk to re-offend, but we have no idea when or how this will happen. We can't tell if the next offence is going to be violent or not — although, again, we may have to rely on probabilistic statements. Assigning a percentage value to the risk to re-offend and then making a vague statement about services or resources is confusing. Why not just focus on what we need to do?

Risk-need measures could provide direction with respect to the provision of timely and appropriate services. The proper use of risk-need measures is to inform the case plan for a youth who is presenting with a number of needs that are thought to be related to future offending but also to self-perceived needs and needs that are related to the youth's level of adjustment and reintegration into their community. How the plan will be implemented and who will be assisting with this plan is also specified.

Often, youth receive unjust classifications. This will continue as long as adequate validation for risk-need measures is not undertaken, and as long as practitioners have a poor understanding of potential discriminatory effects, particularly where these tools touch on the requirements of youth from different cultures and youth with mental disabilities.

Conclusions

The Preamble to the *Youth Criminal Justice Act* proclaims the joint responsibility of various sectors of Canadian society to forge interventions for crime prevention, at-risk youth, and youth involved with the justice system — "members of society share responsibility to address the developmental challenges and the needs of young persons and to guide them into adulthood" — but the YCJA is silent on how we might work together toward these goals. What the YCJA does not tell us is that there is little funding for forging such interventions. The evaluation of programming is not a priority in organizations whose budgets are already stretching to maintain basic services. Those agencies that are evaluating their interventions have so far kept the information in-house; it is not disseminated to the public, or is not published.

This is not to say that many of these interventions are not effective; we just have no real way of knowing. Sometimes we are flying by the seat of our pants.[46] This is not to criticize the many well-thought-out efforts and programs currently available, nor to discount the extensive literature on actuarial assessment in Canada and other countries and the importance of these findings for issues of public safety and the effective management of offenders, especially for adults.[47] Rather, it is to remind us that the field is young, and we have much to learn and much to explain. Let us be cautious in our use of risk-need measurements and the interventions we propose for young offenders.

Practitioners in youth justice need to apply their critical thinking skills and approach risk-need evaluations with a modicum of scepticism, but we should not throw out the baby with the bath water. We need to temper our criticisms of the "what works" agenda — and the risk-need technology that is part of that agenda — by examining the evidence critically and recognizing the importance of using risk-need assessments with care.

The agenda of risk-need assessment and the *Youth Criminal Justice Act* are not necessarily driven by the same principles. Principles of sentencing must focus on proportional sentencing with a view to rehabilitation and reintegration as well as with a view to determining the least restrictive alternatives for youth. The danger of statements about a particular youth's risk to re-offend is that they could prejudice the judge, and others who work with the youth. The law states that the sentence must be proportional to the offence, and it must consider the underlying circumstances of the youth being sentenced. The *needs* portion of the risk-need assessment is still germane to sentencing; risk-need assessors and legal professionals share a common interest in the rehabilitation and reintegration of young offenders. Risk-need assessments play an important role in helping youth manage their custody and probation successfully, and they also provide a means by which we can ensure the safety of youth — and the community — to the greatest extent possible.

We must not abandon risk-need measures, but we must use them in an ethically defensible manner with young offenders.

CHAPTER TEN

Easing the Alliance

In world mythologies, the young hero frequently receives critical help from wise benefactors — sages, goddesses, and supernatural aides. Without their help, the hero's journey is probably doomed. We should not be misled, therefore, into thinking that myth making is a solitary quest. . . . We come to know who we are through relationships and social setting. To depart from the past is not to leave the world behind. It is rather to move from one world to another.

— Dan McAdams
The Stories We Live By

Most young offenders are dependent on and under the legal jurisdiction of their parents or guardians. This poses a challenge for the administration of justice, because the circumstances of each youth must be considered, and there may be competing concerns and interests. Justice sanctions often rely on parents or guardians to implement the conditions of release or probation and support their children who are in custody. While we know that parents play an important role in the psychosocial adjustment of adolescents, less is known about the role of parents whose children are caught up in the justice system. Few researchers have examined its aftermath in parent-child relationships.[1] The fields of criminology, family studies, and developmental psychology have progressed in relative isolation. What we do know suggests that police and court contact changes the parent-child relationship.[2]

A growing body of literature supports what clinicians have always known: adolescents are deeply affected by their relationships with their parents.[3] During periods of rapid development, the sensitivity and support that parents provide are critical in "scaffolding"[4] young people to the next level of functioning. However, in the adolescent phase, the parent-child relationship is thrown into flux as children strive toward autonomy and parents struggle to find new ways of supporting and guiding them. How emotional support is defined and conveyed during this time is key to adolescents' emotional functioning and adjustment.[5]

There is no magic moment when parents step out of the picture. Many people would argue that the parent-child attachment continues well into adulthood. Nonetheless, adolescents tend to be ambivalent about their relationship with their parents. Disengagement from the family during adolescence is normal and does not mean an emotional cut-off between parent and child. It is a period of transformation, and includes various processes of negotiating rules and developing communication patterns.[6] Parents are in a uniquely powerful position to contribute to their child's growth toward independence and individuality.

Adolescence isn't an easy time. Young people navigate various relationships, all of them reflecting common concerns about autonomy, psychological security, and intimacy,[7] but it is parents who often set the tone for the process.

Dependence during adolescence takes on a different flavour than it did during childhood, leaving some parents feeling out of their depth. At the same time, youth are likely to be at different levels of physical dependence. Those who have come up against the law may be living in foster homes, custody facilities, or in independent living arrangements. In these cases, parents do not exercise direct control over their children, who are clearly beyond their jurisdiction. Nonetheless, they continue to play an important role in determining adolescents' values, which is reflected in what they do and how they think.[8] The internal working models youth construct of their relationships with others are generally a reflection of their relationship with their parents. This will influence their expectations for other relationships, and their own parenting capacities in the future.[9]

Adolescents' perceptions about how their parents view them and the type of support their parents provide influence their adjustment. Even in complicated situations in which youth are separated from their parents because of interfamilial abuse, they may continue to desire a positive relationship with their parents. Many youth are generous in reference to their parents and cling to their parents' positive qualities even when their parents have repeatedly discounted their needs or abandoned them. The emotional ties are so strong that authorities are often powerless to keep youth and their parents apart.

Parents are often blamed for mismanaging their children when they come up against the law. People tend to be judgemental about families whose son or daughter commits a crime, though they soften their stance when their own son or daughter is caught. I always remind parents that, statistically, for every crime committed by their son or daughter, at least ten other youths are simultaneously committing crimes in other parts of the neighbourhood. I try to empower them to use this opportunity in a positive, forward-looking manner. I tell parents that, despite our best efforts, there are influences out there that result in our children making wrong choices.

I also challenge the concept of normality in families when it comes up, as it inevitably does when parents are blaming themselves for their children's mistakes. It is normative for adolescents to engage in some sort of antisocial behaviour. We all aspire to functional normality, but there is great diversity in how families develop and in the values they hold.[10] There is no perfect or normal family, and we tend to be too hard on parents when their son or daughter comes into contact with the justice system.

The assumption that young people don't understand the difference between right and wrong and must be taught is behind many punitive reactions to a child's delinquency. It is the rationale behind "tough love," but the idea that punishment can drum a moral conscience into a young person is completely misguided. Parents are sometimes so alarmed at the behaviour of their children that they become prone to catastrophic thinking: they fear that their child has a fundamental character flaw, or is even a psychopath who, left to run wild, could become a violent predator. Or they fear that if they don't do something drastic now, while they can still handle the child, the child will soon be six feet tall and handling them instead. The image is one of a giant-sized child bursting out of his clothes and stepping on his pea-sized parents with unrepentant glee. Of course, we want parents to be firm with their children and we want their children to respect them, but instilling fear in either the parent or the child rarely proves effective. Prognostications about the future are notoriously inaccurate and often divert us from dealing with present issues.

Once parents develop a rationale and implement strategies to set clear expectations and follow through appropriately, they really start to feel more effective. They benefit not from advice, *per se*, but from being encouraged to exercise their own judgement and approaches.

It is normal for youth to engage in some kind of criminal behaviour during adolescence. Most of them get over it fairly quickly. Any theory about the causes of youth crime, therefore, needs to consider why most adolescents engage in some form of it and why there is a peak period for offending. Similarly, it is important to know why the majority of adolescents are likely to grow out of it.[11]

The reason youth grow out of crime is because, as they mature, their responses to situations become more socially desirable and less antisocial. Research tells us that a combination of reduced supervision by parents and increased demands on adolescents may be related to the increase in delinquency between middle and late adolescence.[12] A reduction in supervision during adolescence happens quite naturally as parents encourage their children to become more independent and trustworthy. This means that parents relax the rules, allowing adolescents more freedom. Resources such as money and transportation further reduce the parents' control. One estimate suggests that over 40 per cent of an adolescent's time is unstructured and free from adult oversight.[13] Unstructured time is usually after school and on weekend nights, and these are the times that most youth crime occurs.

The consequences of reduced supervision are that adolescents can engage in delinquency with less chance of detection and sanction. This reduces the apparent cost of crime, and they may be less likely to hold the belief that crime is bad, and less likely to exercise self-restraint because their parents are not in a position to provide external control. In fact, diminished parental supervision has been found to be one of the strongest predictors of association with delinquent peers.[14]

Youth Stress

Adolescents face increasing personal stress as they mature. They must learn to adapt to many different people and social situations. Educational and occupational futures are stressed. School becomes more demanding: there is more emphasis on evaluation, and a climate of greater competitiveness. Adolescents often have difficulty meeting these demands, not only because of their lack of experience but also owing to the physical and social changes that accompany puberty.

Participation in a larger, more diverse, peer-oriented social world is a source of strain for some youth. Adult privileges, the desire for material gain, and an increase in social comparison increase the level of pressure on adolescents. Statuses change. Young people lose old friends as they move from elementary to secondary school, and they must make new ones. They move from a position of high status in elementary school to one of low status in high school. Peers continue to be a major source of status, and exclusion from popular cliques can cause psychological distress. Youth are also at increased risk for negative treatment by others. Less supervision by adults means more chance of getting into conflict with others and being victimized. Adolescents are often victimized or provoked by their peers, and they may respond to such victimization with crime.[15]

Both parent strain and parenting practices contribute to a youth's level of strain. In clinical settings, youth typically bring issues related to their relationships with their parents and talk about their parents' discipline practices. It is well known that marital conflict is related to delinquency, especially when the conflict involves abusive behaviour between parents. Parental lifestyles can be an additional source of strain.

People like to be treated in a fair, just, and predictable manner, so inconsistent discipline and discipline that is seen as unjust contribute to both psychological distress and delinquency in youth.[16] At the same time, excessive discipline is associated with higher levels of delinquency,[17] as it interferes with the autonomy goals of many adolescents. The deleterious effects of overly strict parenting are exacerbated by the style of discipline, particularly threatening, ridiculing, nagging, hitting, and other abusive behaviours.

Youth cope with stress in different ways. Some try to escape their parents' authority. They may run away, skip classes, use drugs, violate curfews, or steal. They engage in delinquency to get revenge or to rebel against their parents. Some attempt to reduce their obvious financial dependence by stealing. When parents mistrust their children's motives, some youth retaliate by fulfilling their parents' beliefs.

The failure of children to satisfy parental expectations can be a major source of strain, but rather than taking out their anger on their parents, youth will often take it out on others, sometimes with little regard for their personal safety. Some manage their negative feelings through illicit drug use, and once this pattern of coping is established, addiction takes on a life of its own.

There has been little research into the role that supportive parental behaviour plays among youth who come into contact with the justice system. Parental support of adolescents embraces a number of dimensions, including emotional concern such as empathy and love, instrumental assistance in the form of goods and services, information about the environment, and information relevant to self-appraisal and evaluation.[18]

The literature illustrates that parental support reduces not only delinquency but a host of other problems, including depression and social anxiety. It is considered by clinicians and researchers alike to be a key and universal factor in buffering youth from a range of negative outcomes. "Supportive parenting," according to one team of researchers, "has been associated with positive outcome across time, method, stage of development, and culture."[19] It is how parents and adolescents maintain their attachment bond.

Supportive parent-child transactions promote prosocial and altruistic behaviour and provide insulation to children in high-risk environments. Parental forgiveness of youthful misconduct may actually reduce delinquency. Young people who enjoy their parents' support report more outings with them, more supportive communications, and more sharing of confidences. They also tend to seek more help from their parents. The absence of parental support, on the other hand, has been statistically shown to exceed the importance of parental criminality, marital discord, parental absence, parental health, and family size in predicting delinquency. As one researcher put it, "It is as if parents' responsiveness, affection, and obvious commitment to their children's welfare gave them the right to make demands and exercise control."[20]

Parental Stress

Studies investigating the onset, persistence, and desistance of antisocial and criminal lifestyles reveal important clues about the role of parents.[21] Antisocial children cause stress to their parents, leading parents to be more irritable and consequently less effective in their discipline. They tend to withdraw their support and attention, which seems, in turn, to accelerate children's antisocial behaviour, which precipitates further deterioration in parenting.

Research has shown that the reactions of mothers toward normal children and children with conduct disorders are different, not because of the mother but mostly because of the children.[22] Parenting styles are critically different when mothers have to deal with children who have conduct disorder, and the resultant negative and coercive parenting style may play a key role in children developing antisocial behaviours such as aggression.

Parents of children who are challenging to manage experience a great deal of stress in their lives. Parents of delinquent youth feel ashamed of the behaviour itself and of the need to seek help. Both fathers and mothers suffer reductions in overall health and happiness, and the marital relationship may deteriorate. Some of the research suggests that mothers may be uniformly more negatively affected than fathers. They are more likely to experience difficulties with other relatives, friends, and coworkers, more likely to seek counselling, and more likely to be blamed and to feel shame, especially if the adolescent has been arrested several times and exhibits multiple behavioural problems.[23]

Some research suggests that delinquency actually gets worse as parents attempt to deal more directly with their child's behaviour, particularly in early adolescence. The increased involvement is likely to result in negative interactions between parents and child, eroding the quality of supervision and monitoring. As the relationship bonds weaken, the youth appears to be less influenced by the parents, resulting in more defiance and delinquency.[24] Another interpretation might be that awareness of delinquent behaviour in early adolescence may increase parental supervision and monitoring during a time when youth are seeking greater independence.

Divorce, separation, single parents, large families, teenage parents, economic hardship, and marital conflict are just some of the factors that have been studied in reference to parental strain.[25] A central variable in much of this research is the impact of parental strain on the emotional climate of the home. Strain leads to negative emotions and increases negative affect until everyone feels badly and the situation seems to call for corrective action. Parents may increase coërcive pressure on their son or daughter, or they may withdraw, emotionally and physically. Sometimes the child is seen as the source of the stress, and becomes the scapegoat of the family. The child's behaviour then becomes a justification for negative parenting; it is easier to withdraw from or attack others when they are seen to be at fault. Negative emotions are manifested in a variety of ways. Withdrawal and neglect are more likely when depression dominates, harsh and abusive parenting when anger dominates, and inconsistent parenting when depression and anger occur together.

Encounters with the legal system create pressures and embarrassment for parents as their child's behaviour becomes public and they have to invest time and resources to deal with it. Delinquency is more likely to have a negative impact on family relationships when it results in criminal sanctions.[26] After all, parents of adolescents who are engaging in delinquent behaviour are largely unaware of it; it goes on covertly or it goes unnoticed. Once the law is involved, however, parents not only become aware of their child's delinquency, but it is now framed as criminal behaviour. They may blame themselves, but they are also extremely disappointed in their child. Trust becomes a huge issue.

Themes from Parents' Experiences

A qualitative study done in 2003 gives us a glimpse into the experiences of ten middle-class Caucasian families who had a son involved with the justice system in the late 1990s on Vancouver Island. The themes that emerged from the interviews are instructive and thought-provoking.[27]

Stress and Loss

The stress that parents felt appeared to be proportional to the behaviour problems exhibited by their son and the time, energy, and nature of his involvement with the justice system. Parents described some of their experiences in traumatic terms — "shell shocked," "emotionally drained," "having the wind knocked out of their sails"[28] — noting especially assaults on their self-esteem and identity as parents. They also described a great deal of worry and guilt, as well as grief and loss "in relation to health, safety, and well-being, material possessions, social life, family relationships, and a sense of control over their own lives, self-esteem, future expectations, and time."[29]

When parents were interviewed by probation officers or mental health professionals, they were required to reveal their personal stories to strangers. Their past lives became an open book, and they were forced to struggle with emotional baggage, "with what they had done wrong or failed to do right. They worked to maintain an identity and to cope with various emotions, including anger, feeling overwhelmed, and wanting to escape."[30]

Many of the parents I have seen over the years have been struggling with their marriages, and have been divided for some time on how to deal with their children. A youth's involvement with the justice system can be the straw that breaks the camel's back for worn-down family relationships. Many parents reported symptoms of depression, sleep disorder, and anxiety. They often found their extended families polarized, with one or the other left blamed and isolated. If there were other children in the home with high needs, such as infants or toddlers, the parent supporting the offender was often taxed to the limit, and such stress may trigger mental health or addiction problems.

Hard Work

Parents of young offenders spent a great deal of time, effort and money waiting, attending court, looking for services, contacting lawyers and probation officers, accessing services, bringing youth to appointments, and sometimes organizing every minute of the day to provide the structure their child needed. They were less able to attend to their spousal relationships, and friendships were put on hold. Their work may have deteriorated because they had difficulty concentrating, or they fell behind because they had to miss work to attend appointments. Financial stress added to their burdens if they were unable to maintain their employment.

Limited Support

Parents experienced varying levels of support from the community and family, and many felt unsupported by agencies outside the justice system. Faced with contradictory advice, they had to make difficult decisions on their own and suffered the often negative consequences in their family or the community:

> The message seems to be that society provides family support within limited parameters and on terms dictated by the state, leaving parents with the choice between coping individually with the burden of managing challenging young people and losing their rights as parents. Social workers become gatekeepers for scarce resources rather than facilitative agents of family support, and parents and social workers are then portrayed as at fault when things go wrong.[31]

Support without judgement was hard to come by for some parents interviewed in the Vancouver Island study. Maintaining their emotional equilibrium in the face of misunderstanding and negativity was overwhelming for some. On the other hand, even small gestures of support were appreciated, and professionals who were efficient and effective, and who showed empathy toward their situation, were highly valued.

System Constraints

Another theme that emerged from the parents' experiences with the youth justice system was a lack of clarity about the role they were expected to play. They didn't always know when to step in or when to hold back; sometimes they felt their input was valued and other times it was not.

Many parents I have seen over the years have been similarly ambivalent about how much they should intervene in the legal process. On the one hand, they are trying to get their child to take responsibility for his or her behaviour; on the other, they do not want to be the cause of more onerous sanctions. At times, too, the justice system simply disregards parents' views, suggesting that the system is unaccustomed to dealing with them. On the other hand, I have found that some parents simply withdraw and remain passive throughout the process, even if their opinions are solicited. Some have no problem relating information about their lives and giving opinions in public forums, while others feel constrained by the public nature of court and conferencing process and will not say things they might say in a more private interchange.

Another system constraint identified was staffing and the levels of stress experienced by staff. Probation officers have huge caseloads and multiple roles to play, limiting the amount and quality of time they spend with individual clients. Waiting times and a lack of resources were both factors:

> Inadequate staffing . . . was perceived as the reason why parents had to wait so long for the court process to unfold, and why police, probation officers, and forensic psychologists seemed so overworked. Inadequate staffing meant that a prompt response to offending behaviour was often missing, as was timely information sharing in numerous instances. Parents also identified a lack of comprehensive assessment and treatment facilities and a shortage of alternatives to custody. [32]

Diminished Participation

While parents express uncertainty about when or how to voice their opinions, evidence shows that they have little involvement overall, with only a small number being involved throughout the process.[33] Most are involved during bail or sentencing hearings, where they are perceived as playing an instrumental role. At other times, however, it is their children who seem to control the extent to which they are involved. Sometimes youth fail to appreciate that they can request their parents to be present during police questioning; sometimes they are in conflict with their parents and do not want them involved. Often parents are willing and able to participate, but they know little about the justice system generally and lack specific information about their son or daughter's case.[34]

In the Vancouver Island study, parents who gave positive evaluations of their experience with the justice system reported that their participation contributed to feelings of competency, empowerment, and control over their lives. Feelings of powerlessness in relation to dealing with their often difficult son during the process appeared to be mitigated by the experience of working with others as allies rather than foes. At the same time, parents who were highly competent in many areas of their lives were not immune to feelings of incompetence in dealing with their child's behavioural problems and with the justice system, and deeply appreciated the times when they were given positive feedback about their ability to cope or their concern and commitment to their child.

Emotions run high when difficult youth become involved with the justice system. Parents reported feelings of intense aloneness, not fitting in, and what the researchers called "internalized conditioning of self-blame."[35] Such feelings may be intensified when parents are not kept informed or are not directly encouraged to participate. Many parents in the Vancouver Island study had a great deal of anger, which remained unexpressed because they felt ashamed about their current circumstances, and felt they had failed: "It seems a paralysis sets in, perhaps influenced by assumptions about the system and the sense of not having the power to act. Unfortunately, the judgemental public eye sees such behaviour as evidence of poor parenting."[36]

Youth with Mental Disabilities

Themes of system constraints, diminished participation, limited support, hard work, stress, and loss are likely to be amplified in situations where youth present with mental disabilities. There are no studies that address this issue, but clinical observation indicates that such families are much more at risk should they have to navigate the youth justice system. A great deal depends on whether the young person already has a diagnosis and the family has a support network to buffer their involvement with the justice system. Most families do not.

Sometimes, parents have received a diagnosis and been offered services, perhaps during the child's early or middle years. They watch their child's problems growing during grade 7 and 8, and finally blossoming in high school. Many of the parenting techniques that seemed to be working are now failing miserably, and the youth is more and more out of control. They have no desire to see their child arrested and brought to court, and they are just as shocked as any other parents when it happens.

Parents in this scenario sometimes appreciate the involvement of the justice system, but their reasons differ. Some see it as a respite from constant conflict and monitoring. Others believe that their children will finally get the help they need. Still others may have decided that the situation is beyond their control and the justice system should take over. In this last scenario, parents may be dismissive of family therapy and see the problem as being with the youth and not themselves. There are other, finer nuances to these scenarios, but these three are common, and they all stem from unrealistic expectations about what the youth justice system has to offer.

Over time, these parents may come to experience the youth justice system as those in the Vancouver Island study did — only more negatively. The system has difficulty dealing with the average young offender, much less one with special needs.

Many parents are not aware that their child has a mental disability until he or she comes into contact with the law. They often hear about it for this first time when the youth undergoes a court-ordered psychological assessment or psychiatric evaluation. In these situations, parents are overwhelmed by the information and unsure how to proceed. Many go through a process that is analogous to grieving. A delayed diagnosis can arouse feelings of anger over recollections of injustices and missed opportunities. Youth who receive a delayed diagnosis are "system failures," in the sense that they have fallen between the cracks; for one reason or another they were misidentified as developmentally delayed but within the normal range, idiosyncratic rather than disordered. Some are clearly struggling in their late elementary years, but parents and teachers are not overly concerned; they adopt a wait-and-see approach. As the youth grow older, their difficulties become more serious because of the widening gap between their capabilities and the demands of their daily lives.

Families differ widely in their reactions to the specific diagnosis as well. If a young person has been diagnosed with a mild intellectual disability, a family with high academic expectations may be much more devastated than one whose thinking is more flexible and can visualize normal adult roles for children with intellectual disabilities. Some families simply have more tolerance for differences, and are less likely to define certain behaviours as deviant. As one study concluded: "Although parents and professionals from middle- and upper-class backgrounds may regard mild mental retardation as a devastating condition, lower-class parents may not even define it as a disability."[37] In my experience, however, parents can be so accepting that they may not notice the functional implications of their son or daughter's disabilities. They may have unrealistic expectations and allow the child far more independence or privileges than the youth is capable of handling. There is, inevitably, greater propensity for these children to come to the attention of the justice system.

Helping Families Cope

Parents whose son or daughter has been caught breaking the law vary in their reactions and coping skills. Some theories propose that families can be categorized on a continuum from mastery to passivity in their reactions to crises.[38] Masterful families are more likely to move toward problem resolution, to shape their circumstances and to take active control of the situation. They expect that they can overcome the crisis and that the family can return to normality. Other families are much more pessimistic and passive. They seem to expect to fail, and are less likely to take action to solve their problems. They accept rather than shape their circumstances.

Not surprisingly, masterful families manage stress much more effectively, are less likely to devolve from stress into crisis, and are more likely to recover from stressful events, situations, or states of crisis.[39] These families tend to present as informed consumers who are aware of their rights and freedoms. They will question police practices, speak up about the pace or content of criminal proceedings, and may not be appeased by placating assurances that their case is proceeding with fairness. Families like this are sometimes thought to pose special challenges, as they do not fit well with a system that tends to operate on its own agenda and timelines.

Many forces and factors will shape the parents' role, including the law, which is very clear: parents play a key role in all aspects of youth justice. But the system is not a surrogate parent. It clearly aspires to keep the parents informed and hear their concerns, but it must strive at the same time to establish a clear boundary between the role of youth justice and the role of parents.

Maintaining this boundary is not always easy, because the parents and the system may not have the same understanding of each other's role: parents may not understand what the system expects of them, while the system may not understand the concerns and needs of parents. When expectations are clear, parents are much more likely to understand their role. When the system understands the needs, capacities, and concerns of parents, it is also more likely to be responsive to them, and will be in a better position to support rather than undermine their role.

Conclusions

According to the limited data we have about parent's involvement in the youth justice system, many parents are not clear about their role. At the same time, while some parents may be aware of their role, there is a disconnect between what they aspire to do and what they actually do.[40] There are both physical and psychological barriers to involvement for some parents, whereas others may feel that they have little or no voice. It might be helpful to suggest some ground rules for people who work in the system:

- Exert efforts toward "keeping an active focus on the vitality of"[41] the parent-child relationship.
- Model an attitude of support, not blame.
- Parents need to be rewarded for taking positive steps and following through on plans.
- Find opportunities for parents to be heard and validated.
- Provide assistance with stress management.
- Find culturally relevant supports for the parents, including interpreters and elders who can accompany them to court or meetings.
- Help parents gauge appropriate expectations.
- Ensure that victimization and substance abuse issues in the home and community are addressed.

- Provide parents with strategies and services that are not onerous to access and are timely, given the current crisis.
- Consult with parents about the conditions and plans for their youth; ensure that they are aware of their own role in implementing them.
- Keep communication between parents and probation officers open and clear, so that everyone knows what probation officers will take on and what they will not, and so that parents will be encouraged to follow through on their commitments and refrain from falling back on the youth worker for parenting their son or daughter.

Parents wishing to be effective advocates for their children if and when they come to the attention of the legal system might consider the following suggestions:

- Avoid alliances with your child against the youth worker or others.
- Find strategies for parenting that do not rely on sanctions from the justice system.
- Determine if siblings are under undue stress and request assistance for them.
- Make your opinions known to the lawyer and the judge in matters of importance.
- Request education about the justice system to assist you with your role.
- Request medical or psychological assessments if you feel your child might have a mental disability.
- Provide instrumental assistance to your child, such as transportation to and from appointments.
- Request opportunities to meet with justice staff to stay informed of your child's progress.
- Ensure that your child receives adequate counsel and procedural fairness; never encourage your child to speak with authorities about incriminating matters unless his or her lawyer is present; never persuade your child to waive the rights to counsel or silence.
- Request all relevant information about your son or daughter — including previous medical, educational, or psychological assessments — and keep it in a dossier; if you do not understand something, request an appointment with the writer of the report or assessment to clarify it.
- Inquire if your workplace allows leave time to attend appointments and court dates.
- Inquire about employee assistance programs for family counselling.
- Consult with your family physician about stress-related symptoms you

or your children are experiencing;

- Be aware that you have rights and responsibilities involving your child; if you are unsure of them, consult with your child's lawyer or youth worker.
- Access counselling or parenting classes to help manage your own emotions.
- Seek professional support if you suspect your child is suicidal or engaging in a harmful or high-risk lifestyle.
- At all times, model respect and patience for the justice system, the processes that follow from it, and the staff who are working with you.

Following these suggestions will not guarantee a successful resolution to involvement in the youth justice system. Hopefully, however, they will assist in making the involvement less stressful and, potentially, more productive.

CHAPTER ELEVEN

Justice as Therapy

Those who believe that everything is solid and real are stupid, like cattle, but those who believe that everything is empty are even more stupid. Everything is changing all of the time, and we keep wanting to pin it down, to fix it. So whenever you come up with a solid conclusion, let the rug be pulled out.

— Pema Chodron
Start Where You Are

Can criminal law be therapeutic? It definitely affects people's emotional and so-cial lives, but could we imagine that it sometimes affects a person's well-being in a positive manner? Can the law have a therapeutic effect on people who are subject to criminal sanctions?[1]

The definition of "therapeutic" is telling. According to the *Oxford English Dic-tionary*, it means "contributing to the cure of disease" or "contributing to general, especially mental, well-being." "Therapeutics," in turn, can be defined as "the action of remedial agents." Law is one remedial agent in our society. Health and education are two more.

The type of therapy envisioned is based on the idea that law can become thera-peutic by incorporating the insights of the behavioural sciences.[2] Therapeutic jurisprudence provides a philosophy of law that attempts to ally the behavioural sciences with legal processes and procedures:

This approach suggests that the law itself can function as a therapist. Le-gal rules, legal procedures, and the roles of legal actors, principally lawyers and judges, may be viewed as social forces that can produce therapeutic or anti-therapeutic consequences. The prescriptive focus of therapeutic juris-prudence is that, within important limits set by principles of justice, the law

162

ought to be designed to serve more effectively as a therapeutic agent. . . . The therapeutic jurisprudence "lens" enables us to ask a series of questions regarding legal arrangements and therapeutic outcomes that likely would have gone unaddressed under other approaches. Therapeutic jurisprudence leads us to raise questions, the answers to which are empirical and normative. The key task is to determine how the law can use behavioural science information to improve therapeutic functioning without impinging upon concerns about justice.[3]

The approach has applications in terms of guidance to the legal system at a philosophical level, but also at the individual case level, the court level, and the policy level.

At the individual level, the judge may incorporate principles from the behavioural sciences into the legal process by requiring that sentenced persons acknowledge and describe their offences, using the principles of behavioural contracting, or engaging offenders in the process of problem-solving to encourage their adherence to the conditions of their probation.[4] Like the "teachable" or "therapeutic" moment that can occur in educational and mental health interventions, therapeutic jurisprudence seizes on what have been dubbed "psychojudicial soft spots" — areas in which the judicial system's unchecked actions could lead to negative consequences — when interacting with individuals in the court-room.

At the court level, it may mean the development of special programs or specialized courts whose underlying legal theory is related to concepts from therapeutic jurisprudence, reflecting "a more responsive and involved judiciary."[5] Examples of these "therapeutic courts" would include mental health courts, drugs courts, and restorative justice programs, whose "intent is to reduce criminal behaviour and recidivism by treating the illness that is causing illegal behaviour. . . . Mental health courts, by embracing the principles of therapeutic jurisprudence, become dual agents, representing both treatment and justice concerns."[6]

This requires a change in the paradigm traditionally used by the law:

Traditional Process	Therapeutically Informed Process
Dispute resolution	Problem solving and dispute avoidance
Legal outcome	Therapeutic outcome
Adversarial process	Collaborative process
Case oriented	People oriented
Rights-based	Interest- or needs-based
Emphasis on adjudication	Emphasis on alternatives and post sentencing
Interpretation and application of law	Interpretation and application of social science
Judge as arbiter	Judge as coach

Traditional Process	Therapeutically Informed Process
Backward looking	Forward looking
Precedent-based	Planning-based
Few participants/stakeholders	Wide range of participants/stakeholders
Individualistic	Interdependent
Legalistic	Common-sensical
Formal	Informal
Efficient	Effective[7]

The Therapeutic Youth Court

Cognitive and Behavioural Principles

Cognitive principles focus on the way youth think about other people, the experiences of their life, and their offences. When working with young people in the forensic context, we are always interested in their thinking errors and distortions as well as the attitudes they convey about themselves, their behaviour, and others. A major component of cognitive restructuring involves increasing their mental acuity to these issues. This means teaching them to pay attention to their own thinking, a form of self-monitoring. They become experts on themselves by bringing information to the sessions about their thoughts, feelings, and behaviour and drawing connections between them. The advantage of this approach is that they become active participants in the assessment and intervention process.

Many do not believe, at first, that thinking precedes either feelings or reactions, but they soon learn that feelings and behaviours do not come out of nowhere, and that their mind is a powerful tool in many ways. Many sophisticated young people quickly recognize that the sequence from thought to behaviour is quite simplistic, and they note that sometimes behaviours and emotions lead to thoughts, and vice versa. Cognitions, feelings, and behaviour are functionally related: a change in one can cause a change in the others. More importantly, when you modify one, you can produce a desired outcome in another.

Cognitive interventions are premised on two assumptions about the relationship between thinking and criminal behaviour in youth: first, that their thinking almost invariably shows errors or cognitive distortions in specific areas; and second, that they have a tendency toward uncritical thinking in relation to these distortions. The focus then turns to identifying and correcting the errors.

Cognitive therapy is an active form of both education and remediation. It involves learning to distinguish between errors in thinking (what they tell themselves) and what is actually going on in the real world (including what is likely to happen if they choose a particular course of action). It means developing the ability to step outside their thinking long enough to gather facts, weigh them, draw sensible conclusions, plan a realistic course of action, and assess their plan's effectiveness. Some of the methods used to encourage identifying and correcting thinking patterns may include homework assignments and Socratic questioning that explores thinking.

Behavioural interventions focus on how a person behaves in a given situation and how it leads to desirable consequences or not. The goal is to help the young person develop more appropriate behaviours and to reduce the frequency and severity of problem behaviours. The approach is based on the principle that consequences shape behaviour: we want to do things we will be rewarded for and avoid things we will be punished for. Therefore, we are more likely to repeat actions we have been rewarded for and avoid actions that have resulted in punishment. It is true that people are sometimes rewarded for the wrong things and punished for the right things, but behaviour therapy takes this into account by focussing on specific situations; behaviour leads to success or failure in a given situation that the youth is able to identify. The youth learns, too, that successes (the desired outcome) feel good. A side effect is that they feel good about themselves and their world.

Behavioural principles rarely occur in isolation from cognitive principles in designing interventions. Restructuring a person's mental acuity or thinking skills results in more permanent and generalizable skills than those that are learned solely using behavioural principles, but many youth are less responsive to cognitive approaches initially, depending on their maturity and cognitive abilities. The key is to find naturally occurring reinforcers that the youth has reliable access to, and to teach the youth how to reinforce him or herself for desired behaviours. Motivators play a huge role in generalizing behaviours that have been learned in one setting and transferred to others — custody to community, for example — and takes the place of motivation which is often lacking in youth. Adults in the youth's life must therefore ensure that the youth has appropriate supports and incentives for staying with the program.

Behavioural interventions always start with an analysis of the antecedents and the consequences of a particular behaviour, and they always focus on observable behaviour. This is one reason it is successful with people in controlled environments, such as custody facilities: the antecedents and consequences can be manipulated in a controlled manner. Behavioural interventions will not work if there is no reliable way of manipulating antecedents and consequences. The generalizability of these intervention have poor predictive validity for uncontrolled or natural settings unless there is some element of transfer in the intervention that can be maintained following the change of environment.

Behavioural interventions can have a powerful effect on the emotional climate of schools or custodial facilities. This is because they rely on contingencies that also shape the emotional tone of the environment. This aspect of behavioural interventions is often overlooked, but it is important to recognize that the value of apparently simplistic programs designed to increase the likelihood of a particular behaviour has the side effect of making care-givers and educators more consistent and positive in their overall approach. Behaviour principles have played a huge role in turning parents and educators away from a punitive model toward a more positive model of interaction with youth who are challenging to manage.

Cognitive behavioural interventions are useful for youth involved in the justice system because they focus on the exacerbating or reducing factors evident in problem behaviours, encouraging youth to focus on issues of personal control. Again, the intervention must be sensitive to the youth's maturity and cognitive abilities. The cognitive approach in tandem with the behavioural approach also teaches youth important lessons in mental acuity and locus of control. Asking them to monitor their thoughts and feelings or describe the circumstance surrounding a problem behaviour helps them identify the environmental events that can prompt or maintain the behaviour. The negative triggers can then be avoided, and the positive triggers sought out.

Locus of Control

Locus of control is a concept that comes up frequently when working with youth in the justice system. Essentially, it asks, "Who's in charge?" It is based on a theory of learning that emphasizes the link between how an individual feels about certain events and his or her sense of control over things that happen. People who feel victimized by circumstances or the events of life are referred to as having an external locus of control. Alternatively, people who feel they are in control of a situation have an internal locus of control.

The notion is apt in the youth justice context because the nature of the process is to take charge of a young person who is apparently not in control of him or herself. Interventions based on locus of control issues are aimed at helping youth distinguish what is under their control and what is not, and to help them recognize that they often misperceive locus of control as externally driven when in fact it is internal. Such misattributions can lead to difficulties with self-control in tempting situations involving illegal activities or in complying with probation orders.

Control issues of a more generic variety are also relevant, as youth involved in the justice system often attribute a negative valence — something to be avoided — to the issue of control, when in fact the capacity for power and influence is the cornerstone of good mental health and a healthy lifestyle. All people have an innate capacity for influencing others and exercising power. It varies with situations and expectations, but it is always there. Youth who are in conflict with the law frequently under- or over-estimate their level of control; they misconstrue risky situations because they are unable to gauge their power in particular circumstances or with particular people, and are often unrealistic about how to apply it.

Many youth (and many more children) are chronically power-deprived or power-saturated; by virtue of their status relative to adults, they are often unable to exercise power. Power-saturated youth often have an over-developed sense of entitlement, and struggle with accepting the authority of others. Maturation and the acceptance of the privileges and responsibilities of adulthood are accompanied by an increase in personal power for most people. By focussing on how to gain power in prosocial ways, youth are less likely to act out in ways that are harmful to themselves or others.

Relapse Prevention

Relapse prevention principles as applied to young offender treatment are based on treatment models used in the area of addictions. The basic strategy is to teach youth to anticipate problems and rehearse alternative, prosocial responses to cope with difficult situations. Significant others in the youth's life may also be trained to offer support in the process. The emphasis in interventions is on recognizing the patterns that lead to offending. The elements of relapse prevention therapy are adapted to the youth's particular pattern and offense, but the training typically involves identifying specific triggers — people, places, special times or events. These triggers are related in some way to the offending pattern and, once identified, can be managed in a number of ways. When youth have better insight into their triggers, and when their offences are only associated with particular triggers, their offending pattern or negative coping patterns can be broken.

Learning to manage the troublesome situations using relapse prevention training can be related to mental health problems such as depressive feelings or anxiety reactions, substance abuse as well as offending. It includes learning how to create emotional distance from a trigger as well as establishing alternative lifestyle values. New skills and experiences disconnect old triggers so they become less powerful. Some will simply need to be avoided, but finding alternatives that are not related to the trigger situation can then be reinforced and encouraged.

Solution-Focused Principles

Solution-focused principles are useful in working with youth who have been the chronic recipients of negativity, pathologizing, and rejection.[8] There are few people around them who model optimism and problem-solving. Most of these youth and their families have accessed multiple services in the past and are stuck in a negativistic and pessimistic condition. Involvement with the justice system always marks a significant event for the youth and the family, who experience a heightened level of sensitivity and awareness. The youth's anxiety sometimes makes him or her more willing to look at issues and explore alternatives. The parents' anxiety can lead them to ask questions and evaluate their response to the dilemma.

With the spotlight on the youth and the family, there is an opportunity for self-reflection and intervention at a moment when everyone is feeling shaken and vulnerable. It would be easy to use the situation for punishment and negativity, but there is also an opportunity to harness the youth's and the family's strengths to encourage their self-determination and develop problem-solving skills. The solution-focused stance is positive and optimistic, broadening the way a situation is viewed, building enduring personal resources, strengthening protective factors and coping abilities, and loosening the grip of negative emotions.[9]

The goal of the therapeutic court is to be democratic and Socratic, rather than paternalistic or authoritarian, and thus, solution-focussed principles are useful. Socratic or presuppositional questioning can be a powerful tool in working with justice-involved youth. Sometimes referred to as "Columbo tactics," asking questions to which the youth already has the answers can amplify the positive changes that have already taken place. They can identify exceptions to negative behaviours and convey a sense that change is inevitable and expected. "Miracle" questions create expectations for change and goal-setting. "Scaling" questions assist with understanding the youth's confidence level in making a change in an identified area, or in setting a reasonable goal. "Externalizing" questions assist with separating the problem behaviour from the person by first identifying the negative consequences of the behaviour and then establishing a sense of controllability and defiance toward the problem as something that can be challenged and overcome.

Solution-focussed approaches use our knowledge about how people change, including how they rise above adversity. Harnessing these natural coping abilities — sometimes called protective factors — is closely related to the notion of resilience. Resilience derives from the observation that some youth confronted with multiple-risk factors do not suffer the negative consequences observed in others who experience the same risk factors. Individual protective factors thought to be related to resilience include simple optimism, a sense of humour, self-efficacy, strong social skills, cognitive competence, an agreeable temperament, perseverance, involvement in creative activities, strong problem-solving skills, good emotional management, and a sense of self-awareness. Family protective factors include caring and supportive parents, strong parent-child relationships, low levels of family conflict, and optimistic explanatory styles. Extrafamilial factors include a nurturing support system (relative, friends, teachers, neighbours, and inspirational significant others), church or community involvement, and successful school experiences. A positive home environment and prosocial peer associations are examples of variables that have been identified as serving a protective function in the case of delinquency.[10]

Buying into the Program

Many offenders never complete the programming they are supposed to undertake, either in the community or in the correctional facility.[11] One line of research has begun to explore the factors related to treatment adherence, particularly among offenders who are at high risk to re-offend and require more intensive services.[12] For example, some findings suggest that the academic abilities required for a program are a significant factor, which lead to suggestions as to how the program could be more responsive for individuals with lower academic achievement.

Many youth are simply not motivated to work on the factors related to their offending. In the past, they would have been considered "treatment resistant," posing a real predicament for forensic mental health and youth court staff, raising questions about public safety and individual deterrence. Even when treatment was mandated, however, these youth proved resistant and difficult to work with, leading to further prognostications about their untreatability.

Currently, there is less focus on forcing youth to change (or else!) and labelling them resistant. Motivation for change is seen on a continuum, which provides a way to conceptualize the complex interaction between youth and those who want to help them. The model, based on research about adult addictions, is predicated on assumptions about how people naturally make changes.[13] The framework is relevant for many treatment situations. In work with young offenders, it provides a means of placing those who appear untreatable on a conceptual continuum along which change occurs. Rather than working at odds with the youth, this approach helps service providers understand their role, depending on where the youth falls on the continuum. Identifying where youth fall on this continuum provides clues to providing stage-matched interventions:

1. Precontemplation   Raise doubt; increase perceptions of risk and
                           problems with current behaviour.
                           Helper's Stance: nurturing care-giver

2. Contemplation   Tip balance: evoke reasons to change, risks of
                           not changing, strengthen the youth's
                           confidence in the ability to change
                           the current behaviour.
                           Helper's Stance: Socratic teacher

3. Preparation   Assist the youth to determine the best course
                           of action to take in seeking change.
                           Helper's Stance: experienced coach

4. Action/Maintenance   Assist the youth to take steps toward change.
                           Helper's Stance: facilitator

5. Relapse   Assist the youth to renew the processes above
                           without becoming stuck or demoralized
                           because of relapse.
                           Helper's Stance: consultant

6. Recyle through the stages.[14]

Youth are at different stages of change, depending on what behaviours are targeted: some may not want to stop smoking, but they may be questioning whether they should cut down on their drinking, given that their previous offences were incurred while they were under the influence of alcohol. Others may be ready to take a plan of action with respect to violence, and so a structured approach can be used to give them the skills they need. These same young people may be unwilling to take any steps toward reducing their use of marijuana, however, so it is pointless to devise an elaborate plan to reduce their marijuana use until they are ready to commit to it. The practitioner need not abandon the client on these issues, but can continue to raise doubt and ask them to evaluate the cost and problems associated with their current use.

The framework helps the practitioner maintain an organized focus, using strategies that are in keeping with the youth's stage of change, and countering discouragement by setting workable and achievable goals.[15] It also means that the court can set conditions of probation that support these goals, while ensuring the intervention is individualized.

One youth my colleagues worked with fit the description of "treatment resistant" because he did not appear to be responding to any of the interventions in the custody facility:

> A traditional interpretation of this situation would result in T. being viewed as treatment resistant and being denied services or being placed prematurely into an action-oriented treatment program. We believe the success of either approach would have been minimal. Instead, we conceptualized T. as a precontemplative youth, and developed a stage-matched intervention to (1) help T. develop awareness of the costs of his inappropriate sexual behaviours; (2) increase his desire to change in order to move him to the contemplation stage; (3) deliver services in a supportive style to avoid triggering his defensive responses about offending; and (4) co-ordinate services with facility — their role was to encourage T. to journal his thoughts and feelings about offending. This approach helped T. to view treatment as a positive experience; he has been more co-operative in therapy and less obstructive in the facility.[16]

Conclusions

One UK researcher suggests that we need to get over the novelty of therapeutic courts[17] and start thinking about how they might benefit clients. The judge should find the benchmark sentence for the offence and "then adjust the sentence for traditional and aggravating factors," followed by a second adjustment for "therapeutic factors (e.g., mental illness, drug addiction)."[18] For example, in cases where it is clear that the mental illness was related to the criminal act, a number of strategies might be applied to use the sentence as leverage to get the offender to participate in treatment:

> There are several ways the judge might do this. The judge might sentence the defendant to 30 days in jail (the non-therapeutically adjusted bench-mark sentence) but allow days of freedom to be earned back if the individual stays in treatment while incarcerated (the equivalent of good time credits in traditional sentencing). . . . Similar inducement could be crafted for de-fendants on probation or parole, in cases in which time under supervision is tied to the defendant's participation in treatment. . . . Compliance with or participation in treatment could be determined by standards worked out between the court and correctional agencies in close collaboration with mental health providers.[19]

One of the strengths of this approach is that it is derived from empirically based behavioural principles that draw "a clear connection between freedom and com-pliance, and between criminal behaviour and the loss of freedom," and may stop the "cost shifting and hiding game that has long characterized the criminal justice system and mental health system dynamic."[20] Continuity of services, especially to those who have mental disabilities, could be greatly enhanced using such an approach. Detractors may argue that it is tantamount to blackmailing offend-ers to comply with their treatment. Others might argue that forcing offenders to comply with treatment orders will fail on the grounds that the young offender is not "ready" for it. But bargaining with offenders about the choices they can make in regard to judicial as opposed to treatment measures does allow the offender a choice. This in itself can be therapeutic, in that it gives some power back to of-fender. In Canada this approach is heralded as a way to stop the revolving door of justice/mental health/addiction services for some offenders.[21] If they choose treat-ment in exchange for less probation or less custody time, it may tip the balance for offenders at a precontemplative stage of change. They will be more willing to consent to treatment because there is a clear link between their offence and a therapeutic objective, and between the therapeutic objective and the immediate payoff of a reduced sentence.

A therapeutic orientation places increased demands on the youth court sys-tem, which can be costly in a number of ways — by creating a more extended and expensive court process, for example. But there are also positive consequences, including more individualized decisions and outcomes, a non-adversarial climate, more hands-on judicial involvement and flexibility, a clearer delineation of treat-ment programs, and a team approach that brings together the judge, prosecutor, defence counsel, treatment providers, and correctional staff.

In one model of drug court, individuals attend treatment programs following their arrest, with prosecutions deferred, or after their conviction, with sentences deferred. The aspects of this model that reflect therapeutic jurisprudence include early identification, assessment, and community placement for offenders; continuous judicial supervision during the individual's participation in the program; clear communication of program requirements to the individual and confirmation of the individual's agreement to comply; the imposition of intermediate (and timely) sanctions when program requirements are violated; and an emphasis on overcoming denial and promoting personal responsibility as well as self-esteem. As one researcher noted, "The combination of a valid treatment approach within a supportive legal framework could have the capacity to produce a 'synergistic' effect in terms of potential outcomes."[22]

The New Era

Balance depends upon some insight into the variety of our contradictory impulses and feelings and the capacity to come to terms with these inner conflicts... The need for integration, moreover, derives from the unconscious knowledge that hate can only be mitigated by love... Integration also has the effect of tolerance towards one's own impulses and therefore also towards other people's defects.

> — Melanie Klein
> "On Mental Health"
> From *Envy and Gratitude* and *Other Works, 1946 – 1963*

Perceptions about the restrictiveness or intrusiveness of therapeutic interventions have changed throughout history. Interventions can be placed on a continuum from low- to high-risk, depending on how intrusive or restrictive they are considered to be. But our consideration may be a judgement based on a particular case. What may be restrictive or intrusive in one instance may not be in another. Risk analysis weighs the alternatives: the amputation of an infected limb would be extremely intrusive and result in highly restrictive consequences, but the risks appear less important when compared to the possible alternatives, one of which is death.

Lobotomies and other neurosurgeries were at one time considered effective treatments for mental disorders. Like a limb amputation, they were highly invasive, with irreversible consequences. They permanently altered the person's thinking, feeling, and behaviour. The neurological knowledge base was in its infancy, and many unintended side effects resulted.[1] Imagine the risk-benefit calculus that occurred when families had to make decisions about whether to consent to this operation.

Interventions can also be invasive when they involve many intrusions into a person's life, essentially robbing the person of privacy and self-determination. People confined in mental institutions had virtually no personal freedom, and few choices about their treatment. Many have been seriously harmed by the interventions used on them: medication, physical restraint, isolation, procedures not yet refined or validated. The decisions to have people committed to these institutions were motivated by concerns about the safety of the person and the community, and at the time there may have been few alternatives. But many such interventions were later seen as human rights infringements, and countless people who were once confined to institutions are now leading productive lives in the community.

The point is, it is extraordinarily easy to bias our risk-benefit calculus; so much depends on how we interpret the particular characteristics of the particular person we are dealing with. We are further biased by our knowledge base regarding the risks and benefits of an intervention, as well as the availability of alternatives when making a decision. The more alternatives that are available to us, the more likely we are to choose interventions that are relatively less intrusive and restrictive. Depending on our interpretation of the risk factors, we are more likely to tolerate higher-risk interventions — more intrusive, more restrictive — for people we perceive as having a higher risk of doing harm to themselves or others. The risk we perceive in the person mitigates our judgement about the risk of the intervention itself.

When interventions apparently do not deter a youth from re-offending, he or she will be seen as less amenable to interventions and at higher risk to re-offend. Resulting decisions about this young person may be based partially on the availability — or the non-availability — of resources. A young person's past history of poor follow-through will influence perceptions about risk and amenability. Obviously, young people who have little or no motivation to access services, especially when there are few available, are at higher risk, particularly if their risk assessments are framed in terms of access to timely and suitable interventions.

Risk factors are seen to multiply, with a concomitant shrinking of available resources, when a young person is diagnosed with a mental disability. The placement of these youth in restrictive environments is partly based on a perceived threat associated with mental disabilities, and partly on the time and resources it would take to manage them effectively. Young people with mental disabilities are at risk of extended placements in highly restrictive environments or subject to court orders and conditions as a result of the perceived link between their disorder and probable future violence.[2] Often, when they are perceived as being at risk for violence, they are barred from therapeutic settings, even those designed to provide high levels of supervision and intervention. When these options are denied them, they find themselves in unsuitable and often inadequately supervised situations, setting them up for further failure and extended or repeated periods in custody facilities. To many, it seems to be the only alternative. Indeed, to the young offender caught in a cycle that never seems to end, it appears to be the only option available.

The youth justice system has traditionally been relied on as a gateway to services for young people with high needs and those who need to be kept safe. The *Youth Criminal Justice Act* attempts to curtail this practice, partly because custody increased rather than decreased recidivism. But the belief that custody provides protection and rehabilitation has its roots in the welfare orientation of earlier legislation and youth justice strategies, and it dies hard. I can understand why. Many times I see troubled youth in extremely unsafe circumstances with little adult support. There does not appear to be any easy or accessible solution to the immediate situation. Would not a short period of custody — just a few days to buy us time to come up with a plan — be better than leaving the youth in such a high-risk environment? The YCJA rejects this type of thinking, and with good reason. It is simply inappropriate to place a young person in jail based on child welfare or mental health concerns. "Buying time" is a red herring; it always takes more than "a few days" to come up with a suitable treatment plan for these youth.

It is a sad statement about society if young people with mental disabilities can have their needs met only in custody. It might be less sad if it were true, but it is simply not the case. It is true that some youth — the more astute ones — become more motivated in jail, as they realize that they need to make a good impression on the judge or youth worker in order to get back into the community. In some cases, too, a young person may feel a deep sense of shame about the offence, and this can translate into a desire to save face and accept some services as a way to show that he or she is genuinely remorseful. But it rarely lasts.

Of course, we all need a wake-up call from time to time to alert us to the fact that we need to make changes in our lives. There is clearly a role for mental health services to help young people through this difficult time in their lives. But is custody the best place for it to happen? Many custody facilities across Canada provide quality programs, with well-trained and well-intentioned staff, but they cannot possibly provide the treatment or support that many professionals and parents imagine. Few judges and lawyers, let alone parents, have first-hand experience of what custody facilities can offer to young people.

It is true that some youth may be willing to access mental health services while in custody, but most will not. Why would they trust anyone in a system that has effectively taken them hostage? People working in these environments are not doing a bad job; they are simply working in an impossible dynamic: adolescents will have great difficulty reconciling extreme forms of social control with personal growth and change. Beyond these issues, the fact remains that many youth will not make a connection between their criminal offence and their need for treatment. They have limited ability to plan for the future, and they cannot imagine how the treatment is going to help them in the world they must face once they get out, or how it will help them get along better with peers and staff they may never see again.

Research into the experiences of youth and families in Canada does not inspire confidence in the custody-as-therapy philosophy.[3] Adults who were interviewed about their memories of lifetime stresses reported that being incarcerated as a youth was one of the most traumatic experiences they had ever had, ranking at the same level as the death or divorce of parents.[4]

The institutions themselves and the people running them, their methods and curricula, are not to blame. Custody is never a pure intervention. There are many confounding variables, many unexpected and uncontrollable factors.[4] Judges who commit youth to custodial dispositions cannot possibly control the environment of custody. Neither can the lawyers, youth workers, and parents who may have convinced the judge that custody was warranted. Custody provides the youth with structure, supervision, shelter, and food — but rehabilitation? The claim is highly suspect. They will, almost by default, mature somewhat during their stay, and this will help them when they get out. But no treatment in custody is likely to have a lasting effect. Mental health workers can be called in to help them navigate the system, but the best the custody facility can do is help them cope with their current circumstances.

Some people take the view that custody might help young people by keeping them away from negative peers and not allowing them to smoke or use drugs. But as I have learned from the many youth who come into my office, those in custody are rarely engaged in any kind of activity I would judge to be rehabilitative. On the contrary, they make friends with other antisocial youth, and they form alliances and plans that continue when they return to the community.

One young man I saw over a year had had minimal experience with custody at the beginning, but through repeatedly breaching his curfew and abusing alcohol he got more and more experience with it over the course of the year. He later received a sentence for minor theft which led to more custody time, this time in open custody. His frequent breaches and remands in custody for breaches meant that he missed more and more school. He explained to me that the experience of custody had undermined his confidence in his ability to cope in the real world. He told me that some of his peers felt they could no longer cope "on the outside," and tried to get re-arrested so they could come back to custody. Within two weeks of being in open custody, this young man told me he wasn't sure he wanted to come out. "It feels like home to me," he said. He was tired of the revolving door and felt maybe he should just stay inside. This young man came from a caring and functional home, but now he tells me, "I don't feel like I fit in any more. I'm the criminal of the family."

I have heard many versions of this story. They are compelling as anecdotes, but they are also supported by empirical data. Placing young people in custody may provide some respite to parents, but family relationships suffer as a result, and parents are often derailed in their parenting when the justice system takes over.

It is clearer to me how rehabilitation could occur after custody. According to the dictionary definition, rehabilitation means to "restore to effectiveness or normal life by training, etc., especially after imprisonment or illness." Given that many young people's experiences in custody are deleterious, counterproductive, and demoralizing, they will more than likely require rehabilitation when they get out. Most youth go into custody in poor shape and come out angry, hostile, and hurt.

Youth who have been in custody are much more likely to re-offend than those who have not. There are a number of reasons for this. Aside from the damaging effects of custody itself, placing young people in custody does not address the underlying reasons for their offending in the first place. Community, family, and individual factors are what put youth at risk for offending, and none of these can be properly addressed in custody. In fact, encounters with the system may increase the likelihood of inadequate parenting and increased disconnection from community supports. The youth fall further behind in school, and they miss important transitional events. Further, we cannot guarantee that their rights are being protected or that procedures in custody are implemented in a fair and unharmful manner. Young people may be victimized or mistreated in custody. Those with pre-existing difficulties, such as a mental disability, are at much higher risk of negative consequences from custody and other justice sanctions.

The questions we ask about youth crime are critically important in determining the direction we take in dealing with young offenders. If we ask questions that are concerned about how to manage groups of young people in custody and provide efficient services to them, we may frame our inquiries in terms of how best to classify them and help the system process them more efficiently. The emphasis is on efficient classification and prediction.

Youth who are at moderate to high risk to re-offend, who have serious or persistent patterns of offending, who have previous dispositions, or are currently in custody are candidates for individual and group forensic mental health interventions. Those who are deemed to have committed minor offences and are at low risk to re-offend are left alone. Developmental and educational research shows, however, that intervening early can prevent delinquency or escalations in delinquency. Many apparently low-risk offenders have high needs in areas that place them at risk for ongoing adjustment problems.

In my experience, when the probation system abdicates from these cases with no relevant supports or services, these youth sometimes get worse and end up re-offending — which is the opposite of what the risk-need paradigm predicts. When these youth re-offend, they usually get another risk assessment and receive a medium-risk rating. Now their probation officer has the official go-ahead to do something. This makes sense from the perspective of management and economics — with limited resources, we need to be clear about where we focus our efforts — but the ethics of the situation are questionable. Professionals should be encouraged to use their judgement and training to make a case for providing services to youth on the basis of their needs, not just their risk to re-offend.

The youth justice system in Canada has undergone tremendous evolution over the past 100 years. Under current legislation, the use of the justice system for child welfare or mental health agendas is fundamentally disconnected from the principles of proportional sentencing and other principles of youth justice. Addressing the underlying issues of a youth's offending remains as important as it was under previous legislation, but statutes clearly state that these objectives must still be subservient to the higher principle of proportionality.

In this new era of youth justice, the use of the justice system for minor cases and the over-reliance on custody and other criminal sanctions for social and emotional problems is simply wrong. The justice system must pull back. Other systems must step in and begin to share the responsibility for dealing with the social and emotional causes and consequences of youth crime.

NOTES

Introduction — pp. 9-14

1 Callahan, 2004; Cocozza and Skowyra, 2000; Conry and Fast, 2000; Hagell, 2002; Mears and Aron, 2003; Osher *et al.*, 2002; Otto *et al.*, 1992.

2 Grisso and Underwood, 2004, p. 1.

3 Bill C-68, the first version of the *Youth Criminal Justice Act* (YCJA), was introduced in the House of Commons in March 1999. After several delays it was re-introduced as Bill C-7 in Feb. 2001. It received royal assent Feb. 19, 2002, and the statutes came into force April 1, 2003. The complete text of the YCJA can be found at http://laws.justice.gc.ca/en/Y-1.5/216604.html#rid-216633.

4 Billinghurst and Hackler, 1982; Endicott, 1991.

5 Wolff, 2002.

6 Callahan, 2004; Grisso, 1998a, 2003; Hayes, 2000; Repucci *et al.*, 2002; Rich, 2003.

7 *Supra*, note 1.

8 Mears and Aron, 2003.

Chapter 1 — pp. 15-31

1 *Criminal Code of Canada* (R.S., 1985, c. C-46).

2 *Youth Criminal Justice Act* (2002, c.1).

3 *R. v. R. C.* [2005] 3 S.C.R. 99; 2005 SCC 61.

4 Section 487.04 of the *Criminal Code of Canada* lists some 26 separate offences which can be defined as a "primary designated offence," ranging from acts of piracy and hijacking to murder, aggravated assault and kidnapping.

5 *Supra* note 3. The facts are summarized from the headnote.

6 *Ibid.* at para. 39.

7 *Ibid.* at para. 36 and 37.

8 2005 SCC 78

9 *Supra* note 8 at para. 21

10 The *Young Offenders Act* was repealed upon the enactment of the YJCA.

11 *R. v. Demers*, [2004] 2 S.C.R. 489, 2004 SCC 46.

12 A review board is an administrative body established by the *Criminal Code* to make decisions concerning people the courts have found not criminally responsible or unfit to stand trial. Federal and provincial legislatures create review boards when there is a need for an adjudicative body to make independent decisions in areas requiring special expertise. The *Criminal Code* requires review boards to be appointed in every province and territory of Canada. Each board must have at least five members and be chaired either by a judge or by someone qualified to be a judge. At least one member of the board must be qualified to practice psychiatry. The board customarily includes members whose qualifications are unspecified, typically professionals with experience in mental health, medicine, psychology, social work, or criminology.

13 *Supra* note 11 at para. 55 of 2004 SCC 46.

14 R. v. W. A. L (1), (2004), 245 Sask. R. 98, 2004 SKPC 40.

15 *Ibid.* at para. 3 of 2004 SKPC 40.

16 *Ibid.* at para. 86 of 2004 SKPC 40.

17 R. v. B (D.) (2004), 118 C.R.R. (2d) 141, 2004 SKPC 43.

18 *Ibid.* at para. 77 of 2004 SKPC 43.

19 *Ibid.* at para. 44 of 2004 SKPC 43.

20 *Ibid.* at para. 47 of 2004 SKPC 43.

21 *Supra* note 11 at para. 89 and 90 of 2004 SCC 46.

22 *Supra* note 11 at para. 64 of 2004 SCC 46.

23 Barnhorst, 2004, p. 233.

24 Doob, 2001, p. 9.

25 Barnhorst, 2004, p. 236.

26 The 1999 Supreme Court decision in *R. v. Gladue* [1999] 1 S.C.R. 688, CanLII 1999 SCC 679 is pivotal in raising awareness about Aboriginal peoples and the criminal justice system: "[Y]ears of dislocation and economic development have translated for many aboriginal peoples, into low incomes, high unemployment, lack of opportunities and options, lack or irrelevance of education, substance abuse, loneliness and community fragmentation. These and other factors contribute to a higher incidence of crime and incarceration" (cited in Green and Healy, 2003, pp. 90-91).

27 Under s. 2 of the *Youth Criminal Justice Act*, a presumptive offence is defined as first or second-degree murder, manslaughter, attempted murder, aggravated sexual assault, or when a person has committed two previous serious violent offences in addition to the one currently under proceedings. A serious violent offence is defined as an offence for which an adult is liable for imprisonment for a term of more than two years and means "an offence in the commission of which a young person causes or attempts to cause serious bodily harm."

28 Most provinces have not put this provision into force.

29 Under the YCJA, a provincial director is defined as "a person, a group or class of persons or a body appointed or designated by or under an Act of the legislature of a province or by the lieutenant governor in council of a province or his or her delegate to perform in that province, either generally or in a specific case, any of the duties or functions of a provincial director under this Act." In other words, the provincial director is a person who has been granted authority, under a provincial legislature, to render legal judgements and opinions relative to the *Youth Criminal Justice Act*.

30 Roberts, 2004.

31 Quebec (Minister of Justice) v. Canada (Minister of Justice), 2003 CanLII 52182 (QC C.A.)

32 *Ibid.* at paras. 139, 145-47.

33 *Ibid.*, para. 246.

34 *Ibid.*, para. 249.

35 *Ibid.*, para. 256.

36 *Ibid.*, para. 253.

37 *Ibid.*, para. 6.

Chapter 2 — pp. 32-40

1   "The quintessential characteristic of adolescence is change." Moretti and Peled, 2004, p. 551.

2   Spear, 2000; Weisz and Hawley, 2002.

3   Petersen *et al.*, 1996.

4   Vasta *et al.*, 1995, p. 199; see also Tanner, 1990.

5   Moretti and Peled, 2004.

6   Spear, 2000; Tamm *et al.*, 2002; Case, 1985; Selman, 1980; Harter, 1990; Marsh, 1989.

7   Chak, 2001.

8   Baldry and Winkel, 2004; Chrouses and Gold, 1992; Cohen and Herbert, 1996; Glantz and Leshner, 2000; Graber and Peterson, 1991; McNeill, 1991.

9   Moffitt, 1994; Reijone *et al.*, 2003; Romerl and Stanton, 2003.

10 Beyth-Marom and Fischhoff, 1997; Chrousos, 1998; Chrousos and Gold, 1992.

11 Von Hirsch, 2000, cited in Roberts, 2004, p. 304.

12 Agnew, 2001; Brier, 1989; Cauffman and Steinberg, 2000; Dishion *et al.*, 1995; Dishion *et al.*, 1996; Hartup, 1996.

13 Stephens *et al.*, 1999.

14 Mann *et al.*, 1989; Steinberg, 2001; Steinberg and Scott, 2003.

15 Kazdin, 2000; Keating, 1990.

16 Ge *et al.*, 1996.

17 Agnew *et al.*, 2000; Haggerty *et al.*, 1994.

18 Simmons *et al.*, 1988; Marsh 1989.

19 *Ibid.*, 1988.

20 Steinberg and Belsky, 1996.

21 Rutter *et al.*, 1976.

22 Haggerty *et al.*, 1994; Melberg Schwier and Hingsberger, 2000.

23 Reijone *et al.*, 2003.

24 Larson and Richards, 1994.

25 Spear, 2000.

26 Watson and Clark, 1984.

27 Larson and Richards, 1994.

28 Millstein, 1993.

29 Steinberg and Belsky, 1996; this reward deficiency in adolescence may also be linked to changes in the limbic system around puberty.

30 *Ibid.*, 1996.

31 Graber and Petersen, 1991.

32 These differences are associated with prefrontal cortex development.

33 Cauffman and Steinberg, 2000; Chesney-Lind and Shelden, 2004.

34 Agnew, 2001; Dishion *et al.*, 1995; Kaplan *et al.*, 1987.

35 Irwin and Millstein, 1992; McCord, 1990; Glantz and Leshner, 2000.

36 Beyth-Maron and Fischoff, 1997; Evans *et al.*, 2001; Haggerty *et al.*, 1994; Hayes, 2000; Irwin, 1989.

37 Spear, 2000, p. 446.

38 McNeill, 1991.

39 Estroff *et al.*, 1989.

40 Clark *et al.*, 1998.

41 Hein, 1987.

42 Moffit, 2003, uses this term in her work in developmental criminology; see also Johnson *et al.*, 2004.

43 Bonnie and Grisso, 2000; Grisso and Underwood, 2004; Woolard *et al.*, 2001.

44 Adams *et al.*, 2003; af Klinteberg *et al.*, 1992; Davis *et al.*, 2004; Dembo *et al.*, 1987; Doob and Cesaroni, 2004; Green and Healy, 2003; Hagell, 2002; Pasternoster and Iovanni, 1989.

45 Barber and Doob, 2004; Doob, 2001; Doob *et al.*, 1995; Havemann, 2000; von Hirsch, 2000.

Chapter 3 — pp. 41-55

1 Allerton *et al.*, 2003; Bailey, 2003; Burrell and Warboys, 2000; Cocozza and Skowyra, 2000; Correctional Service of Canada, 1991; Department of Justice Canada, 1998; Lader *et al.*, 2000; Lyons *et al.*, 2001; Mears and Aron, 2003; Mulford *et al.*, 2004; Smith *et al.*, 2002; Thompson *et al.*, 2003; UNICEF *Innocenti Digest*, 2001; U.S. Department of Justice, 2000; World Health Organization, 2001.

2 Conway, 2003.

3 Mears and Aron, 2003, p. 23.

4 Cohen and Herbert, 1996.

5 Lasser *et al.*, 2000.

6 Goodman and Capitman, 2000.

7 Castellanos *et al.*, 1994.

8 Boney-McCoy and Finkelhour, 1995, 1996; Chaimowitz, 2000; Cohen *et al.*, 2000; Cole *et al.*, 1994; Downs, 1993; Odgers and Moretti, 2002; Zingraff *et al.*, 1993.

9 Health Canada, 2002, p. 20.

10 Chudley *et al.*, 2005, p. 51.

11 Graham-Bermann and Edleson, 2001; Hamilton *et al.*, 2002; Hiday *et al.*, 2001; Shaffer and Ruback, 2002; Spohn, 2000; Stirpe and Stermae, 2003.

12 Scott, 1992, suggested the following estimates: 3.8 for any affective disorder, 5.2 for drug abuse or dependence, 2.1 for alcohol abuse or dependence, 3.4 for phobia, and 3.4 for depression. See also Boney-McCoy and Finkelhor, 1995, 1996.

13 DuRant *et al.*, 1995; Singer, *et al.*, 1995.

14 Finkelhor, 1984, 1994.

15 Chapell, 2003.

16 Mulford *et al.*, 2004.

17 Cicchetti *et al*, 1995.

18 Shipman *et al.*, 2000, p. 57.

19 Baldry, 2003; Rigby, 2000.

20 Cole and Putman, 1992; Spohn, 2000.

21 Evans *et al.*, 2001.

22 Finkelhor and Hashima, 2001.

23 Chapell, 2003.

24 Finkelhor and Hashima, 2001.

25 Graham-Bermann and Edleson, 2001; Hamilton *et al.*, 2002.

26 See Rossman, 2001, p. 39, citing the ideas put forward by Perry, 1994, 1997.

27 *Ibid.*, 2001.

28 Lader *et al.*, 2000.

29 Bardone *et al.*, 1996.

30 Allerton *et al.*, 2003, note that 20 per cent of males and females reported a history of physical abuse; 20 per cent of the males and 45 per cent of the females reported that they had been emotionally abused; and four per cent of the males and 22 per cent of the females reported they had been sexually abused.

31 McManus *et al.*, 1984.

32 Chesney-Lind and Shelden, 2004; Dishion *et al.*, 1995; Hamilton *et al.*, 2002; Leschied *et al.*, 2001; White, 2001; Williams and Hollis, 1999; Wolfe *et al.*, 2003.

33 Fagan *et al.*, 1987.

34 Correctional Service Canada, 1995a.

35 Loeber and Farrington, 2000.

36 Shaffer and Ruback, 2002.

37 Falshaw *et al.*, 1996; Hamilton *et al.*, 2002.

38 Skuse *et al.*, 1998; Widom, 1989; Watkins and Bentovim, 1992; Skuse estimated that between one in six physically abused youth go on to commit a violent offence. Widom, 1989, and Watkins and Bentovim, 1992, draw attention to the finding that one in five sexually abused males later commits sex offences. They also suggest a cumulative effect of sexual victimization in boys, and that family violence may be related to future sexual offending. However, we await empirical validation for this hypothesis.

39 Abel *et al.*, 1995.

40 Correctional Service Canada, 1995a, 1995b; Broidy *et al.*, 2003; Davis *et al.*, 2004; Doob and Cesaroni, 2004; Farrington, 1995; Irwin and Millstein, 1992; Nieland *et al.*, 2001.

41 Stirpe and Stermac, 2003.

42 Zingraff *et al.*, 1993, 1994. Victims of neglect are at the greatest risk of delinquency (1 in 10), whereas victims of physical abuse had a 1 in 11 probability, but they found no difference in probability between victims of sexual abuse and those who had not experienced it.

43 Ney *et al.*, 1994.

44 Hawkins *et al.*, 2000; Lauritsen *et al.*, 1991; Fagan *et al.*, 1987.

45 Baldry and Farrington, 2000; Cosden *et al.*, 2005; Henggeler *et al.*, 1998; Ovaert *et al.*, 2003; Perkins-Dock, 2001; Rigby, 2000; Stirpe and Stermae, 2003.

46 Burgess *et al.*, 1988; Cohen *et al.*, 2000; Boney-McCoy and Finkelhor, 1996.

47 Endicott, 1991; See also Barron *et al.*, 2002; Cullen *et al.*, 1997; French, 1993; Garcia and Steele, 1988; Reed, 1989; Santamour and West, 2000.

48 American Psychiatric Association, 2000, p. xxii.

49 Hiday, 1995, 1997; Link *et al.*, 1992; Link and Stueve, 1994; Silver *et al.*, 1999; Steadman *et al.*, 1998.

50 Ewing, 1990; Hiday *et al.*, 2001; Litwack, 2002.

51 Borum, 2000; Catchpole and Gretton, 2003; Conway and McCord, 2002; Corrado *et al.*, 2003; Jung and Rawana, 1999.

52 Monahan, 1992, 1996; Mulvey, 1994; See Borum *et al.*, 2002; their *Structured Assessment of Violence Risk in Youth* (SAVRY) includes dynamic risk and protective factors in the prediction of violence.

53 Mears and Feld, 2000; Sprott, 2004; Zingraff *et al.*, 1994.

54 LaPrairie, 1992, 2002.

55 Watkinson, 1999, p. 110; see also Peters, 2004.

56 UNICEF, *Innocenti Digest*, 2001; cited in *Saskatchewan Children's Advocate*, 2003, p. 7.

Chapter 4 — pp. 56-63

1 Brier, 1989; Eggleston, 1996; Mears and Aron, 2003.

2 *Ibid.*

3 Endicott, 1991; McAfee and Gural, 1988.

4 Pope and Feyerherm, 1995; Sampson and Lauritsen, 1997.

5 Burrell and Warboys, 2000.

6 Conry and Fast, 2000; Farrington, 1995; Government of Canada, 1992; Roberts and Nanson, 2000; Streissguth, 1997; Streissguth and Randels, 1988; Kazdin, 2000.

7 French, 1983, p. 60.

8 Billinghurst and Hackler, 1982.

9 Reed, 1989.

10 Garcia and Steele, 1988; Shields and Simourd, 1991.

11 Santamour and West, 1982, p. 30.

12 French, 1983, p. 59.

Chapter 5 — pp. 64-79

1 Prenatal factors may include genetic disorders, teratogens, infections, nutritional and metabolic disorders, accident, or injury. Perinatal factors may include premature or prolonged labour and delivery, placenta previa, and multiple or high-risk pregnancies. Postnatal factors include infections, toxins, accident/injury, malnutrition, and social/emotional factors such as deprivation and neglect.

2 Gresham and MacMillan, 1997.

3 American Psychiatric Association, 2000.

4 Osher *et al.*, 2002.

5   Barron *et al.*, 2002; Cockram, 2005; McGloin and Pratt, 2003; Mulford *et al.*, 2004.

6   Chudley *et al.*, 2005, p. 51.

7   Gideon Koren, director of the Motherrisk program at Toronto's Hospital for Sick Children, quoted in *MacLean's Magazine*, Sept. 6, 2004, p. 80.

8   Blakley, 2003; Roberts and Nanson, 2000; Streissguth, 1988, 1997.

9   Fast *et al.*, 1999.

10 Federal-Provincial-Territorial Task Force on Youth Justice: A Review of the *Young Offenders Act* and the Youth Justice System in Canada, Aug. 1996. See also Government of Canada, 1992.

11 Conry and Fast, 2000, p. 2.

12 Chudley *et al.*, 2005.

13 *Ibid.*

14 FAS can be diagnosed in the absence of confirmed maternal drinking during pregnancy if all the other causes of the child's impairment have been ruled out and the child meets the other three criteria required.

15 Chudley *et al., 2005.*

16 Blakley, 2003; Streissguth, 1988, 1997

17 Streissguth *et al.*, 1997; Streissguth and Randels, 1988.

18 Turgay, 2005.

19 Barkely, 1997.

20 *Ibid.*

21 *Ibid.*

22 *Ibid.*, p. 335.

23 Levine, 1994, is an excellent resource for developing strategies for youth with these difficulties.

24 Moeller *et al.*, 2001, p. 1784.

25 Yapko, 1997, p. 59.

Chapter 6 — pp. 80-84

1   Grisso, 2003.

2   Anand and Robb, 2002.

3   Jaffe *et al.*, 1987.

4   Lawrence, 1983.

5   Peterson, 1988; Peterson-Bedali and Abramovitch, 1992; Ribordy, 1986.

6   Peterson-Bedali and Koegl, 1998.

7   Grisso, 2003.

8   Grisso and Pomicter, 1977; Grisso, 1981; Grisso and Ring, 1979.

9   Grisso, 1998a, 1998b.

10 Conry and Fast, 2000; Gudjonsson, 1992; Gudjonnson *et al.*, 1995; Gudjonsson and Sigurdsson, 1995, 1996.

11 Grisso, 2003.

12 Fulero and Everington, 1995; Grisso, 1998b; Viljoen and Roesch, 2005; Viljoen et al., 2005.

13 Grisso, 1981; Peterson-Badali and Broeking, 2004; Viljoen et al., 2002.

14 Cited in Conry and Fast, 2000, p. 42.

15 S. 146(4) YCJA.

16 S. 146(5) YCJA.

17 S. 146(7) YCJA.

Chapter 7 — pp. 85-111

1   Cited in Viljoen et al., 2003, p. 371-372.

2   Viljoen et al., 2003, p. 376.

3   Grisso, 2003, p. 20.

4   Ibid.

5   Borum and Grisso, 1996; Grisso et al., 2003.

6   Fulero and Finkel, 1991; Rogers, et al., 1990; Rogers and Shuman, 2000.

7   Borum, 2003, p. 209.

8   Saunders, 2001.

9   Truscott and Crook, 2004.

10 Ibid., p. 30.

11 Roesch et al., 2004; See also Cowden and McKee, 1995.

12 See Ibid., 2004, regarding research using the FIT as well as the earlier edition of the FIT by Roesch et al., 1984.

13 Ibid., 2004.

14 Ibid., p. 16.

15 R. v. Taylor (1992) 59 O.A.C. 43 (ON. C. A.).

16 Roesch et al., 2004, p. 5.

17 R. v. S. L. (2004), 181 Man R. (2nd) 251 (MB P.C.).

18 Ibid. at para. 32.

19 Ibid. at para 36.

20 Supra note 15 at para. 50.

21 McGaha et al., 2001.

22 R. v. Cooper (1979) 31 N.R. 234 at para. 7.

23 R. v. R. F. (2002). S. J. No. 742, cited in the Power Point presentation, "FASD and Criminal Justice," by Judge Sheila Whelan, presented Sept. 9, 2005, La Ronge, SK.

24 Borum, 2003, p. 203.

25 Ibid., p. 206.

26 Ibid., p. 206.

27 Borum, 2003, notes that the R-CRAS (Rogers, 1984) was designed to provide insanity assessment using the American Law Institute standards, but has also been used for the McNaughton standard and for the Guilty But Mentally Ill (GBMI) standard in the U.S.

28 Borum, 2003, p. 218.

Chapter 8 — pp. 112-124

1 Hoge, 2001.

2 Borum, 2003.

3 Fried and Repucci, 2001; Cauffman and Steinberg, 2000; Scott, 2000; Gudjonsson *et al.*, 1996.

4 Moffit, 2003.

5 Statistics Canada, 1994, 2000a, 2000b.

6 System-generated charges are those charges that are related to the youth's compliance with his or her conditions of probation or undertaking and usually include such things as breaches of curfew, school attendance, and non-contact clauses.

7 Kempf-Leonard and Peterson, 2000; Scraton and Haydon, 2003.

8 Roberts, 2004, footnote 12, p. 319.

9 Roberts, 2004.

10 National Task Force on Juvenile Sexual Offending, 1993, p. 20; See also Worling and Curwen, 2000.

11 *Ibid.*, p. 19.

12 Baumbach, 2002; Gudjonsson and Sigurdsson, 1996.

Chapter 9 — pp. 125-147

1 Andrews and Bonta, 2003, p. 27.

2 *Ibid.*, 2003; Andrews *et al.*, 1990a; 1990b; Andrews and Dowden, 1999; Hoge and Andrews, 1996.

3 Martinson, 1974.

4 Gendreau, 1996; Gendreau *et al.*, 2001, 2004; Gendreau and Ross, 1987; Hoge and Andrews, 1996.

5 Bonta, 2002; Dowden and Andrews, 1999; Hoge, 2002; Kempf-Leonard and Peterson, 2000; Zinger, 2004.

6 The revised version is available as *Level of Service Inventory — Revised* (LSI-R) by Andrews and Bonta, 1995.

7 See Hannah-Moffat and Maurutto, 2003.

8 Hoge and Andrews, 1996, p. 23.

9 Andrews and Bonta, 2003; Andrews and Kiesling, 1980; Andrews *et al.*, 1990a.

10 Bonta, 2002.

11 "Needs" in the risk-needs paradigm are referred to as forensic needs or criminogenic needs.

12 Andrews and Bonta, 2003, p. 262.

13 Adapted from Hoge and Andrews, 1996, p. 10.

14 Andrews and Bonta, 2003.

15 Hoge and Andrews, 1996.

16 Andrews and Bonta, 2003, p. 261.

17 Adapted from Andrews and Bonta, 2003; Gendreau and Andrews, 2001; Gendreau *et al.*, 2004; Hoge, 2001.

18 Hoge, 2001; Latessa *et al.*, 2002.

19 Meta-analysis is "a way of statistically combining the results of a set of research studies on the same general topic to get an overall 'bottom line' conclusion as to what the literature shows." www.hs.ttu.edu/Hdfs3390/meta.htm

20 Andrews and Bonta, 2003; Andrews and Dowden, 1999; Andrews *et al.*, 1990b; Lipsey, 1992.

21 Face validity means that a construct or idea is considered by consensus to ring true to the experience of practitioners or the public; that is, the construct seems relevant despite the fact that it does not have empirical validity.

22 "Prosocial behaviour occurs when someone acts to help another person, particularly when they have no goal other than to help a fellow human." www.changingminds.org/explanations/theories/prosocial_behavior.htm

23 Hoge and Andrews, 1996; Hoge, 2001.

24 Bonta, 1995; Latessa *et al.*, 2002.

25 Andrews and Kiesling, 1980; Gendreau and Andrews, 2001; Gendreau *et al.*, 2004; Mulvey, 1984.

26 Gendreau *et al.*, 2001.

27 Abel *et al.*, 1995; Altschuler, 1998; Johnson *et al.*, 2004; Kurtz, 2002; Leschied *et al.*, 2001.

28 Hoge and Andrews, 2002.

29 Hoge and Andrews, 2002. The YLS/CMI is often used in designing an individual forensic mental health treatment plan. It was developed on the basis of the *Level of Supervision Inventory* (Andrews, 1982), an instrument used to assist in decisions about parole release and parole supervision for adult offenders by assessing the level risk for re-offending. There is a revised version of the LSI-R for adults and a youth version. The YLS/CMI uses an earlier version of the LSI adapted for use with children and adolescents.

30 Terminology and tables from the YLS/CMI are reproduced and adapted with permission from Dr. Robert Hoge, Carleton University, Feb. 2005.

31 Procriminal/antisocial attitudes are characterized by not seeking (or actively rejecting) help, defiance of authority and showing little concern for others.

32 Preamble, YCJA.

33 *R. v. S. M. R.*, 2004; SKPC 131 (CanLII), printed 2005-9-3, p. 17.

34 Cole and Angus, 2003; Doob, 2001.

35 Doob, 2001.

36 Gendreau, 2002.

37 Hannah-Moffat and Maurutto, 2003.

38 *Ibid.*, p. 17; see also Scraton and Haydon, 2003, who discuss the slippage between adult terminology to the youth criminal justice system.

39 Scraton and Haydon also comment on the risk of criminalizing youth by actuarial assessments designed for adults.

40 See the American Psychological Association, *Standards for educational and psychological testing*, 1985; Meehl, 1954; Messick, 1989.

41 Hoge *et al.*, 1996.

42 *Ibid.*, p. 28.

43 Hannah-Moffat and Maurutto, 2003.

44 Jung and Rawana, 1999.

45 Hannah-Moffat and Shaw, 2001.

46 Hoge, 2001; Gendreau *et al.*, 2001.

47 See the special issue of *Criminal Justice and Behaviour*, Vol. 29, No. 4, Aug. 2002, on contemporary risk assessment. See also the Special Report submitted to Parliament, "Protecting their Rights: A Systemic Review of Human Rights in Correctional Services for Federally Sentenced Women," in the Legislation and Policies section of the Canadian Human Rights Commission website (Aug. 23, 2005).

Chapter 10 — pp. 148-161

1 Perkins-Dock, 2001; Peterson-Bedali and Broeking, 2004.

2 Stewart *et al.*, 2000.

3 Larson and Richards, 1994; Farrington, 1995; Smith and Stern, 1997.

4 Moretti and Peled, 2004.

5 Rothery and Enns, 2001.

6 *Ibid.*, 2001.

7 McAdams, 1993.

8 Harris, 1995.

9 Chesney-Lind and Shelden, 2004; Cicchetti *et al.*, 1995; Litten Fox and Benson, 2000.

10 Rothery and Enns, 2001; McCord, 2001.

11 Agnew *et al.*, 2000.

12 Agnew, 2003.

13 U.S. Department of Justice, 2000.

14 Agnew, 2001; Elliott *et al.*, 1985.

15 Agnew, 1997; Osgood *et al.*, 1996.

16 Berkowitz, 1993; Loeber and Farrington, 2000; Patterson *et al.*, 1992.

17 Rankin and Kern, 1994.

18 Wright *et al.*, 2000.

19 *Ibid.*, p. 142.

20 Maccoby, 1980, p. 40.

21 Lahey *et al.*, 2003; Lahey and Waldman, 2003; Rutter, 2003.

22 Snyder *et al.*, 2003.

23 Ambert, 1992.

24 Thornberry *et al.*, 1991.

25 Agnew *et al.*, 2000.

26 Stewart *et al.*, 2000.

27 Hillian and Reitsma-Street, 2003.

28 *Ibid.*, p. 26.

29 *Ibid.*, p. 27.

30 *Ibid.*

31 *Ibid.*, p. 29.

32 *Ibid.*, p. 30.

33 Peterson-Bedali and Broeking, 2004.

34 *Ibid.*, p. 7.

35 Hillian and Reitsma-Street, 2003, p. 33.

36 *Ibid.*

37 Seligman and Benjamin Darling, 1997, p. 174.

38 Wolin and Wolin, 1993.

39 Figley and McCubbin, 1983.

40 Pederson-Bedali and Broeking, 2004.

41 Gavazzi *et al.*, 2000, 2003.

Chapter 11 — pp. 162-172

1   McGuire, 2000.

2   McGuire, 2003.

3   Wexler, 1994, pp. 279-280.

4   Rottman and Casey, 1999; Casey and Rottman, 2000.

5   *Ibid.*, 1999.

6   Wolff, 2002, p. 431.

7   Adapted from Warren, cited in Rottman and Casey, 1999, p. 14; See also Casey and Rottman, 2000.

8   Selekman, 1997.

9   Rothery and Enns, 2001.

10 Hoge, 2002, p. 386.

11 Andrews and Kiesling, 1980; O'Donnell, 1992; Ogloff *et al.*, 1990.

12 Wormith and Olver, 2002.

13 Prochaska and DiClemente, 1984.

14 Adapted from Prochaska and Norcross, 1994, Miller and Rollnick, 1991.

15 Cohen and Hebert, 1996

16 Willoughby *et al.*, 2003.

17 Wolff, 2002.

18 *Ibid.*, p. 435.

19 *Ibid.*, p. 435.

20 *Ibid.*, p. 435.

21 See The Urban Institute, 2005.

22 McGuire, 2000, p. 423.

Conclusion — pp. 173-178

1   See Morley, 2004.

2   Mulford *et al.*, 2004.

3   See Doob and Cesaroni, 2004, p. 233; Hoge, 2001.

4   Frydenberg, 1997; cited in Doob and Cesaroni, 2004, p. 233

5   Petrosino *et al.*, 2000.

REFERENCES

Abel, G. G., Mittelman, M. S. and Becker, J. V. (1995). Sexual offenders: results of assessment and recommendations for treatment. In M. H. Ben-Aron, S. J. Hucker and C. D. Webster (eds.), *Clinical Criminology* (pp. 191-205). Toronto: M and M Graphics.

Adams, M. S., Robertson, C. T., Gray-Ray, P. and Ray, M. C. (2003). Labeling and delinquency. *Adolescence*, 38(149), 171- 186.

af Klinteberg, B., Humble, K., Schalling, D. (1992). Personality and psychopathy of males with a history of early criminal behaviour. *European Journal of Personality*, 6, 245-266.

Agnew, R. (1997). Stability and change in crime over the life course: A strain theory explanation. In T. P. Thronberry (ed.), *Developmental theories of crime and delinquency* (pp. 101-132).

_____. (2001). Building on the foundation of general strain theory: specifying the types of strain most likely to lead to crime and delinquency. *Journal of Research in Crime and Delinquency*, 38, 319-361.

_____. (2003). An integrated theory of the adolescent peak in offending. *Youth and Society*, 34(3), 263-299.

Agnew, R., Rebellon, C. and Thaxton, S. (2000). A general strain theory approach to families and delinquency. *Families, Crime and Criminal Justice*, 2, 113-138.

Allerton, M., Kenny, D., Champion, U. and Butler, T. (2003). 2003 NSW Young people in custody health survey: A summary of some key findings. Paper presented as *Juvenile Justice: From Lessons of the Past to a Road Map for the Future* conference, Sydney, Dec. 1-2.

Altschuler, D. M. (1998). Intermediate sanctions and community treatment for serious and violent offenders. In R. Loeber and D. P. Farrington (eds.), *Serious and violent juvenile offenders: Risk factors and successful interventions* (pp. 367-385). Thousand Oaks, CA: Sage.

Anand, S. and Robb, J. (2002). The admissibility of young people's statements under the proposed *Youth Criminal Justice Act. Alberta Law Review*, 39(4), 771-787.

Ambert, A. M. (1992). *The effect of children on parents.* New York: Haworth.

American Psychiatric Association (2000). *Diagnostic and statistical manual of mental disorders* (4th ed., text revision, Desk Reference). Washington, DC.

American Psychological Association. (1985). *Standards for Educational and Psychological Testing.* Author.

Andrews, D. A. and Bonta, J. (1995). *The Level of Supervision Inventory-Revised.* Toronto: Ontario Ministry of Correctional Services.

Andrews, D. A. and Dowden, C. (1999). A meta-analytic investigation into effective correctional intervention for female offenders. *Forum on Corrections Research*, 11(3), 18-21.

Andrews, D. A. and Kiesling, J. J. (1980). Program structure and effective correctional practices: A summary of the CaVIC research. In R. R. Ross and P. Gendreau (eds.), *Effective correctional treatment* (pp. 439-463). Toronto: Butterworth.

Andrews, D. A. and Bonta, J. (2003). *The psychology of criminal conduct* (3rd ed.). Cincinnati: Anderson.

Andrews, D. A., Bonta, J. and Hoge, R. D. (1990a). Classification for effective rehabilitation: Rediscovering psychology. *Criminal Justice and Behavior*, 17, 19-52.

Andrews, D. A., Zinger, I., Hoge, R. D., Bonta, J., Gendreau, P. and Cullen, F. T. (1990b). Does correctional treatment work? A psychologically informed meta-analysis. *Criminology*, 28, 369-404.

Bailey, S. (2003). Young offenders and mental health. *Current Opinions in Psychiatry*, 16, 581-591.

Baldry, A. C. (2003). Bullying in schools and exposure to domestic violence in Italy: The intra-generational transmission of violence in youngsters. *Child Abuse and Neglect*, 27, 713-723.

Baldry, A. C. and Farrington, D. P. (2000). Bullies and delinquents: Personal characteristics and parental styles. *Journal of Community and Applied Social Psychology*, 10, 17-31.

Baldry, A. C. and Winkel, F. W. (2004). Mental and physical health of Italian youngsters directly and indirectly victimized at school and at home. *International Journal of Forensic Mental Health*, Vol. 3, No.1, 77-91.

Barber, J. and Doob, A. N. (2004). An analysis of public support for severity and proportionality in the sentencing of youthful offenders. *Canadian Journal of Criminology and Criminal Justice*, 46(3), 327-342.

Bardone, A., Moffitt, T., Caspi, A., Dickson, N. and Silvan, P. (1996). Adult mental health and social outcomes of adolescent girls with depression and conduct disorder. *Development and Psychopathology*, 8, 811-829.

Barkley, R. A. (1997). *ADHD and the nature of self-control.* New York: Guilford.

Barnhorst, R. (2004). The *Youth Criminal Justice Act*: New directions and implementation issues. *Canadian Journal of Criminology and Criminal Justice*, 46 (3), 231-250.

Barron, P., Hassiotis, A. and Banes, J. (2002). Offenders with intellectual disability: the size of the problem and therapeutic outcomes. *Journal of Intellectual Disability Research*, Vol. 46, Part 6, 454-463.

Baumbach, J. (2002). Some implications of prenatal alcohol exposure for the treatment of adolescents with sexual offending behaviour. *Sexual Abuse: A Journal of Research and Treatment*, 14(4), 313-327.

Berkowitz, L. (1993). *Aggression: its causes, consequences and control.* Philadelphia: Temple.

Beyth-Marom, R. and Fischhoff, B. (1997). Adolescents' decisions about risks: a cognitive perspective. In J. Schulenberg, J. L. Maggs and K. Hurelmann (eds.), *Health risks and developmental transitions during adolescence* (pp. 110-135). Cambridge, UK: Cambridge.

Billinghurst, J. and Hackler, J. (1982). The mentally retarded in prison: Justice denied? *Canadian Journal of Criminology*, 24, 341-343.

Blakely, P. (2003). FAS and the young offender. Presentation to Child and Youth Program, Saskatoon, SK. Apr., 2003.

Boney-McCoy, S. and Finkelhor, D. (1995). The psychosocial impact of violent victimization on a national youth sample. *Journal of Consulting and Clinical Psychology*, 63, 726-736.

Boney-McCoy, S. and Finkelhor, D. (1996). Is youth victimization related to PTSD and depression after controlling for prior symptoms and family relationships? A longitudinal study. *Journal of Consulting and Clinical Psychology*, 64, 1406-1416.

Bonnie, R. J. and Grisso, T. (2000). Adjudicative competence and youthful offenders. In *Youth on trial: a developmental perspective on juvenile justice*, pp. 73-103. Chicago: University of Chicago.

Bonta, J. (1995). The responsivity principle and offender rehabilitation. *Forum on Corrections Research*, 7, 34-37.

_____. (2002). Offender risk assessment: Guidelines for selections and use. *Criminal justice and behaviour*, 29(4), 355-379.

Borum, R. (2000). Assessing violence risk among youth. *Journal of Clinical Psychology*, 56, 1263-1288.

_____. (2003). Not guilty by reason of insanity. In T. Grisso (ed.), *Evaluating competencies: Forensic assessments and instruments* (2nd ed., 193-227). New York: Plenum.

Borum, R., Bartel, P. and Forth, A. (2002). *Manual for the Structured Assessment for Violence Risk in Youth (SAVRY). Consultation Version*. Tampa, FL: Florida Mental Health Institute at University of South Florida.

Borum, R. and Grisso, T. (1996). Psychological test use in criminal forensic evaluations. *Professional Psychology: Research and Practice*, 26, 465-473.

Brier, N. (1989). The relationship between learning disability and delinquency: A reappraisal. *Journal of learning disabilities*, 22. 546-553.

Broidy, L. M., Nagin, D. S., Tremblay, R. E., Bates, J. E., Brame, B., Dodge, K. A., Ferguson, D., Horwood, J. L., Loeber, R., Laird, R., Lynam, D. R., Moffitt, T., Pettit, G. S. and Vitaro, F. (2000). Developmental trajectories of childhood disruptive behaviors and adolescent delinquency: A six-site, cross-national study. *Developmental Psychology*, 39(2), 222-245.

Burgess, A. W., Hartman, C. R., McCormack, A. and Grant, C. A. (1988). Child victim to juvenile victimizer: Treatment implications. *International Journal of Family Psychiatry*, 9, 403-416.

Burrell, S. and Warboys, L. (2000). *Special education and the juvenile justice system*. Washington, DC: U.S. Department of Justice, Office of Justice Programs, Office of Juvenile Justice and Delinquency Prevention.

Callahan, L. (2004). Correctional officer attitudes toward inmates with mental disorders. *International Journal of Forensic Mental Health*, 3(1), 37-54.

Case, R. (1985). *Intellectual development: Birth to adulthood*. New York: Academic.

Casey, P. and Rottman, D. B. (2000). Therapeutic jurisprudence in the courts. *Behavioral Sciences and the Law*, 18, 445-457.

Castellanos, F. X., Giedd, J. N. and Eckburg, P. (1994). Quantitative morphology of the caudate nucleus in attention deficit hyperactivity disorder. *American Journal of Psychiatry*, 151(12), 1791-1796.

Catchpole, R. E. H. and Gretton, H. M. (2003), The predictive validity of risk assessment with violent young offenders: A 1-year examination of criminal outcome. *Criminal Justice and Behavior*, 30(6), 688-708.

Cauffman, E. and Steinberg, L. (2000). (Im)maturity of judgement in adolescence: Why adolescents may be less culpable than adults. *Behavioral Sciences and the Law*, 18, 741-760.

Chaimowitz, G. (2000). Aboriginal mental health — Moving forward. *Canadian journal of psychiatry*, 45, 605-606.

Chak, A. (2001). Adult sensitivity to children's learning in the zone of proximal development. *Journal of Theory Social Behavior*, 31, 383-395.

Chapell, M. (2003). Violence Again Women with Disabilities: A research overview of the last decade. BC Institute Against Family Violence — Newsletter. Retrieved May 6, 2006, from www.bcifv.org/resources/newsletter/2003/spring/vaw.shtml.

Chesney-Lind, M. and Shelden, R. G. (2004). *Girls, delinquency and juvenile justice* (3rd Edition). Thomson/Wadsworth.

Children's Forum Report (2002). *UN Special Session on Children*. Retrieved Mar. 1, 2005, from www.unicef.org/special/session/docs_new/documentsforumreport_en.pdf.

Chodron, P. (1994). *Start where you are: a guide to compassionate living*. Boston: Shabhala.

Chrousos, G. P. (1998). Stressors, stress and neuroendocrime integration of the adaptive response. *Annals of the New York Academy of Sciences*, 851, 311-335.

Chrousos, G. P. and Gold, P. W. (1992). The concepts of stress and stress system disorders: Overview of physical and behavioural homeostasis. *Journal of the American Medical Association*, 267, 1244-1252.

Chudley, A., Conry, J., Cook, J. L., Loock, T. R. and LeBlanc, N. (2005). Fetal Alcohol Spectrum Disorder: Canadian guidelines for diagnosis. *Canadian Medical Association Journal*, 172(5), 51- 59, S10-S15.

Cicchetti, D., Toth, S. L. and Lynch, M. (1995). Bowlby's dream comes full circle: The application of attachment theory to risk and psychopathogy. *Advances in Clinical Child Psychology*, 17, 1- 75.

Clark, D. B., Kirisci, L. and Tartar, R. E. (1998). Adolescent versus adult onset and the development of substance use disorders in males. *Drug and Alcohol Dependence*, 49, 115-121.

Cockram, J. (2005). Careers of offenders with an intellectual disability: the probabilities of rearrest. *Journal of Intellectual Disability Research*, Vol. 49, Part 7, 525-536.

Cocozza, J. J. and Skowyra, K. (2000). Youth with mental health disorders: Issues and emerging responses. *Juvenile Justice Journal*, 7, 3-13.

Cohen, S. and Herbert, T. B. (1996). Health psychology: Psychological factors and physical disease from the perspective of human psychoneuroimmunology. *Annual Review of Psychology*, 47, 113-142.

Cohen, J. A., Mannarino, A. P., Berliner, L. and Deblinger, E. (2000). Trauma-focused cognitive behavioral therapy for children and adolescents: An empirical update. *Journal of Interpersonal Violence*, 15(11), 1202-1223.

Cole, D. P. and Angus, G. (2003). Using pre-sentence reports to evaluate and respond to risk. *Criminal Law Quarterly*, 47, 302-364.

Cole, P. M. and Putnam, F. W. (1992). Effect of incest on self and social functioning: A developmental psychopathology perspective. *Journal of Consulting and Clinical Psychology*, 60, 174-184.

Cole, P. M., Michel, M. K. and O'Donnell Teti, L. (1994). The development of emotion regulation and dysregulation: A clinical perspective. *Monographs of the Society for Research in Child Development*, 59, 73-102.

Conry, J. and Fast, D. (2000). *Fetal alcohol syndrome and the criminal justice system.* Vancouver, BC: British Columbia Fetal Alcohol Syndrome Resource Society.

Conway, J. (2003). *Saskatchewan Mental Health Sector Study Final Report.* Saskatchewan: Mental Health Work Force, Saskatchewan Learning, Saskatchewan Health.

Conway, K. P. and McCord, J. (2002). A longitudinal examination of the relation between co-offending with violent accomplices and violent crime. *Aggressive Behavior*, 28, 97-108.

Corrado, R. R., Cohen, I. M., Glackman, W. and Odgers, C. (2003). Serious and violent young offenders' decisions to recidivate: An assessment of five sentencing models. *Crime and Delinquency*, 49(2), 179-200.

Correctional Service Canada. (1991). *Report of the Task Force on Mental Health.* Ottawa.

_____. (1995a). *Psychopathy and young offenders: Rates of childhood maltreatment.* CSC Forum Vol. 7, No. 1: Retrieved Nov. 1, 2004 from www.cscscc.gc.ca/text/pblct/forum/e07/e071e_e.shtml.

_____. (1995b) *Young sex offenders: A comparison with a control group of non-sex offenders.* CSC Forum Vol. 7, No. 1: Retrieved Nov. 1, 2004 from www.cscscc.gc.ca/text/pblct/forum/e07/e071e_e.shtml.

Cosden, M., Ellens, J., Schnell, J. and Yamini-Diouf, Y. (2005). Efficacy of a mental health treatment court with assertive community treatment. *Behavioral Sciences and the Law*, 23, 199-214.

Cowden, V. L. and McKee, G. R. (1995). Competency to stand trial in juvenile delinquency proceedings: Cognitive maturity and the attorney-client relationship. *Journal of Family Law*, 33, 629-660.

Cullen, F. T., Gendreau, P., Jarjoura, G. R. and Wright, J. P. (1997). Crime and the bell curve: Lessons from intelligent criminology. *Crime and delinquency*, 43, 387-411.

Davis, M., Banks, S., Fisher, W. and Grudzinskas, A. (2004). Longitudinal patterns of offending during the transition to adulthood in youth from the mental health system. *The Journal of Behavioral Health Services and Research*, 31(4), 351-366.

Dembo, R., La Voie, L., Schmeidler, J. and Washburn, M. (1987). The nature and correlates of psychological/emotional functioning among a sample of detained youths. *Criminal Justice and Behavior*, 14, 311-334.

Department of Justice Canada (1998). *A strategy for the renewal of youth justice.* Ottawa.

Dishion, T. J., Capaldi, D. M., Spracklin, K. M. and Li, F. (1995). Peer ecology of male adolescent drug use. *Development and Psychopathology*, 7, 803-824.

Dishion, T. J., Spracklen, K. M., Andrews, D. W. and Patterson, G. R. (1996). Deviancy training in male adolescent friendships. *Behavior Therapy*, 27, 373-390.

Doob, A. N. (2001). *Youth court judges' view of the youth justice system: The results of a survey*. Ottawa: Department of Justice Canada.

Doob, A. N. and Cesaroni, C. (2004). *Responding to youth crime in Canada*. Toronto: University of Toronto.

Doob, A. N., Marinos, V. and Varma, K. N. (1995). *Youth crime and the youth justice system in Canada: A research perspective*. Toronto: Centre of Criminology, University of Toronto.

Dowden, C. and Andrews, D. A. (1999). What works in young offender treatment: A meta-analysis. *Forum on Corrections Research*, 11(2), 21-24.

Downs, W. R. (1993). Developmental considerations for the effects of childhood sexual abuse. *Journal of Interpersonal Violence*, 8, 331-345.

DuRant, R., Getts, A., Cadenhead, C. and Woods, E. (1995). The association between weapon-carrying and the use of violence among adolescents living in or around public housing. *Journal of Adolescent Health*, 17(6), 376-380.

Eggleston, C. R. (1996). The justice system. In Cramer, S. C. and Ellis, W. (eds.), *Learning disabilities: Lifelong issues*, 197-201. Baltimore: Paul H. Brookes.

Elliot, D. S., Huizinga, D. and Ageton, S. (1985). *Explaining delinquency and drug use*. Beverly Hills, CA: Sage.

Endicott, O. R. (1991). *Persons with intellectual disability who are incarcerated for criminal offences: A literature review*. Ottawa: Correctional Services of Canada.

Epp Buckingham, J. (2000). Human rights. Retrieved Feb. 7, 2005 from Public Legal Education Association of Saskatchewan. www.plea.org/freepubs/hr/hr.htm.

Estroff, T. W., Schwartz, R. H. and Hoffman, N. G. (1989). Adolescent cocaine abuse: Addictive potential, behavioral and psychiatric effects. *Clinical Pediatrics*, 28, 550-555.

Evans, W. P., Marte, R. M., Betts, S. and Silliman, B. (2001). Adolescent suicide risk and peer-related violent behaviors and victimization. *Journal of Interpersonal Violence*, 16(12), 1330-1348.

Ewing, C. P. (1990). Juveniles or adults? Forensic assessment of juveniles considered for trial in criminal court. *Forensic Reports*, 3, 3-13.

Fagan, J., Piper, E. S. and Cheng, Y. T. (1987). Contributions of victimization to delinquency in inner cities. *Journal of Criminal Law and Criminology*, 78, 586-613.

Falshaw, L., Browne, K. D. and Hollin, C. R. (1996). Victim to offender: A review. *Aggression and Violent Behavior*, 1, 389-404.

Farrington, D. P. (1995). The development of offending and antisocial behavior from childhood: Key findings from the Cambridge study in delinquent behavior. *Journal of Clinical Psychology and Psychiatry*, 36, 929-964.

Fast, J. K., Conry, J. and Loock, C. A. (1999). Identifying fetal alcohol syndrome among youth in the criminal justice system. *Developmental and Behavioral Pediatrics*, 20(5), 1-3.

Federal-Provincial-Territorial Task Force on Youth Justice (1996). *A review of the Young Offenders Act and the youth justice system in Canada*. Ottawa: Department of Justice Canada.

Figley, C. R. and McCubbin, H. E. (1983). *Stress and the family: coping with catastrophe* (Vol. 2). New York: Brunner/Mazel.

Finkelhor, D. (1984). *Child sexual abuse: New theory and research.* New York: Free Press.

_____. (1994). Current information on the scope and nature of child sexual abuse. *The Future of Children*, 4(2), 31-53.

Finkelhor, D. and Hashima, P. Y. (2001). The victimization of children and youth: A comprehensive overview. In S. White (ed.), *Handbook of youth and justice* (pp. 49-79). New York: Plenum.

French, L. A. (1983). The mentally retarded and pseudoretarded offender: A clinical legal dilemna. *Federal Probation*, 47, 55-61.

Fried, C. S. and Reppucci, N. D. (2001). Criminal decision making: the development of adolescent judgement, criminal responsibility and culpability. *Law and Human Behavior*, 25, 45-61.

Frydenberg, E. (1997). *Adolescent Coping: Theoretical and Research Perspectives.* London: Routledge.

Fulero, S. and Everington, C. (1995). Assessing competency to waive Miranda rights in defendants with mental retardation. *Law and Human Behavior*, 19, 533-543.

Fulero, S. and Finkel, N. (1991). Barring ultimate issue testimony: An "insane" rule? *Law and Human Behavior*, 15, 495-507.

Garcia, S. and Steele, H. (1988). Mentally retarded offenders in the criminal justice and mental retardation services systems in Florida: Philosophical, placement and treatment issues. *Arkansas Law Review*, 41, 809.

Gavazzi, S. M., Yarcheck, C., Wasserman, D. and Patridge, C. (2000). A balanced and restorative approach to juvenile crime: Programming for families of adolescent offenders. *Families, Crime and Criminal Justice*, 2, 381-405.

Gavazzi, S. M., Yarcheck, C. M., Rhine, E. E. and Partridge, C. R. (2003). Building bridges between the parole officer and the families of serious juvenile offenders: a preliminary report on a family-based parole program. *International Journal of Offender Therapy and Comparative Criminology*, 47(3), 291-308.

Ge, X., Conger, R. D. and Elder, G. H., Jr. (1996). Coming of age too early: Pubertal influences on girls' vulnerability to psychological distress. *Child Development*, 67, 3386-3400.

Gendreau, P. (1996). Offender rehabilitation: what we know and what needs to be done. *Criminal Justice and Behavior*, 23, 144-161.

_____. (2002). We must do a better job of cumulating knowledge. *Canadian Psychology*, 43(3), 205-210.

Gendreau, P. and Andrews, D. A. (2001). *The Correctional Program Assessment Inventory-2000 (CPAI 2000).* Saint John, NB: University of New Brunswick.

Gendreau, P. and Ross, R. R. (1987). Revivication of rehabilitation: Evidence from the 1980s. *Justice Quarterly*, 4, 349-408.

Gendreau, P., Goggin, C., Smith, P. (2001). Implementation guidelines for correctional programs in the "real world." In G. A. Bernfeld, D. P. Farrington and A. W. Leschied (eds.), *Offender rehabilitation in practice* (pp. 247-268). New York: John Wiley.

Gendreau, P., French, S. A. and Gionet, A. (2004). What works (what doesn't work): The principles of effective correctional treatment. *Journal of Community Corrections*, 13, 4-30.

Glantz, M. D. and Leshner, A. I. (2000). Drug abuse and developmental psychopathology. *Development and Psychopathology, 12*, 795-814.

Goodman, E. and Capitman, J. (2000). Depressive symptoms and cigarette smoking among teens. *Pediatrics*, 106(4), 746-755.

Government of Canada. (1992). *Fetal alcohol syndrome: From awareness to prevention.*

Graber, J. A. and Petersen, A. C. (1991). Cognitive changes in adolescence: biological perspectives. In K. R. Gibson and A. C. Petersen (eds.), *Brain maturation and cognitve development: Comparative and cross-cultural perspectives* (pp. 253-279). New York: Aldine de Gruyter.

Graham-Bermann, S. A. and Edleson, J. L. (eds.). (2001). *Domestic violence in the lives of children. The future of research, intervention and social policy.* Washington, DC: American Psychological Association.

Green, R. G. and Healy, K. F. (2003). *Tough on kids: Rethinking approaches to youth justice.* Saskatoon, SK: Purich.

Gresham, F. M. and MacMillan, D. L. (1997). Social competence and affective characteristics of students with mild disabilities. *Review of Educational Research, 1997,* 67(4), 377-415.

Grisso, T. (1981). *Juveniles' waiver of rights: Legal and psychological competence.* New York: Plenum.

_____. (1998a). *Forensic evaluation of juveniles.* Sarasota, FL: Professional Resource Press.

_____. (1998b). *Instruments for Assessing Understanding and Appreciation of Miranda Rights.* Sarasota, FL: Professional Resource Press.

_____. (2003). *Evaluating competencies: Forensic assessments and instruments — Second Edition.* NY: Kluwer/Plenum.

Grisso, T. and Pomicter, C. (1977). Interrogation of juveniles: an empirical study of procedures, safeguards and rights waiver. *Law and Human Behavior*, 1, 321-342.

Grisso, T. and Ring., M. (1979). Parents' attitudes toward juveniles' rights in interrogation. *Criminal Justice and Behavior*, 6, 221-226.

Grisso, T. and Underwood, L. A. (2004). *Screening and assessing mental health and substance use disorders among youth in the juvenile justice system: A resource guide for practitioners* (Report, Dec. 2004). Washington, DC: Office of Juvenile Justice and Delinquency Prevention.

Grisso, T., Steinberg, L., Woolard, J., Cauffman, E., Scott, E., Graham, S., Lexcen, F., Repucci, N. and Schwartz, R. (2003). Juveniles' competence to stand trial: A comparison of adolescents' and adults' capacities as trial defendants, *Law and Human Behavior*, 27, 333-364.

Gudjonsson, G. (1992). *The psychology of interrogations, confessions and testimony.* London: Wiley.

Gudjonsson, G. and Sigurdsson, J. (1995). The relationship of confabulation to the memory, intelligence, suggestibility and personality of prison inmates. *Nordic Journal of Psychiatry*, 49, 373-378.

_____. (1996). The relationship of confabulation to the memory, intelligence, suggestibility and personality of juvenile offenders. *Applied Cognitive Psychology*, 10, 85-92.

Gudjonnson, G., Rutter, S. and Clare, C. (1995). The relationship between suggestibility and anxiety among suspects detained at police stations. *Psychological Medicine*, 25, 875-878.

Hagell, A. (2002). *The mental health of young offenders. Bright futures: Working with vulnerable young people.* London: Policy Research Bureau.

Haggerty, R. J., Sherrod, L. R., Garmez, N. and Rutter, M. (1994). *Stress, risk and resilience in children and adolescents: Processes, mechanisms and interventions.* Cambridge, UK: Cambridge.

Hamilton, C. E., Falshaw, L. and Browne, K. D. (2002). The link between recurrent maltreatment and offending behaviour. *International Journal of Offender Therapy and Comparative Criminology*, 46(1), 75-94.

Hannah-Moffat, K. and Maurutto, P. (2003). *Youth risk/need assessment: An overview of issues and practices.* Ottawa: Department of Justice Canada: Youth Justice Research.

Hannah-Moffat, K. and Shaw, M. (2001). Taking risks: Incorporating gender and culture into the classification and assessment of federally sentenced women in Canada. *Policy Research Report*. Ottawa: Status of Women.

Harris, J. R. (1995). Where is the children's environment? A group socialization theory of development. *Psychology Review*, 102, 458-489.

Harter, S. (1990). Self and identity development. In S. S. Feldman and G. R. Elliott (eds.), *At the threshold: The developing adolescent* (pp. 352-387). Cambridge: Harvard.

Hartup, W. W. (1996). The company they keep: friendship and their developmental significance. *Child Development*, 67, 1-13.

Havemann, P. (2000). From child saving to child blaming: The political economy of the *Young Offenders Act* 1908-1984. In R. Mann (ed.), *Juvenile crime and delinquency* (pp. 36-48). Toronto: Canadian Scholars.

Hawkins, J. D., Herrenkohl, T. I., Farrington, D. P., Brewer, D., Catalano, R. F., Harachi, T. W. and Cothern, L., (2000). *Predictors of youth violence.* Bulletin, Washington, DC: U.S. Deparment of Justice, Office of Justice Programs, Office of Juvenile Justice and Delinquency Prevention.

Hayes, L. M. (2000). Suicide prevention in juvenile facilities. *Juvenile Justice*, 7(1), 24- 33.

Health Canada. (2002). *A report on mental illness in Canada. How do mental illnesses affect people?* Ottawa.

Hein, K. (1987). The use of therapeutics in adolescence. *Journal of Adolescent Health Care*, 8, 8-35.

Henggeler, S. W., Schoenwald, S. K., Borduin, C. M., Rowland, M. D. and Cunningham, P. B. (1998). *Multisystemic treatment of antisocial behaviour in children and adolescents.* New York: Guilford.

Hiday, V. A. (1995). The social context of mental illness and violence. *Journal of Health and Social Behavior, 36,* 122-137.

_____. (1997). Understanding the link between mental illness and violence. *International Journal of Law and Psychiatry, 20,* 399-417.

Hiday, V. A., Swanson, J. W., Swartz, M. S., Borum, R. and Wagner, H. R. (2001). Victimization: A link between mental illness and violence? *International Journal of Law and Psychiatry, 24,* 559-572.

Hillian, D. and Reitsma-Street, M. (2003). Parents and youth justice. *Canadian Journal of Criminology and Criminal Justice,* Jan., 19-41.

Hillian, D., Reitsma-Street, M. and Hackler, J. (2004). Conferencing in the *Youth Criminal Justice Act* of Canada: Policy developments in British Columbia. *Canadian Journal of Criminology and Criminal Justice, 46*(3), 343-366.

Hoge, R. D. (2002). Standardized instruments for assessing risk and need in youthful offenders. *Criminal Justice and Behavior, 29*(4), 380-396.

_____. (2001). *The juvenile offender: Theory, research and applications.* Boston: Kluwer.

Hoge, R. D. and Andrews, D. A. (2002). *The youth level of service/case management inventory manual and scoring key.* North Tonawanda, NY: Multi-Health Systems.

_____. (1996). *Assessing the youthful offender: Issues and techniques.* New York: Plenum.

Hoge, R. D. and Andrews, D. A. and Leschied, A. (1996). An investigation of the risk and protective factors in a sample of youthful offenders. *Journal of Child Psychology and Psychiatry, 37,* 419-424.

Irwin, Jr., C. E. (1989). Risk taking behaviors in the adolescent patient: Are they impulsive? *Pediatric Annals, 18,* 122-133.

Irwin, Jr., C. E. and Millstein, S. G. (1992). Correlates and predictors of risk-taking behavior during adolescence. In L. P., Lipsitt and L. L. Mitnick (eds.), *Self-regulatory behavior and risk taking: causes and consequences* (pp. 3-21). Newbury Park, CA: Sage Publications.

Jaffe, P., Leschied, A. and Farthing, J. (1987). Youth knowledge and attitudes about the *Young Offenders Act:* Does anyone care what they think? *Canadian Journal of Criminology, 29,* 309-316.

Johnson, L. M., Simons, R. L. and Conger, R. D. (2004). Criminal justice system involvement and continuity of youth crime: A longitudinal analysis. *Youth and Society, 36*(1), 3-29.

Jung, S. and Rawana, E. P. (1999). Risk and need assessment of juvenile offenders. *Criminal Justice and Behavior, 26,* 69-89.

Kaplan, H. B., Johnson, R. J. and Bailey, C. A. (1987). Deviant peers and deviant behavior: further elaboration of a model. *Social Psychology Quarterly, 50,* 277- 284.

Kazdin, A. (2000). Adolescent development, mental disorders and decision making of delinquent youths. In T. Grisso and R. Schwartz (eds.), *Youth on trial: A developmental perspective on juvenile justice,* pp. 33-65. Chicago: University of Chicago.

Keating, D. P. (1990). Adolescent thinking. In S. S. Feldman and G. R. Elliott (eds.), *At the threshold: the developing adolescent* (pp. 54-89). Cambridge, MA: Harvard.

Kempf-Leonard, K. and Peterson, E. (2000). Expanding realms of the new penology: the advent of actuarial justice for juveniles. *Punishment and Society*, 2(1), 66-97.

Klein, M. (1975). *Envy and Gratitude and Other Works 1946-1993*. The Hogarth Press and The Institute of Psycho-Analysis.

Kurtz, A. (2002). What works for delinquency? The effectiveness of interventions for teenage offending behavior. *The Journal of Forensic Psychiatry*, 13(3), 671-692.

Lader, D., Singleton, N. and Meltzer, H. (2000). *Psychiatric morbidity among young offenders in England and Wales*. London: Office for National Statistics.

Lahey, B. B., Moffitt, T. E. and Caspi, A. (eds.), (2003). *Causes of conduct disorders and juvenile delinquency*. New York: Guilford.

Lahey, B. B. and Waldman, I. D. (2003). A developmental propensity model of the origins of conduct problems during childhood and adolescence. In B. B. Lahey, T. E. Moffitt and A. Caspi, *Causes of conduct disorder and juvenile delinquency*, (pp. 76-117). New York: Guilford.

LaPrairie, C. (1992). *Dimensions of Aboriginal over-representation in correctional institutions and implications for crime prevention*. Ottawa: Solicitor General of Canada.

_____. (2002). Aboriginal overrepresentation in the criminal justice system: A tale of nine cities. *Canadian Journal of Criminology*, Apr., 181-208.

Larson, R. and Richards, M. H. (1994). *Divergent realities: The emotional lives of mothers, fathers and adolescents*. New York: Basic.

Lasser, K., Wesley Boyd, J., Woolhandler, S., Himmelstein, D. U., McCormick, D. and Bor, D. H. (2000). Smoking and mental illness: A population-based prevalence study. *Journal of the American Medical Association*, 284, 2606-2610.

Latessa, E. J., Cullen, F. T. and Gendreau, P. (2002). Beyond correctional quackery— professionalism and the possibility of effective treatment. *Federal Probation*, 66, 43-49.

Lauritsen, J. L., Sampson, R. J. and Laub, J. H. (1991). The link between offending and victimization among adolescents. *Criminology*, 29, 265-292.

Lawrence, P. A. (1983). The role of legal counsel in juveniles' understanding of their rights. *Juvenile and Family Court Journal*, 34, 49-58.

Leschied, A. W., Cummings, A. L., Van Brunschot, M., Cunningham, A. and Saunders, A. (2001). Aggression in adolescent girls: Implications for policy, prevention and treatment. *Canadian Psychology*, 42(3), 200-215.

Levine, M. (1994). *Educational care: a system for understanding and helping children with learning problems at home and in school*. Cambridge, MA: Cambridge.

Link, B. G. Andrews, H. and Cullen, F. T. (1992). The violent and illegal behavior of mental patients reconsidered. *American Sociological Review*, 57, 275-292.

Link, B. G. and Stueve, C. (1994). Psychotic symptoms and the violent/illegal behavior of mental patients compared to community controls. In J. Monahan and H. Steadman (eds.), *Violence and mental disorder* (pp. 137-159). Chicago: University of Chicago.

Lipsey, M. W. (1992). Juvenile delinquency treatment: A meta-analytic inquiry in the variability of effects. In T. D. Cook, H. Cooper, D. S. Cordray, H. Hartmann, L. V. Hedges, R. J. Light, T. A. Louis and F. Mosteller (eds.), *Meta-analysis for explanation: A casebook* (pp. 83-127). New York: Russell Sage.

Litton Fox, G. and Benson, M. L. (2000). Families, crime and criminal justice: Charting the linkages. *Families, Crime and Criminal Justice*, 2, 1-21.

Litwack, T. R. (2002). Some questions for the field of violence risk assessment and forensic mental health: Or, "back to basics" revisited. *International Journal of Forensic Mental Health*, 1(2), 171-178.

Loeber, R. and Farrington, D. P. (2000). Young children who commit crime: epidemiology, developmental origins, risk factors, early interventions and policy implications. *Development and psycholopathology*, 12, 737-762.

_____. (eds.). (2001). *Child delinquents.* Thousand Oaks, CA: Sage.

Lyons, J. A., Baerger, D. R., Quigley, P., Erlich, J. and Griffin, E. (2001). Mental health services needs of juvenile offenders: A comparison of detention, incarceration and treatment settings. *Children's Services: Social Policy, Research and Practice*, 4(2), 69-85.

Maccoby, E. (1980). *Social development: Psychological growth and the parent child relationship.* New York: Harcourt Brace Jovanovich.

Mann, L., Harmoni, R. and Power, C. (1989). Adolescent decision-making: the development of competence. *Journal of Adolescence*, 12, 265-278.

Marsh, H. W. (1989). Age and sex effects in multiple dimensions of self-concept: Preadolescence to early adulthood. *Journal of Educational Psychology*, 81, 417-430.

Martinson, R. (1974). What works? Questions and answers. *The Public Interest*, 35, 22-54.

McAdams, D. P. (1993). *The stories we live by: personal myths and the making of the self.* New York: William Morrow.

McAfee, J. K. and Gural, M. (1988). Individuals with mental retardation and the criminal justice system: the view from States' Attorney's General. *Mental Retardation*, 26(1), 5-12.

McCord, J. (1990). Long-term perspectives on parental absence. In L. N. Robins and M. Rutter (eds.), *Straight and devious pathways from childhood to adulthood* (pp. 116-134). New York: Cambridge.

_____. (2001). Forging criminals in the family. In S. White (ed.), *Handbook of Youth and Justice* (pp. 223-235). New York: Plenum.

McGaha, A., Otto, R. K., McClaren, M. D. and Petrila, J. (2001). Juveniles adjudicated incompetent to proceed: A descriptive study of Florida's competence restoration program. *The Journal of the American Academy of Psychiatry and the Law*, 29, 427-437.

McGloin, J. M. and Pratt, T. C. (2003). Cognitive ability and delinquent behaviour among inner-city youth: A life-course analysis of main, mediating and interaction effects. *International Journal of Offender Therapy and Comparative Criminology*, 47(3), 253-271.

McGuire, J. (2000). Can the criminal law ever be therapeutic? *Behavioral Sciences and the Law*, 18, 413-426.

_____. (2003). Maintaining change: converging legal and psychological initiatives in a therapeutic jurisprudence framework. *The Western Criminology Review*, 4(2), 1-20. Retrieved July 21, 2004, from www.wcr.sonoma.edu/v4n2/mcguire.html.

McManus, M., Alessi, N., Grapentine, W. and Brickman, A. (1984). Psychiatric Disturbance in serious delinquents. *Journal of the American Academy of Child Psychiatry*, 23, 602-615.

McNeill, A. D. (1991). The development of dependence on smoking in children. *British Journal of Addiction*, 86, 589-592.

Mears, D. P. and Aron, L. Y. (2003). *Addressing the needs of youth with disabilities in the juvenile justice system: the current state of knowledge.* Washington, DC: The Urban Institute.

Mears, D. P. and Feld, S. H. (2000). Theorizing sanctioning in a criminalized juvenile court. *Criminology*, 38, 983-1020.

Meehl, P. E. (1954). *Clinical versus statistical prediction.* Minneapolis: University of Minnesota.

Melberg Schwier, K. and Hingsberger, D. (2000). *Sexuality: Your sons and daughters with intellectual disabilities.* Baltimore: Paul H. Brookes.

Messick, S. (1989). Meaning and value in test validation: the science and ethics of assessment. *Educational researcher*, 18, 5-11.

Miller, W. and Rollnick, S. (1991). *Motivational interviewing: Preparing people to change addictive behavior.* New York: Guilford.

Millstein, S. G. (1993). Perceptual, attributional and affective processes in perceptions of vulnerability through the life span. In N. J. Bell and R. W. Bell (eds.), *Adolescent risk taking* (55-65). Newbury Park, CA: Sage Publications.

Moeller, G. F., Barratt, E. S., Dougherty, D. M., Schmitz, J. M. and Swann, A. C. (2001). Psychiatric aspects of impulsivity. *American Journal of Psychiatry*, 158(11), 1783-1793.

Moffit, T. (1994). Natural histories of delinquency. In E. G. M. Weitekamp and H. J. Kerner (eds.), *Cross-national longitudinal research on human development and criminal behaviour* (pp. 3-61). Netherlands: Kluwer.

_____. (2003). Life-course-persistent and adolescence-limited antisocial behavior: A 10-year research review and a research agenda. In B. B. Lahey, T. E. Moffitt and A. Caspi (eds.), *Causes of conduct disorder and juvenile delinquency,* (pp. 49-76). New York: Guilford.

Monahan, J. (1992). Mental disorder and violent behaviour: Perceptions and evidence. *American Psychologist*, 47, 511-521.

_____. (1996). Violence prediction: The past twenty and the next twenty years. *Criminal justice and behaviour*, 23, 107-120.

Moretti, M. M. and Peled, M. (2004). Adolescent-parent attachment: Bonds that support healthy development. *Paediatric Child Health*, 9(8), 551- 560.

Morley, T. P. (2004). *Kenneth George McKenzie and the Founding of Neurosurgery in Canada.* Markham, ON: Fitzhenry and Whiteside.

Mulford, C. Fried, Dickon Reppucci, N., Mulvey, E. P., Woolard, J. L. and Portwood, S. L. (2004). Legal issues affecting mentally disorders and developmentally delayed youth in the justice system. *International Journal of Forensic Mental Health*, 3(1), 3-22.

Mulvey, E. P. (1984). Judging amenability to treatment in juvenile offenders: Theory and practice. In N. D. Reppucci, L. A. Withorn, E. P. Mulvey and J. Monahan (eds.), *Children, mental health and the law,* pp. 195-210. Beverly Hills, CA: Sage.

Mulvey, E. P. (1994). Assessing the evidence of a link between mental illness and violence. *Hospital and community Psychiatry*, 45, 663-668.

National Task Force on Juvenile Sexual Offending. (1993). Revised report. *Juvenile and Family Court Journal*, 44(4), 1-121.

Ney, P. G., Fung, T. and Wickett, A. R. (1994). The worst combinations of child abuse and neglect. *Child Abuse and Neglect*, 18, 705-714.

Nieland, M., McCluskie, C. and Tait, E. (2001). Prediction of psychological distress in young offenders. *Legal and Criminological Psychology*, 6, 29-47.

O'Donnell, C. R. (1992). The interplay of theory and practice in delinquency prevention: From behavior modification to activity settings. In J. McCord and R. E. Tremblay (eds.), *Preventing antisocial behavior: Interventions for birth through adolescence* (pp. 209-232). New York: Guilford.

Odgers, C. L. and Moretti, M. M. (2002). Aggressive and antisocial girls: Research update and challenges. *International Journal of Forensic Mental Health*, 1(2), 103-119. Ontario Office of the Child and Family Advocacy (1998).

Ogloff, J. R. P., Wong, S. and Greenwood, A. (1990). Treating criminal psychopaths in a therapeutic program. *Behavioral Sciences and the Law*, 8, 181-190.

Osgood, D. W., Wilson, J. K., O'Malley, P. M, Bachman, J. G. and Johnston, L. D. (1996). Routine activities and individual deviant behavior. *American Sociological Review*, 61(4), 635-655.

Osher, D., Rouse, J., Quinn, M., Kandizoria, K. and Woodruff, D. (2002). *Addressing invisible barriers: improving outcome for youth with disabilities in the juvenile justice system.* College Park, MD: Center for effective collaboration and practice, American Institute for Research.

Otto, R. K., Greenstein, J. J., Johnson, M. K. and Friedman, R. M. (1992). Prevalence of mental disorders among youth in the juvenile justice system. In J. J. Cocozza (ed.). *Responding to the mental health needs of youth in the juvenile justice system,* pp. 7-48. Seattle, WA: The National Coalition for the Mentally Ill in the Criminal Justice System.

Ovaert, L. B., Cashel, M. L. and Sewell, K. W. (2003). Structured group therapy for post-traumatic stress disorder in incarcerated male juveniles. *American Journal of Orthopsychiatry*, 73(3), 294-301.

Pasternoster, R. and Iovanni, L. (1989). The labeling perspective and delinquency: An elaboration of the theory and an assessment of the evidence. *Justice Quarterly*, 6, 359-354.

Patterson, G. R., Reid, J. B. and Dishion, T. J. (1992). *Antisocial boys.* Eugene, OR: Castalia.

Perkins-Dock, R. E. (2001). Family interventions with incarcerated youth: A review of the literature. *International Journal of Offender Therapy and Comparative Criminology*, 45(5), 606-625.

Petersen, A. C., Silbereisen, R. K. and Sorensen, S. (1996). Coping with adolescence. In M. E. Colten and S. Gore (eds.), *Adolescent stress: Causes and consequences* (93-110). New York: Aldine de Gruyter.

Peterson, M. (1988). Children's understanding of the juvenile justice system: A cognitive-developmental perspective. *Canadian Journal of Criminology*, 30, 381-395.

Peterson-Bedali, M. and Abramovitch, R. (1992). Children's knowledge of the legal system: Are they competent to instruct legal construct? *Canadian Journal of Criminology*, 34, 139-160.

Peterson-Bedali, M. and Broeking, J. (2004). *Parents' involvement in youth justice proceedings: perspectives of youth and parents*. Ottawa: Department of Youth Justice.

Peterson-Bedali, M. and Koegl, C. J. (1998). Young people's knowledge of the Young Offenders Act and the youth justice system. *Canadian Journal of Criminology*, Apr., 127-152.

Peters, Y. (2004). Twenty years of litigating for disability equality rights: has it made a difference? An assessment by the Council of Canadians with Disabilities. Retrieved Sept. 23, 2005 from www.ccdonline.ca/publications/20yrs.htm.

Petrosino, A., Turpin-Petrosino, C. and Finkenauer, J. O. (2000). Well-meaning programs have harmful effects! Lessons from experiments of programs such as Scared Straight. *Crime and Delinquency*, 46, 354-379.

Pope, C. E. and Feyerherm, W. (1995). *Minority and the juvenile justice system*. Washington, DC: Office of Juvenile Justice and Delinquency Prevention.

Prochaska, J. and DiClemente, C. (1984). *The transtheoretical approach: Crossing traditional boundaries of therapy*. Homewood, IL: Dorsey Professional.

Prochaska, J. and Norcross, J. (1994). *Systems of psychotherapy: A transtheoretical analysis* (3rd ed.). Pacific Grove, CA: Brooks/Cole.

Rankin, J. H. and Kern, R. (1994). Parental attachments and delinquency. *Criminology*, 32, 495-515.

Reed, E. F. (1989). Legal rights of mentally retarded offenders: hospice and habilitation. *Criminal Law Bulletin*, 25, 411-443.

Reijone, J. H., Pratt, H. D. and Greydanus, D. E. (2003). Eating disorders in the adolescent population: An overview. *Journal of Adolescent Research*, 18, 209-222.

Reppucci, N. D., Fried, D. S. and Schmidt, M. G. (2002). Youth violence: Risk and protective factors. In R. R. Corrada, R. Roesch and S.D. Hart (eds.), *Multi-problem youth: A foundation for comparative research on needs, interventions and outcomes*, pp. 3-22. Amsterdam: ISO Press.

Ribordy, F. X. (1986). *Legal education and information: an exploratory study*. Ottawa: Department of Justice.

Rich, P. (2003). *Understanding, assessing and rehabilitating juvenile sexual offenders*. New Jersey: John Wiley.

Rigby, K. (2000). Effects of peer victimization in schools and perceived social support in adolescent well-being. *Journal of Adolescence*, 23, 57-68.

Roberts, G. and Nanson, J. (2000). *Best practices: Fetal alcohol syndrome/fetal alcohol effects and the effects of other substances during pregnancy*. Ottawa: Health Canada. www.cds-csa.com.

Roberts, J. V. (2004). Harmonizing the sentencing of young and adult offenders: A comparison of the *Youth Criminal Justice Act* and Part XXIII of the *Criminal Code*. *Canadian Journal of Criminology and Criminal Justice*, 46(3), 301-326.

Roesch, R., Zapf, P. A., Eaves, D. and Webster., C. D. (2004). *Fitness Interview Test* (Revised Edition). Burnaby, BC: The Mental Health Law and Policy Institute.

Rogers, R. (1984). *Rogers Criminal Responsibility Assessment Scales.* Odessa, FL: Psychological Assessment Resources.

Rogers, R. and Shuman, D. (2000). *Conducting insanity evaluations* (2nd ed.). New York: Guilford.

Rogers, R., Bagby, R., Couch, M. and Cutler, B. (1990). Effects of ultimate opinions on juror perceptions of insanity. *International Journal of Law and Psychiatry*, 13, 225-232.

Romerl, D. and Stanton, B. F. (2003). Feelings about risk and the epidemic diffusion of adolescent sexual behavior. *Prev. Science*, 4, 39-53.

Rossman, B. B. R. (2001). Longer terms effects of children's exposure to domestic violence. In S. A. Graham-Bermann and J. L. Edleson, (eds.), *Domestic violence in the lives of children. The future of research, intervention and social policy* (pp. 35-65). Washington, DC: American Psychological Association.

Rothery, M. and Enns, G. (2001). *Clinical practice with families: supporting creativity and competence.* New York: Haworth.

Rottman, D. and Casey, P. (1999). Therapeutic jurisprudence and the emergence of problem-solving courts. *National Institute of Justice Journal*, July, 13-19

Rutter, M. (2003). Crucial paths from risk indicator to causal mechanism. In B. B. Lahey, T. E. Moffitt and A. Caspi (eds.), *Causes of conduct disorder and juvenile delinquency* (pp. 3-26). New York: Guilford.

Rutter, M., Graham, P., Chadwick, O. F. D. and Yule, W. (1976). Adolescent turmoil: fact or fiction? *Journal of Child Psychology and Psychiatry*, 17, 35-56.

Sampson, R. J. and Laub, J. H. (1997). *Crime in the making: Pathways and turning points through life.* Cambridge, MA: Harvard.

Sampson, R. J. and Lauritson, J. L. (1994). Violent victimization and offending: individual-, situational-, and community level risk factors. In A. J, Reiss and J. A. Roth (eds.), *Understanding and Preventing Violence* (Vol. 3, pp. 1-114). Washingtopn, DC: National Academy.

Santamour, M. and West, B. (1982). The mentally retarded offender: presentation of the facts and a discussion of the issues. In M. Santamour and B. West (eds.), *The retarded offender*, pp. 7-20. New York: Praeger.

Saskatchewan Children's Advocate. (2003). 2003 Annual Report. Saskatoon: Author.

Saunders, J. W. S. (2001). Experts in court: A view from the bench. *Canadian Psychology*, 42, 109-118.

Scott, E. S. (2000). Criminal responsibility in adolescence: Lessons from developmental psychology. In *Youth on trial: A developmental perspective on juvenile justice* (pp. 291-324). Chicago: University of Chicago.

Scott, K. D. (1992). Childhood sexual abuse: Impact on a community's mental health status. *Child Abuse and Neglect*, 16, 285-295.

Scraton, P. and Haydon, D. (2003). Challenging the criminalization of children and young people: securing a rights-based agenda. In J. Muncie, G. Hughes and E. McLaughlin (eds.), *Youth justice: critical readings* (pp. 311-328). London: Sage.

Selekman, M. D. (1997). *Solution-focused therapy with children: Harnessing family strengths for systemic change.* New York: Guilford.

Seligman, M. and Benjamin Darling, R. (1997). *Ordinary families, special children: A systems approach to childhood disability* (2nd ed.). New York: Guilford.

Selman, R. (1980). *The growth of interpersonal understanding.* New York: Academic.

Shaffer, J. N. and Ruback, B. (2002). Violent victimization as a risk factor for violent offending among juveniles. *Juvenile justice bulletin, Office of juvenile justice and delinquency prevention*, Dec., 1-10.

Shields, I. W. and Simourd, D. J. (1991). Predicting predatory behavior in a population of incarcerated young offenders. *Criminal Justice and Behavior*, 18(2), 180-194.

Shipman, K., Zeman, J., Penza, S. and Champion, K. (2000). Emotion management skills in sexually maltreated and nonmaltreated girls: A developmental psychopathology perspective. *Development and Psychopathology*, 12, 47-62.

Silver, E., Mulvey, E. P. and Monahan, J. (1999). Assessing violence risk among discharged psychiatric patients: Toward an ecological approach. *Law and Human Behavior*, 23, 237-255.

Simmons, R. G., Burgeson, R. and Reef, M. J. (1988). Cumulative change at entry to adolescence. In M. R. and W. A. Collins (eds.), *Development during the transition to adolescence* (Vol. 21, pp. 123-150). Hillsdale, NJ: Lawrence Erlbaum Associates.

Singer, M. L., Anglin, T. M., Song, L. and Lunghofer, L. (1995). Adolescents' exposure to violence and associated symptoms of psychological trauma. *Journal of the American Medical Association*, 273(6), 477-482.

Skuse, D., Bentovim, A., Hodges, J., Stevenson, J. Andreou, C., Lanyado, M., New, M., Williams, B. and McMillan, D. (1998). Risk factors for development of sexually abusive behavior in sexually victimized adolescent boys: Cross-sectional study. *British Medical Journal*, 137, 175-179.

Slobogin, S., Melton, G. and Showalter, C. (1984). The feasibility of a brief evaluation of mental state at the time of the offense. *Law and Human Behavior*, 8, 305-320.

Smith, C. E., Esposito, J. and Gregg, S. (2002). *Advocating for children with cognitive disabilities in the juvenile justice system.* College Park, MD: Center of Effective Collaboration and Practice, American Institute for Research.

Smith, C. A. and Stern, S. B. (1997). Delinquency and antisocial behavior: A review of family processes and intervention research. *Social Service Review*, Sept., 383-420.

Snyder, J., Reid, J. and Patterson, G. (2003). A social learning model of child and adolescent antisocial behavior. In B. B. Lahey, T. E. Moffitt and A. Caspi, *Causes of conduct disorder and juvenile delinquency,* (pp. 27-48). New York: Guilford.

Spear, L. P. (2000). The adolescent brain and age-related behavioral manifestations. *Neuroscience and Biobehavioral Reviews*, 24, 417-463.

Spohn, R. E. (2000). Gender differences in the effect of child maltreatment on criminal activity over the life course. *Families, Crime and Criminal Justice, Contemporary Perspectives in Family Research*, 2, 207-231.

Sprott, J. B. (2004). The development of early delinquency: Can classroom and school climates make a difference? *Canadian Journal of Criminology and Criminal Justice*, Oct., 553-572.

Statistics Canada. (1994). Youth Court Statistics. Ottawa: Canadian Centre for Justice Statistics.

_____. (2000a). Youth Court Statistics 1996-1997. Ottawa: Canadian Centre for Justice Statistics.

_____. (2000b). Youth Court Statistics 1998-1999. Ottawa: Canadian Centre for Justice Statistics.

Steadman, H. J., Mulvey, E. P., Monahan, J., Robbins, P. C. and Appelbuam, P. S. (1998). Violence by people discharged from acute psychiatric inpatient facilities and by others in the same neighborhoods. *Archives of General Psychiatry*, 55, 393-401.

Steinberg, L. and Belsky, J. (1996). An evolutionary perspective on psychopathology in adolescence. In D. Cicchetti and S. L. Toth (eds.), *Rochester symposium on developmental psychopathology, Adolescence: Opportunities and challenges* (Vol. 7, 93-124). Newbury Park, CA: Sage.

Steinberg, L. (2001). Adolescent development. *Annual Review of Psychology*, 52, 83- 110.

Steinberg, L. and Scott, E. S. (2003). Less guilty by reason of adolescence: developmental immaturity, diminished responsibility and the juvenile death penalty. *American Psychologist*, 58(12), 1009-1018.

Stephens, T., Dulberg, C.S. and Joubert, N. (1999). Mental health of the Canadian population: A comprehensive analysis. *Chronic diseases in Canada*, 20(3), 118- 126.

Stewart, E. A., Simon, R. L. and Conger, R. D. (2000). The effects of delinquency and legal sanctions on parenting behaviors. *Families, Crime and Criminal Justice*, 2, 257-279.

Stirpe, T. S. and Stermae, L. E. (2003). An exploration of childhood victimization and family-of-origin characteristics of sexual offenders against children. *International Journal of Offender Therapy and Comparative Criminology*, 47(5), 543-555.

Streissguth, A. P. (1997). *Fetal alcohol syndrome: A guide for families and communities.* MD: Pearl H. Brooks.

_____. (1988). Long term effects of fetal alcohol syndrome. In G. C. Robinson and R. W. Armstrong (eds.), *Alcohol and Child/Family Health* (pp. 135-150). Vancouver: University of British Columbia.

Streissguth, A., Barr, H., Kogan, J., Bookstein, F. (1997). Primary and secondary disabilities in fetal alcohol syndrome. In A. P. Streissguth and J. Kanter (eds.), *The challenge of fetal alcohol syndrome: Overcoming secondary disabilities* (pp. 25-39). Seattle: University of Washington.

Streissguth, A. P. and Randels, S. (1988). Long term effects of fetal alcohol syndrome. In G. C. Robinson and R. W. Armstrong (eds.), *Alcohol and Child/Family Health* (pp. 135-147). Vancouver: University of British Columbia.

Stueve, A. and Link, B. G. (1997). Violence and psychiatric disorders: results from an epidemiological study of young adults in Israel. *Psychiatric Quarterly*, 68, 327-342.

Tanner, J. M. (1990). *Fetus into man: physical growth from conception to maturity* (2nd ed.). Cambridge, MA: Harvard.

Tamm, L., Menon, V. and Reiss, A. L., (2002). Maturation of brain function associated with response inhibition. *Journal of American Academy of Child and Adolescent Psychiatry*, 41, 1231-1238.

Thompson, M. D., Reuland, M. and Souweine, D. (2003). Criminal justice/mental health consensus: Improving responses to people with mental illness. *Crime and Delinquency*, 49(1), 30-51.

Thornberry, T. P., Lizotte, A. J., Drohn, M. D., Farnworth, M. and Jang, S. J. (1991). Testing interactional theory: an examination of reciprocal causal relationships among family, school and delinquency. *Journal of Criminal Law and Criminology*, 82, 3-35.

Truscott, D. and Crook, K. H. (2004). *Ethics for the practice of psychology in Canada*. Edmonton: University of Alberta.

Turgey, A. (2005). The diagnosis of disruptive behavior disorders. *Paediatric Child Health*, 9, Suppl. B, 4b-7b.

UNICEF *Innocenti Digest*. (2001). *Independent Institutions Protecting Children's Rights*. Florence.

Urban Institute. *A decade in development, juvenile drug courts are growing in popularity, but do they work?* Retrieved Mar. 9, 2005 from www.urban.org/urlprint.cfm?ID=9063.

U.S. Department of Justice (2000). Office of Juvenile Justice and Delinquency Prevention. *OJJDP statistical briefing book*. Retrieved Feb. 8, 2004 from ojjp.ncjrs.org/ojstatbb/qa251.html.

Vasta, R., Haith, M. M. and Miller, S. A. (1995). *Child psychology: The modern science* (2nd ed.). New York: John Wiley.

Viljoen, J. L. and Roesch, R. (2005). Competence to waive interrogation rights and adjudicative competence in adolescent defendants: cognitive development, attorney contact and psychological symptoms. *Law and Human Behavior*, Vol. 29, No. 6, Dec., 723-742.

Viljoen, J. L., Roesch, R. and Zapf, P. A. (2002). An examination of the relationship between competency to stand trial, competency to waive interrogation rights and psychopathology. *Law and Human Behavior*, Vol. 26, No. 5, Oct., 481-506.

Viljoen, J. L., Klaver, J. and Roesch, R. (2005). Legal decisions of preadolescent and adolescent defendants: Predictors of confessions, pleas, communication with attorneys and appeals. *Law and Human Behavior*, Vol. 29, No. 3, June, 253-277.

Viljoen, J. E., Roesch, R., Ogloff, J. R. and Zapf, P. A. (2003). The role of Canadian psychologists in conducting fitness and criminal responsibility evaluations. *Canadian Psychology*, 44(4), 369-381.

Von Hirsch, A. (2000). Proportionate sentences for juveniles. *Punishment and Society*, 3, 221-236.

Watkins, B. and Bentovim, A. (1992). The sexual abuse of male children and adolescents: A review of current research. *Journal of Child Psychology and Psychiatry*, 33, 97-248.

Watkinson, A. M. (1999). *Education, student rights and the Charter*. Saskatoon, SK: Purich.

Watson, D. and Clark, L. A. (1984). Negative affectivity: The disposition to experience aversive emotional states. *Psychological Bulletin*, 96, 465-490.

Weisz, J. R. and Hawley, K. M. (2002). Developmental factors in the treatment of adolescents. *Journal of Consulting and Clinical Psychology*, 70(1), 21-43.

Wexler, D. B. (1994). Therapeutic jurisprudence and the criminal justice courts. *William and Mary Law Review*, 35, 278- 299.

Whelan, S. P. (2005). *FASD and Criminal Justice: Strategies for working with FASD*. Presented in La Ronge, SK, Sept. 9, 2005.

White, S. (2001). Understanding victimization and offending. In S. White (ed.), *Handbook of Youth and Justice* (pp. 3- 47). New York: Kluwer.

Widom, C. (1989). The cycle of violence. *Science*, 244, 160-166.

Williams, R. A. and Hollis, H. M. (1999). Health beliefs and reported symptoms among a sample of incarcerated adolescent females. *Journal of Adolescent Health*, 24, 21-27.

Willoughby, T., Perry, G. P. and Vandergoot, M. (2003). Transtheoretical model of change: An approach to the treatment of violent youth. In L. Vandecreek and T. L. Jackson (eds.), *Innovations in clinical practice: Focus on children and adolescents* (pp. 37-49). Sarasota, FL: Professional Resource.

Wolfe, D. A., Crooks, C. V., Lee, McIntrye-Smith, A. and Jaffe, P. G. (2003). The effects of children's exposure to domestic violence: A meta-analysis and critique. *Clinical Child and Family Psychology Review*, 6, 171-187.

Wolff, N. (2002). Courts as therapeutic agents: Thinking past the novelty of mental health courts. *Journal of American Psychiatry and Law*, 30, 431-437.

Wolin, S. J. and Wolin, S. (1993). *The resilient self: How survivors of troubled families rise above adversity*. New York: Villard.

Woolard, J. L., Fried, C. S. and Reppucci, N. D. (2001). Toward an expanded definition of adolescent competence in legal situations. In R. Roesch, R. R. Corrado and R. Dempster (eds.), *Psychology in the courts: International advances in knowledge* (21-39). New York: Routledge.

World Health Organization (2001). *Mental Health: New Understanding, New Hope*. Retrieved Feb. 2004 from www.who,int/whr/2001/main/en/index.htm.

Worling, J. R. and Curwen, T. (2000). Adolescent sexual offender recidivism: Success of specialized treatment and implications for risk prediction. *Child Abuse and Neglect*, 24(7), 965-982.

Wormith, J. S. and Olver, M. E. (2002). Offender treatment attrition and its relationship with risk, responsivity and recidivism. *Criminal Justice and Behavior*, 29(4), 447-471.

Wright, J. P., Cullen, F. T. and Woolredge, J. D. (2000). Parental support and juvenile delinquency. *Families, Crime and Criminal Justice*, 2, 139-161.

Yapko, M. D. (1997). *Breaking the patterns of depression*. New York: Random House.

Zinger, I. (2004). Actuarial risk assessment and human rights: A commentary. *Canadian Journal of Criminology and Criminal Justice*, Oct., 607- 620.

Zingraff, M. T., Leiter, J., Myers, K. A. and Johnsen, M. C. (1993). Child maltreatment and youthful problem behavior. *Criminology*, 31, 173-202.

Zingraff, M. T., Leiter, J., Johnsen M. C. and Myers, K. A. (1994). The mediating effect of good school performance on the maltreatment delinquency relationship. *Journal of Research in Crime and Delinquency*, 31, 62-91.

INDEX

A

abandonment, parental 48, 149

Aboriginal youth 24, 52, 145

absenteeism 34

abstract reasoning/thinking 37, 38, 66, 68, 69, 78, 83

abuse 11, 48, 49, 50, 51, 120, 151; maltreatment 47, 49. *See further* interfamilial abuse; physical abuse; sexual abuse; verbal abuse.

academic issues 35, 41, 52-53, 66-67, 68, 71, 90, 93, 99, 108, 110, 133-34, 158, 168-69

accountability 22-24, 30, 112, 119-120, 121, 140

adaptive behaviours 37, 65-66, 68, 69

addiction 38-39, 52, 133, 135, 137, 139, 152, 154, 167, 169, 171; counselling 135; drug 44, 115, 170. *See further* addictions assessment.

adolescents development 32-34, 35-37; different from adults 34-49, 120, 124, 143

adult sentences 25, 28, 29-30, 112, 118-19, 124

adult sex offender 49, 120

adults and the law 15, 21, 51, 105, 112

advocacy 10, 27, 89; advocacy system 23, 82

advocates 11, 59, 81, 105, 160; human rights 54

aggravated assault 97, 98, 132

aggression 49, 70, 72

alcohol 38, 60, 67, 68-69, 83, 96, 102, 103, 104, 110-111, 170; driving under the influence 38

alcohol abuse 35, 69, 133, 137, 176

amenability 58, 59, 174; to treatment 26, 58

anger 39, 69, 82, 89, 133, 135, 139, 152, 153, 154, 158

angry 70, 83, 107, 113, 115, 177

anhedonia 36

antisocial 49, 71, 105, 114, 130, 135, 150, 152; activities 34, 52; behaviours 38, 49, 59, 70, 130, 150, 153; patterns 48, 140; peers 130, 170

anxiety 11, 36, 43, 46, 56, 60, 62, 66, 71, 73, 74, 76, 83, 98, 106, 108, 123, 152, 154, 167

anxiety disorder 9, 11, 36, 42, 44, 45, 107-109

appeal 15, 16, 17

ARND: *see* Fetal Alcohol Spectrum Disorder.

assessment 17-19, 27-28, 59, 61, 67, 85-87, 90-91, 94-95, 97, 98-99, 101, 103, 104-105, 105-106, 107, 109, 111, 125, 130-31, 146, 156, 157, 160, 164, 172; addictions 135, 137, 139, 140; child welfare 24; court ordered 17, 38, 41, 85-89. *See further* psychological assessment; risk assessment; risk-need assessment.

assertiveness skills 46

asthma 44

attention deficits/difficulties 41, 44, 52, 66, 68, 71, 75. *See also* concentration difficulties.

Attention Deficit Hyperactivity Disorder (ADHD) 9, 12, 26, 44, 45, 69, 70-71, 76, 84, 111, 121

Attorney General 27, 28, 29

Australia 41, 48

authority 17, 60, 73, 90, 117, 135, 139, 167; parental 61, 152

authority figures 58-59, 62, 80, 93, 138

autism 42, 43, 69

avoidance behaviours 65, 93

education system 10, 12, 42, 52, 54-55, 162

educational: assessment 160; intervention 69, 163, 177; professional 69; rights 13

emotion 34, 35, 40, 46, 55, 84, 88, 93, 101, 106, 149, 152, 153, 155, 156, 161, 162, 164, 165, 167, 168

emotional: arousal 34-35, 47, 60, 89; control 46, 62; disabilities 13; disturbance 18, 26; functioning 33, 34, 149; problems 35-36, 39, 41, 43, 45, 63, 66, 104, 107, 113-14, 137, 154, 178

empathy 49, 59, 60, 66, 73, 74, 120, 123, 152, 155

employment 25, 26, 53, 132, 134, 139, 155; unemployment 46

ethical policies in psychology 87-89, 125

ethics 12, 86, 178

extended family 22, 23, 126, 137, 154

extrajudicial (out-of-court) measures 13, 22-23, 27, 30, 58-60, 78, 88, 141; sanctions 23, 59. See also community supervision.

F

false accusations of abuse 50-51

family 22, 35, 39, 51, 53, 59, 61, 62, 67, 89, 100, 106, 107-8, 116, 119, 120, 129, 131, 133-34, 136-37, 149, 150, 152, 154, 158-59, 167-68, 176, 177; family involvement 22, 25; rights of family 23

family support 27, 43, 155, 157

family violence 47, 48, 50, 60

fatigue 43, 83

fear 51, 54, 56, 60, 62, 73, 83

federal: government 19, 30-31, 54; laws 53; penitentiary 28

Federal-Provincial-Territorial Task Force on Youth Justice 67

Fetal Alcohol Spectrum Disorder (FASD) 9, 19, 20, 26, 44, 45, 67-7-, 72; Alco-hol-Related Neurodevelopmental Disorder (ARND) 68, 69; Fetal Alcohol Syndrome (FAS) 12, 67, 68, 96; partial FAS (pFAS) 26, 67, 68, 69

Fitness Interview Test (FIT) 99

fitness: to plead 95-96, 111; to stand trial 18, 19, 27, 82, 85-86, 90-91, 93, 95-99, 101, 111; permanently unfit 20-21. *See further* Unfit to Stand Trial (UST); Not Criminally Responsible (NCR).

frontal cortex 32-33

forensic 67, 85, 86, 87-88, 165; intervention 122-23, 128; mental health 14, 125, 169, 177; needs 127, 132; services 93; treatment 125-127

foster: care 50; homes 50, 149; parents 51, 94, 110, 116; placements 51, 69, 110

friends 39, 43, 49, 89, 134, 151, 153, 168

functional: capacities 41-42, 90, 95, 124; competencies 55, 96; deficits/impairments 43, 62, 65, 67-69, 111; issues 20, 32, 41, 43, 55, 65, 78-79, 158

funding 68, 146

G

genetic: disabilities 65; factors 45, 54

government: *see separately* federal; provincial.

H

headache 36

Health Canada 45, 67-68

homicide 38

honesty and integrity, of youth 78, 84

hormones 35-36, 38

youth justice 159, 166; court 17-18, 19,
27, 84, 88-89; legislation 26, 30; practitioners 146; principles 112, 124, 141;
strategy 125, 140, 175; system 22-23,
26, 30, 32, 39-40, 42, 51, 57, 68, 70,
78, 84, 104, 111, 118, 121, 124, 155,
157, 159, 161, 175, 178

YLS/CMI: *see Levels of Supervision Inventory* (LSI).